HARDPRESS.NET
HOME OF HARD-TO-FIND BOOKS

The Bible in the Middle Ages
by Leicester Buckingham

Address:
HardPress
8345 NW 66TH ST #2561
MIAMI FL 33166-2626
USA
Email: info@hardpress.net

יהוה

The Bible in the Middle Ages.

THE
Bible in the Middle Ages;

With Remarks on the

Libraries, Schools, and Social and Religious Aspects

of

Mediæval Europe.

By

Leicester Ambrose Buckingham.

London:

THOMAS CAUTLEY NEWBY,

Welbeck Street, Cavendish Square.

mdcccliii.

CONTENTS.

THE BIBLE

IN

THE MIDDLE AGES.

THE BIBLE

IN

THE MIDDLE AGES.

By most men, at the present day, the Bible in the Middle Ages is regarded in much the same light with the scattered spots of verdure which lie in the heart of the vast sandy deserts of the eastern world. They believe, indeed, that copies of the Scriptures then existed; but they deem that they were few and far between, as green oases in the arid waste; their abiding-places, not in spots freely open to the access of mankind, but in the locked chests of Churches, guarded from the general eye with the jealous secrecy of priestly care; their precepts, not freely promulgated as the code of active daily life, but hidden from laic apprehension, and wholly concealed from the knowledge of the people. That there were Bibles in the libraries of Churches and Monasteries, none will be found sufficiently hardy to deny; but that these Bibles were really, all circumstances considered, very abundantly dispersed, that they were read and studied alike by clerk and by layman, and placed within the reach of the humblest member of the Church of Christ, are propositions most vehemently and pertinaciously denied by those who are ever ready to denounce the Middle Ages as eras of darkness

B

and superstition, remarkable chiefly for the intellectual degradation and spiritual abasement of mankind.

In the investigation of this deeply interesting and hitherto most ill-examined question, we must be careful at the outset to moderate the nature of our expectations; since, if we do not attain to a clear conception of the limits which must be reasonably assigned to the extent of our anticipations, we shall be subject to painful disappointment. The ages of which we treat, were not ages of printing presses; no giant engines threw off hundreds of printed sheets per hour; no steam power cast into the shade the boldest feats of human energy; no metal types rendered needless the laborious toiling of the copyist's hand. How many Bibles should we find in existence now—if, instead of paying a few shillings for a printed copy of the Scriptures, each person were compelled to support a scribe during some months of continuous labour, to give him adequate reward for his exertion, and to furnish him with the multitudinous skins of parchment necessary for the performance of the required transcription? At the present day, the copying of the Catholic Canon of Scripture on parchment, in the ordinary engrossing hand, would cost, with the parchment, more than £200;[1] is it probable that at this price it would, or indeed could, find very many purchasers? It is not for us to seek to show that in the Middle Ages Bibles were as widely diffused as at the present day; nor is this demonstration necessary to the vindication of the character of our fore-

---

[1] The Catholic Canon of Scripture contains 35,877 verses, making 12,783 folios. This would fill 427 skins of parchment, on both sides, costing £85, and the cost of the copying would be £133; the total expense being therefore £218.

fathers. Not in the extent of advantages enjoyed, but in the use made of those actually possessed, lies the true glory of humanity. With the increase of our blessings comes a fearful augmentation of the weight of our responsibility; happier he, who, with small facilities within his reach, toils unceasingly to make them fruitful of rich results—than he, who, gifted with abundant means of exertion, contents himself with the reflection that he has achieved as much as his less fortunate predecessor, and leaves but half-developed the agencies which have been entrusted to him for the benefit of mankind.

We are not to expect, then, that we shall discover that there was a Bible in every house, or even one for every twenty houses; and this, not because the people were indifferent to the possession of the Scriptures, or the Clergy opposed to their circulation, but simply because one Bible then cost as much as many hundred Bibles at the present day, and it was therefore obviously impossible for the poor to possess for themselves the Sacred Volume. That they had ample facility of access to it, we shall have occasion hereafter to perceive; but that they should own it for themselves, was clearly beyond the limits of possibility.

Nor should we fail to recollect that the Church, while She placed no restrictions on the free perusal, by the pious and well-disposed, of the authentic versions of the word of God, yet did not require as an indispensable essential, that each one of Her children should possess and read for himself the Sacred Volume. And it must be considered fortunate for the happiness of mankind, even by those who are most opposed to the teaching of the Church, that those ages were not enlightened by the theory which arose in later times, that the knowledge of spiritual truth could be attained only by the reading of the Bible, and the application of private judgment to the interpretation of its inspired contents ; for then, indeed, the avenue to the acquirement of religious knowledge would have been closed to the vast majority of mankind. Had such a dogma prevailed during those early centuries, when the various portions of the sacred writings, yet scattered and dispersed, had not been collected into a single volume, so that the whole of the inspired record could be possessed by none ; and had it been the object of general acceptation during the ages to which we are referring, when the cost of a Bible rendered it an inaccessible possession to the poor,—how many pious souls must have passed from the scene of their earthly pilgrimage in utter and hopeless ignorance of God's law, who, in the happy days when this figment of the brains of modern dreamers was unknown, received from the lips of the anointed servants of the sanctuary the precious truths which the Church had cherished as the rich inheritance of which She was guardian for the benefit of the world. That He, who has called the poor especially His own, should have appointed as the only mode of attaining to a knowledge of His will, a means which for fourteen hundred and fifty years the poor could never use, and that the designs of Omnipotence were compelled to await the advent of an invention of man before they could arrive at full developement, were ideas which entered not into the philosophy of our mediæval ancestors. The world has grown wiser with the lapse of years ; to the sectaries of our own day it is sufficiently clear that the printing press is an essential portion of the machinery needed for working out man's redemption, and that the scheme of providence received its completion, not upon Calvary, but at Mentz, in the fifteenth century ; but the Ages of Faith had not witnessed this sublime discovery of modern wisdom, and the Church imposed not upon Her children a command with which they would have found it impossible to comply.

We shall proceed, then, with expectations neither immoderate nor irrational, to investigate the actual state of the evidence on the question which is before us ; and beginning with the class in whose hands we should most naturally look first for the inspired writings, the first question for our consideration will be : Did the Monks and Clergy themselves possess the Sacred Volume? and, possessing it, did they habitually devote themselves to its perusal ?

The matter of possession is capable of easy demonstration. In the first place, we find that all Priests—and a very large number of the Monks were in holy orders—were compelled to have in their possession, before they could be ordained, a considerable portion of the sacred writings. The canons of Ælfric, about 950, decree that " every Priest before he is ordained must have the arms belonging to his spiritual work, that is, the holy books, namely, the Psalter, the Book of Epistles and the Book of Gospels, the Missal, the Book of Hymns, the Manual, the Calendar, the Passional, the Penitential, and the Lectionary ; for these books a Priest requires, and cannot do without, if he would properly fulfil his office, and desires to teach the law to the people under his care ; and let him carefully see that they are well written ;"[2] the constitutions of Reculfus of Soissons, addressed by that Bishop to his clergy in 879, say, " We admonish that each one of you

[2] Wilkins, Conc. i. 250.

should be careful to have a Missal, a Lectionary, a Book
of the Gospels, a Martyrology, an Antiphonary, a Psalter,
and a Book of Forty Homilies of St. Gregory, corrected
and pointed by our copies which we use in the holy Mother Church ; and also fail not to have as many sacred and
ecclesiastical books as you can get; for from them you
shall receive food and condiment for your souls ; our Lord
himself having said, ' Man doth not live by bread alone,
but by every word that proceedeth out of the mouth of
God.' If, however, any one of you is not able to obtain
all the books of the Old Testament, at the very least let
him diligently take pains to transcribe for himself the first
book of the whole sacred history, which is Genesis, by
reading which he may come to understand the creation of
the world ;"[3] and many other passages might be cited to
the same effect. From the provisions of these canons,
requiring the possession of various portions of the Scriptures by the clergy, as indispensable to the due discharge
of their sacred duties, it might safely be inferred that they
invariably constituted a part of the possessions of every
Church and Monastery ; and this inference is amply sanctioned by the various incidental notices which are scattered throughout the annals of mediæval history. When
the Normans attacked Nantes in 843, killed the Bishop in
the Cathedral, put to death many of the clergy and monks
and laity who had sought refuge within its walls, and
carried off a large number of prisoners, one of the captives,
taking advantage of a quarrel among the victors, seized
upon the great Bible which had been taken from the Cathedral, and ultimately succeeded in reaching Nantes,
having saved only this, which the narrator designates

[3] Conc. ix. 418.

"their greatest treasure," from the wreck.[4] We meet, too, with innumerable mentions of the presentation of Bibles, and of separate portions of the Scriptures, to Churches and Monasteries. Pope Leo III. gave to one Church a copy of the Gospels, bound in pure gold and studded with precious gems ;[5] and to another, one so richly adorned that it weighed more than seventeen pounds. Hincmar, Archbishop of Rheims, in the ninth century, caused the Gospels to be written for his Cathedral in letters of gold and silver, and bound in plates of gold, resplendent with jewels ;[6] and ordered another, equally splendid, to be prepared especially for the crypt, which contained the remains of St. Remigius.[7] Pope Leo IV., in the same century, gave copies of the Gospels, the Psalms, and the Books of Kings to the Church of the Blessed Virgin near Rome,[8] and to another Church a copy of the Gospels bound in silver.[9] Pope Benedict III., his successor, presented to the Church of St. Calistus a copy of the Gospels, adorned with plates of gold and silver, and weighing nearly seventeen pounds.[1] About the same period, the Emperor Michael sent, as a present to St. Peter's at Rome, a copy of the Gospels bound in pure gold and adorned with precious stones.[2] The Emperor Henry II., of Bavaria, in the early part of the eleventh century, presented a richly decorated copy of the Gospels to the Church of Mersburg.[3] Paul, Abbot of St. Albans, gave to his Church two copies of the Gospels adorned with gold and silver and gems ;[4] Duke

[4] Frag. Hist. Armor. ap. Martene, iii. 830.   [5] Conc. vii. 1083.

[6] Flodoardi Hist. Rem. l. iii. c. 5, ap. Sismondi, Op. iv. 113.

[7] Ibid. c. 9, ap. Sismondi, Op. iv. 119.   [8] Conc. viii. 22.

[9] Ibid. 27.   [1] Ibid. 230.   [2] Dach. Spicileg. ii. 877.

[3] Ditmar ap. Leob. i. 399.   [4] Matt. Paris, Hist. Abbat. S. Alb. i. 5.

Hugh of Burgundy, in endowing, in 1077, the Monästery
of Clugni, with the possessions of the Church of Analon,
gave at the same time three copies of the Gospels;[5] Ralph,
Bishop of Rochester, in 1114, gave a copy of the Gospels
to his Church,[6] and his successor in the same see, Bishop
Walter, made a similar donation to the same Cathedral;[7]
among the articles belonging to his chapel which King
Robert bequeathed, in the eleventh century, to the Church
of St. Aman, in Orleans, were six copies of the Gospels,
two of which were bound in gold and two in silver;[8] and
it would be easy to go on filling page after page with such
examples, for it is impossible to peruse the lives of any
of the Popes, or the biographies of distinguished Priests
and laymen of the Middle Ages, or to open a volume of
ecclesiastical or monastic history, without encountering innumerable instances of such donations.   Nor must it be
imagined that the gift of a Bible, or a copy of the Gospels
to a Church, is to be taken as evidence that it was previously
destitute in this respect, for it seems to have been by no
means unusual for one Church to possess a large number of
copies of the various portions of the sacred writings.
William de Longchamp, Bishop of Ely, in order to raise the
sum of a hundred and sixty marks, which he contributed towards the ransom of Richard Cœur de Lion from captivity,
pledged the precious covers of thirteen copies of the
Gospels belonging to his Church;[9] and at a visitation of
the treasury of St. Paul's Cathedral, in 1295, by Ralph de
Baudoke, the Dean, there were found there twelve copies
of the Gospels bound in silver, some of them decorated
with precious stones, one encased in silver gilt plates,

---

[5] Dach. Spicileg. iii. 412.   [6] Anglia Sacra, i. 342.   [7] Ibid.
345.   [8] Fleury, xii. 491.   [9] Anglia Sacra, i. 633.

adorned with relics, and four others presenting no peculiar features, six copies of the Epistles, glossed copies of the Epistles of St. Paul, the Twelve Prophets, and the Gospels of St. Luke and St. John, two copies of the gospels of St. Matthew and St. Mark with the commentary of St. Thomas Aquinas, and two entire Bibles.[1] Many, too, of these ancient copies of the Scriptures have survived the ravages of time, and the influence of the various causes tending to promote their destruction, and still remain in the Churches which originally possessed them. "At the cathedral of Rheims," says Martene, "are still to be seen many ancient MSS., and among others a copy of the Gospels written upon purple vellum, and a Bible of the time of Archbishop Hincmar.[2] At Metz," he remarks, "are seen, among others, a very fine Bible, seven or eight hundred years old, and a copy of the Greater and Lesser Prophets in Saxon characters;"[3] at Verdun he found the Canons in possession of "two beautiful texts of the Gospels, one written in capitals and more than nine hundred years old, and the other about seven years of age;"[4] and his researches in other Churches were attended with similar results. In the examination of the archives of various Monasteries, these precious relics of antiquity were discovered in still greater abundance. At La Grasse, in Languedoc, there was, when Martene visited it, "a copy of the gospels asserted to have been given to the Monastery by the Emperor Charlemagne;"[5] at the priory of St. Lupucin he found "a fine copy of the Gospels written in silver, in uncial letters, upon purple vellum, about nine hundred years old."[6] At Luxeuil he "found

[1] Dugdale, Monast. iii. 309—324.   [2] Mart. Voy. Litt. (1717) i. 177.   [3] Ib. ii. 110   [4] Ib. 93.   [5] Ib. 55.   [6] Ib. i. 175

in the sacristy a beautiful copy of the Gospels, which had been presented to the Monastery by the abbot Gerard in the eleventh century."[7]   At Jouarre he discovered " two copies of the Gospels covered with plates of gold, the one seven hundred, the other eight hundred years old ;"[8] at Hautvillers, he found " a copy of the Gospels written in letters of gold, and of striking beauty, of the time of Archbishop Ebon ;"[9] at St. Michel, " a very fine copy of the Psalms in a Greek version ;"[1]   at St. Riquier, " a copy of the Gospels written in letters of gold upon purple vellum, given by the Emperor Charlemagne to St. Angilbert ;"[2] at St. Vincent, at Metz, "a very fine copy of the Gospels ;"[3] at St. Medard, at Soissons, " an ancient copy of the Gospels, presented by Louis le Debonnaire to that Monastery ;"[4] at St. Vaasts, at Douay, "a copy of the Psalms ;"[5] at Eptenac, " two very remarkable copies of the Gospels ;"[6] and many pages might be filled with similar citations ; although, from the nature of his researches, he was induced to notice only those examples which presented striking features from their antiquity, their beauty, or the remarkable circumstances of their history.   It must not be imagined that these surviving relics of antiquity consist only of separate portions of the sacred writings ; it is undoubtedly true that the labour and expense involved in the transcription of the entire Bible, caused the Gospels alone to be multiplied much more extensively than the inspired volume in its integrity, and that these are therefore much more frequently encountered ; yet we find many notices of

---

[7] **Mart.** Voy. Litt. (1717) i. 168.   Mabillon Annal. Ord. S. Bened. iv. 237.   [8] Mart. Voy. Litt. (1717) ii. 74.   [9] Ibid. 78. [1] Ibid. 129.   [2] Ibid. 175.   [3] Ibid. 112.   [4] Ibid. (1724.) 17. [5] Ibid. 76.   [6] Ibid. 297.

entire Bibles still remaining in the monastic libraries. At St. Claude, Martene found " a very fine Bible, eight hundred years old ;"[7] in the Monastery of St. Mary, at Pont à Mousson, " two fine Bibles, about five hundred years old ;"[8] at St. Jean de Vigores, " a Bible, with concordance ;"[9] at Stavelo, " a very fine Bible, in two large volumes ;"[1] at Malmidi, "a Bible, in two volumes ;"[2] at La Val Dieu, "a fine Bible ;"[3] at Grimberg, " two Bibles ;"[4] at St. Pantaleon, at Cologne, " a very fine Bible ;"[5] at the Abbey of Esterboie, " a Bible ;"[6] and so on with numerous other Monasteries, whose libraries he visited with similar results. It would naturally be expected, by any one in the slightest degree versed in monastic history, that such would be found to be the case, since the annals of religious houses present innumerable instances of the donation to their libraries of the whole, or of separate portions, of the sacred writings. Among the books which the Abbot Grimbald gave to the Abbey of St. Gall, were copies of the Gospels and of the Epistles of St. Paul ; in the list of the volumes presented to the Monastery of Fontanelle, by the Abbot Ansegisius, in the ninth century, we find noted " a fine Bible, containing the whole of the Old and New Testament, with prefaces, and having the initial letters richly illuminated ;"[7] in a return of the property of the Monastery of St. Riquier, made in 831, we find included two Bibles, one of which was in fourteen volumes, and four copies of the Gospels ;[8] the chronicle of the Bishops of Hildesheim mentions the existence, in the twelfth century, of a Bible which Bishop

---

[7] Mart. Voy. Litt. (1717) i. 117.   [6] Ibid. ii. 128.   [9] Ibid. (1724) 24.
[1] Ibid. 149.   [2] Ibid. 171.   [3] Ibid. 199.   [4] Ibid. 112.
[5] Ibid. 264.   [6] Ibid. 270.   [7] Chron. Fontan. ap. Dach.
Spicileg. ii. 280.   [8] Chron. Centul. ap. Dach. Spicileg. ii. 311.

Wicbert had written with his own hand for the use of the Monastery in the ninth century;[9] and the library in which this was preserved, was subsequently enriched by two other Bibles, each containing the whole of the sacred books, and carefully glossed, the one presented by Bishop Bruno, in 1153,[1] the other by Bishop Berno, in 1190.[2] Thierry, Abbot of St. Ebreuf, in the eleventh century, caused to be written for his Monastery, among other books, a copy of the entire Bible, containing all the books of the Old and New Testament;[3] and Stephen, Abbot of Beze, in the same century, gave to his Monastery "a Bible, containing the whole of the Old and New Testament."[4] When the Abbot Angilbert restored the Abbey of St. Riquier, in 841, he gave to it, in addition to two hundred other books, a copy of the Gospels, written in letters of gold, and bound in silver plates, studded with gems;[5] and Ansegisius Abbot of Fontanelle, in addition to the Bible already mentioned, which he caused to be prepared for his Monastery, presented to it a copy of the Gospels, in Roman characters, written in letters of gold, upon purple vellum.[6] When the remains of St. Sebastian and St. Gregory were removed to the Monastery of St. Medard, at Soissons, in 826, Louis le Debonnaire presented to it, among other things, a copy of the Gospels, written in letters of gold, and bound in plates of the same precious metal,[7] the same, undoubtedly, which Martene found there upon visiting the Monastery in 1724;[8] in 1022, the Emperor Henry of Bavaria, on his recovery from a severe illness at the

---

[9] Chron. Ep. Hild. ap. Leib. Scr. Br. i. 743.   [1] Ibid. 747.
[2] Ibid. 749.   [3] Mabillon, Act. SS. Ord. S. Bened. ix. 136.
[4] Chron. Bes. ap. Dach. Spicileg. ii. 435.   [5] Mabillon. Act. SS. Ord. S. Bened. v. 110.   [6] Ibid. vi. 597.   [7] Ibid. viii. 398.
[8] Mart. Voy. Litt. (1724) 76.

Monastery of Monte Casino, presented to it a magnificent copy of the Gospels, covered on one side with gold, studded with the most precious gems, and gorgeously adorned with illuminations.[9] Desiderius, who was Abbot of Monte Casino, and who subsequently became Pope Victor III., gave to its library copies of the Epistles and Gospels, together with many other literary treasures,[1] and the Empress Agnes presented to the same Monastery a copy of the Gospels, bound in silver, and adorned with valuable jewels.[2] Brethwold, Bishop of Salisbury, in the eleventh century, gave to the Abbey of Glastonbury, in which he had been a Monk, two copies of the Gospels;[3] and Olbert, Abbot of Gembloux, in the same century, wrote out with his own hand an entire Bible, which he presented to his Monastery, together with four copies of the Gospels, one bound in gold, and three in silver, and one copy of the Epistles, encased in plates of silver.[4] At the destruction of Hyde Abbey, near Winchester, in the twelfth century, there were found ten copies of the Gospels belonging to the Monastery;[5] and when William Rufus imposed a heavy tax to pay for the purchase of Normandy, Godfrey, Abbot of Malmsbury, was compelled to strip the precious covers from twelve copies of the Gospels, in order to pay the amount which was levied upon his Abbey.[6]

Various other incidental evidences of the possession of the Scriptures by the Monks and Clergy present themselves to our notice, which it is difficult to include under any dis-

---

[9] Mabillon. Act. SS. Ord. S. Bened. viii. 400.   [1] Ibid. ix. 594.
[2] Chron. Cas. iii. c. 30. p. 609.   [3] Guil. Malms. ap. Gale. iii. 325.
[4] Mabillon. Act. SS. Ord. S. Bened. viii. 530.   [5] Dugdale Monast. i. 210.   [6] Vit. Ald. ap. Anglia Sacra. ii. 44.

tinct classification. Among these may be enumerated
the frequent mention of the sacred writings among the
books which missionaries carried with them on their journies into heathen countries, and which both Monks and
Priests habitually took with them, when travelling, and
had constantly in their possession. Thus when St. Boniface visited Friesland, where he received the crown of
martyrdom, a copy of the Gospels was one of the treasures
which fell into the hands of his murderers ;[7] an ancient
copy of the Gospels, brought by Augustine into England,
is still preserved in the library of Corpus Christi College,
at Cambridge ;[8] Odo, afterwards Abbot of Clugni, carried
with him, when travelling, a copy of the Scriptures, "according to the general custom," to use the words of his
biographer ;[9] and when Nigel, Bishop of Ely, was plundered
in the reign of Stephen, a valuable copy of the Gospels
were among the spoils which fell into the hands of his assailants.[1] We meet, too, with very frequent notices of the
bequest of Bibles to Churches and Monasteries by distinguished ecclesiastics, such as the Bible in twelve volumes
which was bequeathed by the Bishop of Cambray to the
Carthusians of Macour, in the thirteenth century,[2] and the
Bible which Gennadius, Bishop of Astorga, left at his death
to a Monastery which he had founded ;[8] instances of such
legacies being very numerous in the annals of mediæval
history. Nor should we omit to notice the casual proofs
of the existence of Bibles in Churches and Monasteries,
which may be perceived in the records of donations of lands

[7] Vit. S. Bonifac. ii. 177.   [8] Wanley.   [9] Mabillon Act.
SS. Ord. S. Bened. vii. 756.   [1] Anglia Sacra, i. 622.
   [2] Mart. Thes. Nov. Anecdote. i. 1314.
   [8] Fleury, l. liv. c. 54.   Mabillon. Act. SS. Ord. S. Bened. vii. 36.

to such establishments. When moveable property of any description was thus bestowed, the pious donors, regarding the gift as made, not to the Monks or Priests, who were the humble stewards of Heaven, but to God and the patron Saint, laid it upon the altar in token of its solemn consecration to the uses of religion: thus when a child was dedicated to the Church, his hand was wrapped in the hangings of the altar;[4] the same practice prevailed at the profession of a novice;[5] and many instances are recorded in which books and other articles were thus deposited by those who gave them: but land could not be thus treated; and when tracts of territory, or houses, or mills, were given to the Church, the Bible was frequently laid upon the altar as the representative of the donation. Two such instances are recorded in the charters of the single Monastery of St. Maur on the Loire;[6] another is presented in a charter relating to the Church at Beze, in the twelfth century;[7] and these incidental evidences, peculiarly valuable, on account of that feature in their character, are sufficiently numerous to constitute an important branch of testimony.

It will scarcely be denied that the proof of the possession of the Scriptures by the Monks and Clergy is sufficiently clear and conclusive, and that this first step in our argument is established beyond the possibility of contradiction. Still the question arises: Having the Bible, did they read it?

It is not necessary to contend that both Priests and Monks devoted a large portion of their time to the study of the writings of the Fathers; indeed, far from being

---

[4] Reg. S. Bened. c. 59.   [5] Ibid. 58.   [6] Du Cange in v. *Bibliotheca.* Baluz. Capit. Reg. Franc. ii. 1456.
[7] Chron. Bes. ap. Dach. Spicileg. ii. 436.

contravened, this very custom has been made a ground of
accusation against them, by many who evidently have no very
clear ideas respecting the Fathers, and who furnish us with
indisputable evidence that they, at least, are guiltless of the
heinous crime of cultivating a knowledge of Patristic literature. It is conceded, then, that these holy men read and studied
the works of the illustrious doctors of the ancient Church ;
and no one who is conversant with Christian literature can
fail to perceive that, in so doing, they must have secured
a very enlarged acquaintance with the Scriptures, since
the writings of these venerable sages consist almost wholly
of commentaries on the Bible, whether in the form of sermons, or homilies, or critical dissertations, and are copiously
interspersed with citations from the Sacred Volume. .

But we are not compelled to have recourse to evidence of
such indirect reading of the Bible by the Monks and Clergy,
since we possess ample proof of their constant and diligent
perusal of the inspired writings.   The most eminent monastic writers were zealous and untiring in their inculcation
of this practice upon their disciples.   " St. Benedict," says
Mabillon, "after modestly declaring that his Rule is but a
guide to Christian perfection, avows that those who aspire
to the highest excellence must learn the means of attaining
to it in the books of the Old and New Testament, which
contain, in every page, a perfect rule of Christian life ;"⁸
St. Anthony referred his monks to the same sacred source
for the principles which should regulate in all respects
their conduct ;⁹ St. Jerome says, " Cultivate with diligent

---

⁸ Mabillon Tr. des Etudes Monast. 55. " Quæ enim pagina aut
quis sermos divinæ auctoritatis veteris ac novi Testamenti non est
rectissima norma vitæ humanæ."   Reg. S. Bened. c. 72.

⁹ S. Athanas. Vit. S. Anton. c. 15.

affection a knowledge of the Scriptures, and you will easily overcome the lusts of the flesh ;"[1] and the various monastic rules uniformly and urgently inculcate the reading of the Bible, as one of the most essential duties incumbent upon those who had assumed the habit of religion. In the ordination of deacons, the Bishop, having placed the stole upon the left shoulder of the candidate as he knelt before him, delivered into his hands the Book of the Gospels, saying, "Receive this volume of the Gospels, read and understand it, teach it to others, and in thine own actions fulfil all its precepts ;"[2] and the canons of the Council of Pavia, in the ninth century, inculcating the same practice upon the highest dignitaries of the Church, present at the same time, were an interesting picture of the daily life of a Bishop in the Middle Ages. "The holy synod has decreed that the domestic and private life of a Bishop ought to be above all scandal and suspicion, so that we may, according to the apostles, provide things honest, not only before God, but before all men. It is meet, therefore, that in the chamber of a Bishop, and for all more private service, priests and clerks of sound judgment should be in attendance, who, while their Bishop is engaged in watching, praying, and searching the Scriptures, may constantly wait on him, and be witnesses and imitators, and, to the glory of God, setters-forth of his holy conversation. We decree that Bishops shall offer mass not only on Sundays and on the principal festivals, but that, when possible, they shall attend the daily sacrifice ; nor shall they neglect to offer private prayers, first for themselves, then for their brethren in the priesthood, for Kings, for all the rulers of the Church of God, for those who have particularly com-

[1] St. Hieron. Epist. ad Rustic.   [2] Martene Pont. Egb. 35. Pont Gemet. 39.

mended themselves to their prayers, and, above all, for the poor ; and let them offer the sacrifice of the altar to God with that pious compunction and deep feeling of holy devotion which belongs to more private ministrations, that the Priest himself may become a living offering, a sacrifice to God of a broken spirit.   It is our pleasure that a Bishop shall content himself with moderate entertainments, and shall not urge his guests to eat and drink, but shall rather, at all times, show himself a pattern of sobriety.   At his table there shall be no frivolous subjects of discourse, and let no ridiculous exhibitions, no nonsense of silly stories, no buffoon tricks, no foolish talking of the unwise, be admitted.   Let the stranger, the poor, and the infirm be his guests, who, blessing Christ, may receive a blessing from the sacerdotal table.   Let there be sacred reading during the meal ; let pious exhortation follow ; then the guests may rejoice in having been replenished and refreshed, not only with temporal food for their bodies, but with the nourishment of spiritual discourse ; and that God may be glorified in all things through Christ."[3]

The precepts thus urgently inculcated appear to have been very generally obeyed by both Monks and Priests, and the practice of Scriptural reading is amply demonstrated by the records of mediæval history.   The rule of St. Benedict provided that the whole of the Psalms should be gone through every week ;[4] but so far did the Monks exceed the obligation imposed upon them by their founder, that we learn from the biographer of Abbot Odo, of Clugni, that they had in his time, on account of the weakness of some of the brethren, abated fourteen out of the one hundred

---

[3] Conc. viii. 61.   [4] Reg. S. Bened. c. 18.

and thirty psalms which they had been accustomed to recite every day ;[5] and of Wolphelm, Abbot of Brunwillers, in the eleventh century, we are told that he caused the whole of the Old and New Testament to be read through every year.[6]   But the most striking view of the extent to which the reading of the Scripture was practised by the Monks, may be derived from the account which is left to us of the usage of the Benedictines by Abbot Ulric of Clugni, in a book which he wrote at the request of Abbot William of Hirschau, detailing the customs of Clugni, one of the most renowned of the Benedictine Monasteries, and in all its observances a model establishment of that illustrious order. " To begin," he says, " with the most ancient of all the books, that is the octateuch, this according to general custom, and as it is in other Churches, is appointed to be commenced on Septuagesima. On the Sunday itself then are read short lessons, except that for the first the whole of the prologue of St. Jerome is read ; but during the following nights the lessons are so much increased that in one week the whole book of Genesis is read through in the Church only. On Sexagesima Exodus is begun, and, together with the other books which are read, it also is read both in the Church and in the refectory, in such manner that where the lesson finished one day shall be the beginning of the lesson for the next ; and the whole octateuch is read through, if not before, at least by the beginning of Lent. Lessons are, however, taken from it for the Sundays in Lent. In the Passion of our Lord the prophet Jeremias is read, and, as before, the prologue forms the first lesson ; it is, however read in the Church only; and before Holy Thursday it is finished as far as Lamen-

---

[5] Mabillon Act. SS. Ord. S. Bened. vii. 159.   [6] Ibid. ix. 686.

tations. In Easter week the Acts of the Apostles are read, and for one week only, during which, from the shortness of the nights, it is impossible that much should be read. After this, for two weeks we read the Apocalypse and the Canonical Epistles, finishing them by Ascension Day; then the Acts of the Apostles are again appointed, and are again read from the beginning, as if they had not been read before, until Pentecost. These same books, however, are not the less read regularly, and throughout in the refectory, where also are read, in their appointed season, the Books of Kings, of Solomon, Job, Tobit, Judith, Esther, Ezra, and the Maccabees, which are read only in the refectory, and not at all in the Church, except the short extracts which may be made from any of them for the Sundays. From the calends of November, the lessons for common nights are doubled. The prophet Ezekiel is appointed to be read in the Church only, and is customarily finished before the feast of St. Martin; and although we celebrate the octave of that feast with singing and with other solemnities, yet the prophetical lessons are not changed, nor, indeed, are they on other octaves, unless they would make twelve lessons. Then we commence the prophet Daniel and the twelve minor prophets, which would not suffice to fill up the necessary time, if we did not add, after the last of them, the homilies of the blessed Pope Gregory on Ezekiel. In Advent, Isaias, the prophet, is appointed, and when I inquired about this, and wished to learn in how many nights it ought in strictness to be read through, I could not learn from anybody, and I can only say what I recollect to have seen and heard; when I was there it was sometimes read through in six common nights. After this, follow the epistles of Pope Leo on the Incarnation of our Lord, and other discourses of the holy fathers, chiefly of St. Augustine. The canonical Epistles are appointed for that Sunday which first occurs after Innocent's day, provided that that day is not the feast of the Circumcision; and here again I must say as I did of the Prophets, and state simply what I saw; such an epistle as that of the Romans was read through in two nights, and when one of the monks who had portioned out the lessons had made them shorter, he was reproved by our seniors in chapter. If, however, it should happen that the Epistles were finished before Septuagesima, they read St. John Chrysostom's exposition of the Epistle to the Hebrews. Now, you see, I have in some fashion gone round the circle of the year." [7]

It may reasonably be doubted whether many of those who are most vehement in their condemnation of the Monks, as enemies to the reading of the Scriptures, surpass those against whom their hostility is directed, in their diligent perusal of the Sacred Volume, as pourtrayed in this simple narrative; and the customs thus described, far from being confined to a single Monastery, were of universal prevalence, [8] and were, indeed, the natural result of the observance, not only of the spirit, but of the letter of the rule of St. Benedict, which was followed in the greater number of the Monasteries of Europe. [9] After this evidence it will scarcely be contended that the Monks did not read the Scriptures; in this respect their practice was in entire conformity with the spirit of their teaching, and, as they inculcated the perusal of the sacred writings as the sure method of attaining to spiritual perfection, so

[7] Ulric, ap. Dach. Spicileg. i. 650.   [8] Mart. Voy. Litt. (17 7) ii. 139.   [9] Calmet Comm. in Reg. St. Bened. i. 141, ii. 17.

they endeavoured by the same means to promote their own salvation.

But they were not content with reading the Bible ; with some special portions of the Scriptures they cultivated a yet more intimate acquaintance. The rule of St. Pachomius, the earliest of the Monastic patriarchs, says, "There shall be no one whatsoever in the monastery who will not learn to read and get by heart some part of the Scriptures, at the very least the New Testament and the Psalms ;"[1] the rule of St. Basil says, " If any one who is in good health shall neglect to offer prayers and to commit the Psalms to memory, let him be separated from the society of the others ;"[2] the rule of St. Ferreol declares that " No one who claims the name of a Monk can be allowed to be ignorant of letters, and moreover he must know all the Psalms by heart ;"[3] the Regula Tarnatensis mentions the school in which the younger Monks exercised their memory in learning the Psalms ;[4] and the rule of St. Benedict decrees that the Lessons shall be read and the Psalms recited ;[5] thereby plainly intimating that the latter are to be said from memory.[6] The canons of the Church were equally urgent in inculcating this practice upon the clergy. At the eighth Council of Toledo, which was held in 835, it was decreed that no one should be admitted to the priesthood who did not know by heart the whole of the Psalms, the Hymns of the Church, and the office of Baptism, and that those who had been ordained without possessing such knowledge should forthwith acquire it ;[7] and it was required that each Bishop should, at stated periods, make a

---

[1] Reg. S. Pachom.   [2] Reg. S. Basil.   [3] Reg. S. Ferreol.
[4] Reg. Tarnat. c. 7.   [5] Reg. S. Bened c. 8 to 20.   [6] Martene
de. Antiq. Monach. Rit.   [7] Conc. vi. 406.

regular enquiry throughout his diocese for the purpose of ascertaining, among other things, whether every Priest could rightly interpret the Epistles and Gospels, and whether he knew the whole of the Psalms by heart.[8] In various ways the same precepts were as vehemently enforced. Charlemagne, in the Capitulary of Aix-la-Chapelle, in 789, says, "In all Monasteries and schools let them learn the Psalms, the musical notes, the chants, the mode of making the calendar, and grammar;"[9] again, in the Capitula data Presbyteris, in 804, he says, " I would admonish you, my brethren and sons, to give attention to these few capitula which follow : First, that a Priest of God should be learned in Holy Scripture, and rightly believe and teach to others the faith of the Trinity, and be able properly to fulfil his office ; secondly, that he should have the whole of the Psalms by heart," and so on with other branches of sacerdotal duty;[1] and the Constitutions of Reculfus, Bishop of Soissons, in 889, admonish the clergy " to have by heart correctly the Psalms, the Discourse on the Catholic Faith which begins ' Quicunque vult,' the Canon of the Mass, the Chants, and the Calendar."[2] We meet, too, with numerous examples of Monks and Priests who went far beyond the simple observance of these precepts, and distinguished themselves by a very remarkable extent of scriptural knowledge.   John, Abbot of Gorze, being appointed officiating priest at the nunnery of St. Peter, at Metz, "immediately," says his biographer, " began with these holy hand-maidens of God a course of divine reading, and having first read through the whole of the Old and New Testament, he committed to memory

[8] Regin. Prum.   [9] Capit. Reg. Franc. edit. Baluz. i. 237.
[1] Ibid. i. 417.   [2] Conc. ix. 418.

accurately, so that no one could have done it better, all
the lessons which are appointed for certain times in the
Church ;[3] " Wilfred," says Beda, " came to the Island of
Lindisfarne, and there giving himself up to the service of
the Monks, he took care diligently to learn and to perform
those things which belong to monastic purity and piety,
and being of an acute understanding, he very soon committed to memory the Psalms and some other books
before he was shorn,"[4] and when at Rome he studied
under St. Boniface, and then learned the four Gospels by
heart,[5] as Beda remarks, " according to the general custom."[6]   Peter the Venerable, we are told, " retained the
whole of the holy Scriptures of both Testaments in his
memory ;"[7] Anselm, Bishop of Lucca, in the eleventh
century, " knew almost all the Holy Scriptures by heart,
and as soon as he was asked, would tell what each and all
of the holy expositors thought on any particular passage ;"[8] Wulstan, Bishop of Worcester, when going on a
journey, began to recite the Psalms when he mounted his
horse, and continued this pious exercise until he reached
his destination ;[9] Thierry, Abbot of St. Hubert, in the
Ardennes, " was so diligent in the reading of the Holy
Scriptures that he retained them all in his memory, and
quickly resolved the most obscure and difficult questions
of interpretation ;"[1] Wolphelm, Abbot of Brunwillers, in
the eleventh century, " so profited by the reading of the
Scriptures, that what he had once read never passed from
his recollection ;"[2] and the same thing is noted of a vast

3 Mabillon Act. SS. Ord. S. Bened. vii. 370.
4 Beda. Eccles. Hist. l. v. c. 19.   5 Eddius. Vit. Wilf. c. 5.
6 Beda Eccles. Hist. l. v. c. 19.   7 Bib. Clun. 619.
8 Mabillon Act. SS. Ord. S. Bened. ix. 480.   9 Ibid. 834.
1 Ibid. 565.   2 Ibid. 686.

number of Monks and Ecclesiastics, whose names are recorded with praise in the annals of mediæval history.

Still it has been maintained by some writers, that this reading and committing to memory was a purely mechanical operation, and that the religious, even when they perused or recited the various portions of the Scriptures, performed a mere lip-service, and did not devote their minds to the study of the book, in the reading of which their time was thus extensively employed. Thus, Tyndale, one of the most prominent of the English Reformers, says, " The Abbots took the Scriptures from their Monks, lest some should ever bark against the Abbots living, and set up such long service and singing withal, that they should have no time to read in the Bible but with their lips;"[9] and other writers have given utterance to similar imputations. Were we disposed to be critical, it might be objected that if the Abbots ".took away the Scriptures from their Monks," it was clearly a work of supererogation to " set up long service and singing," to prevent them from reading that which they had not in their possession ; and it might be suggested that the admission of Tyndale, that the Monks were set to " read in the Bible with their lips," clearly overthrows his previous allegation that the Scriptures were taken away from them by their superiors. The evidence which is already before us will enable us at once to perceive the utter falsity of the charge thus brought against our monastic forefathers ; and the spirit of the entire philippic is much akin to that of another passage from the pen of the same amiable and Christian polemic, in which he avers that the custom of continual psalmody was adopted by the Monks merely as a salutary

[9] Tyndale, Practice of Prelates.

C

precaution to favour the digestion of their heavy dinners;
" your singing," he says, " is but roaring, to stretch out
your maws, as do your other gestures and rising at mid-
night, to make the meat sink to the bottom of the stomach,
that he may have perfect digestion and be ready to devour
afresh against the next refection;"[1] the charity of which
imputation can be likened only to its rationality. Certainly,
it would be a very deep and sagacious device, to set men
to the daily perusal of a particular book, and to compel
them to commit a large portion of it to memory, in order
to keep them in entire ignorance of its contents. It is to
be feared that such a scheme would have been almost too
profound for the comprehension of our mediæval ancestors;
and certainly, if it was ever attempted, the testimony of
history fully proves that it failed most signally to achieve
the desired result.

Seriously, however, it may not be amiss to enquire,
whether the reading of the Scriptures by the Monks was
accompanied by a careful and diligent study of the sacred
volume.

That such was required of them, both of those who
were in holy orders, and of those who wore the simple
habit of religion, no one can doubt. The monastic rules
are all sufficiently plain upon this point, and the canons
of many Councils exhort the Priesthood to become learned
in Holy Scripture, as a qualification indispensable to the
due discharge of their sacred duties; nor do we find
that those who were thus admonished, were backward
in the discharge of this obligation. Indeed, no one who
has ever studied the literature of the Middle Ages, can
have failed to perceive in every page of the works of

[1] Tyndale, Expos. on St. Matt. vii. 15.

monastic writers which he may have examined, the strongest evidence of the profound and intimate knowledge of the Scriptures, which the authors of these productions must have possessed. It is not so much in the quotations made from the Inspired Volume, though these are generally abundant, as in the general character of their style, that the extent of their biblical learning is eminently and strikingly displayed. The language employed, the imagery introduced, the entire tone of the composition, is essentially and wholly scriptural, and evinces, more clearly than any other species of testimony could evince, their habit of constantly reading and studying the Bible, until their minds had become so imbued with its contents that new thoughts naturally assumed a form, and arrayed themselves in language drawn from it alone. Many examples of this might be cited, in which the bad taste displayed is indisputable, and in which the passing events of their own day are illustrated by comparisons with incidents recorded in Scripture history which may seem to modern apprehension fantastic and absurd ; but these incongruous applications of their Biblical learning, are perhaps among the best proofs of the deeply rooted and inveterate habit of infusing the fruit of their Scriptural studies into all their productions, the evidences of which pervade the entire body of mediæval literature.

It cannot be deemed singular that this practice should have thus universally prevailed, if we consider how warmly both Monks and Clergy expressed themselves in praise of scriptural learning, and how zealously they addressed themselves to the task of studying and commenting upon the sacred writings. "Nothing is pleasanter," says Trithemius, "nothing more delightful than reading. I have passed nights without sleep studying the Scriptures, and omitted to take my meals in order to save time for reading;"[2] Ruthard, head of the school in the Monastery of Hirschau, refusing the see of Halberstadt which was offered him by the Emperor, said, "Let it be given to one worthy of it; I hesitate not to prefer the monastic quiet, and the studying of the Scriptures, to all the honours and riches of the world;"[3] the Abbess Hilda "obliged those who were under her direction to divide their time between reading the Holy Scriptures and exercising themselves in works of justice, that many might be there found fit for ecclesiastical duties, and qualified to serve at the altar;"[4] Beda says of himself, "When I was seven years old, I was given to be educated to the most holy Abbot Benedict, and then to Ceolfrid; and thenceforth my whole time was spent in meditating on the Scriptures, and observing the regular discipline, and teaching in the Church, and I found it sweet to be always either learning, or teaching, or writing;"[5] St. Pachomius "expounded to his disciples the sacred Scriptures, and desired them to propound to him their difficulties, that he might offer his solution of them;"[6] and in truth the entire religious literature of the Middle Ages may be characterised as one harmonized chorus, in praise of such admirable studies, fruitful of eternal benefits to the student and to the entire family of mankind. The greater portion of the works which the Monks have transmitted to posterity consists of commentaries on various portions of the Sacred Writings; taking our own Beda, than whom few men ever more justly merited the title of "the venerable," as an example: a glorious one it is true,

[2] Trithemius Nepiach. ap Eccard. 11.   [3] Gerbert Hist. Nigr. Silv. i. 123.   [4] Beda Eccles. Hist. l. iv. c. 23.   [5] Smith's Beda. Vit. St. Pachom. 26, 37, 63.

but still an example : we find, that of the one hundred and thirty-nine works from his pen, printed in the Cologne edition of his writings, sixty-four consist entirely of biblical commentary, embracing illustrations of almost every portion of the Inspired Volume ; and among the mediæval MSS. preserved in various libraries, we find, in vast abundance, commentaries on the Scriptures. Nor should we forget that very many of those who did not write professed commentaries employed themselves in composing sermons and homilies which displayed profound biblical learning ; while others engaged in undertakings which required for their completion a yet more intimate acquaintance with the sacred writings. Some devoted themselves to the critical emendation of the text of Scripture ; thus one of the earliest labours which Alcuin undertook, was the revision of the Epistles and Gospels for the year, into which errors of punctuation had crept in the course of multiplied transcriptions, after which he pursued the same course with regard to the whole of the Old and New Testaments, and forwarded a copy of the result of his labours to Charlemagne, in the year 800, on the occasion of his coronation at Rome.[7] Others composed Harmonies and Concordances, some of which still remain, and the existence of which in those ages must be accepted as evidence of an advanced state of scriptural knowledge :, thus in the British Museum are preserved two ancient harmonies of the Gospels, one of which, in French, belonged to Canute ; in the abbey of Morbac Martene found, in 1716, " two beautiful volumes, containing a concordance of the Gospels, nearly a thousand years old ;"[8] at St Jean de Vigorres and other places he found Bibles with concordances, and many of these are

---

[7] Alcuin Op. 154, 258.   [8] Martene, Voy. Litt. (1717) ii. 138.

preserved in various libraries.   In truth, we gain a very just idea of the extent and character of the studies pursued by the Monks, from the account which Beda has left us of his own daily avocations, where he says, " I passed all the time of my life in the retirement of the Monastery, and gave all my labour to the meditation of the Scriptures, the observance of regular discipline, and the daily care of singing in the Church.   From the time of my receiving the order of priesthood until the fifty-ninth year of my age, I have employed myself in briefly noting, from the works of the venerable fathers, those things in the Holy Scriptures most suited to the necessities of me and mine, and adding something to the form of their sense and interpretation."[9] He was, indeed, a splendid example of monastic diligence ; but he differed from his brethren only in the magnitude, and by no means in the nature of his labours.

The Monks, then, it must be conceded, possessed, read, and studied the Sacred Writings.   But did they exert themselves in multiplying copies of the Scriptures, and thus placing within the reach of others, the treasure for which, in their own persons, they manifested so high an appreciation ?   The question is an important one, and by no means difficult of solution.

In the turbulent eras of warlike contention, when so vast a number of books perished in the destruction of the Monasteries, which fell into the hands of the invaders, the MSS. of the Scriptures were exposed to a special peril, yet greater than that which threatened every other class of literary productions.   Our forefathers, anxious to manifest, by every means within their power, their deep and fervent reverence for the Sacred Volume, spared no expense

[9] Smith's Beda, 222.

in the adornment of their copies of the Scripture, with all
the gorgeousness which the most lavish expenditure could
attain; but the means thus employed to give token of
their veneration, increased materially the danger of the
destruction of these precious volumes, and we meet with
frequent instances of the carrying away of copies of the Scriptures by the invaders as the richest portion of their spoil. In
France alone we find recorded three hundred and fifty-one
instances of the destruction of Monasteries in war; can
we wonder, then, that when single copies of the Gospels
were so richly adorned with gold and jewels, as to weigh
seventeen pounds,[1] and others were so gorgeously encased,
that upwards of twenty pounds of gold were used in the
construction of their coverings, as in the copy of the
Gospels in the chapel which King Ina built at Glastonbury,[2] these books were among the first prizes sought for
by the cupidity of the assailants? Great, therefore, as
has been the general destruction of mediæval MSS., there
can be no question that MSS. of the Scriptures have been,
above all others, specially subject to demolition.

Nevertheless, a very large number of these still remain
in preservation. We find them in considerable abundance
in public libraries and private collections; and among the
MSS. in the continental Monasteries the ancient copies of
the Scriptures were still in existence before the French
Revolution of 1793, cherished as their most precious treasures. Even in cases in which time, and war, and fire,
and other causes of destruction, had swept away the ancient libraries, leaving only a few fragments to tell of their
former opulence, we find that the MSS. of the Scriptures were still scrupulously preserved, and yet remained

[1] Conc. vii. 1090.   [2] Guil. Malms. ap. Gale. Scr. xv. 311.

under the same roofs beneath which they had so long reposed. The literary journies of Mabillon and Martene brought to light many such interesting instances, interesting not only from the evidence which they afford of the ancient abundance of the Scriptures, but also from the illustration which they present of the reverence and affection which the Monks ever manifested for the sacred writings. Thus Martene tells us that at Hautvilliers " there remains only a copy of the Gospels, of surpassing beauty, written in letters of gold, of the time of Archbishop Ebon ;"[3] at St. Riquier he found only two MSS., one of which was a copy of the Gospels ;[4] at St. Medard he says, " of all its ancient treasures there remains only a copy of the Gospels ;"[5] at Malmudi, " of all its ancient monuments they have saved only five or six MSS., of which the principal is a Bible in two volumes ;"[6] at La Val Dieu, he " found only one MS., a Bible of considerable beauty ;"[7] at the Abbey of Eisterbach, " all its ancient MSS. having been dispersed by war," he " found there only a Bible ;"[8] at Eptermac, " in consequence of the great revolutions which have taken place," he found only five MSS., of which two were copies of the Gospels ;[9] at Grimberg, " the library having been burnt by the sectaries, all the MSS. were consumed, and there remain only two Bibles, and the ancient synodal statutes of the Church of Cambray ;"[1] at St. Vincent, at Metz, the Monastery having suffered from repeated fires, he " found among the few MSS. which remain, a beautiful copy of the Gospels ;"[2] at Stavelo, " the different convulsions

---

[3] Mart. Voy. Litt. (1717) ii. 78.   [4] Ibid. 175.   [5] Ibid. (1724) 17.   [6] Ibid. 171.   [7] Ibid. 199.   [8] Ibid. 270.   [9] Ibid. 297.   [1] Ibid. 112.   [2] Ibid. (1717) ii. 112.

which have visited it, have greatly diminished the number
of MSS., but there remains, among others, a very fine
Bible, in two volumes;"[3] and in numerous similar instances
the Bible was one of the very few books which had escaped the ravages of warfare. Even in the solitary example which Martene records of the exhibition, by the
Monks, of a want of due appreciation of the value of
works of general literature, the Bible was still preserved
with scrupulous and reverent care;[4] and in all cases they
seem to have clung to this as their most precious possession, amid the convulsions which engulfed their Monasteries in destruction.

That the various books of Scripture, but especially the
Gospels and the Epistles, were copied very frequently, and
multiplied very widely, there cannot be the slightest doubt.
We have already seen that each Priest was compelled to
possess copies of the Gospels, the Epistles, and the Psalms,
before he could be ordained; and, as the Monks were the
only copyists, the supply of all the copies thus required
would have afforded them considerable employment, even
if none had been needed by the monastic libraries; but,
if we take these into account, we shall perceive that the
fruits of their diligence afford an ample demonstration of
their unwearying industry. But we are not compelled to
rest satisfied with such inferential evidence; ample direct
testimony exists in proof of the constant occupation of the
Monks in the transcription of the Sacred Writings. The
learned authors of the Histoire Litteraire de France, in ac-
counting for the neglect of general literature in that country
at the beginning of the eleventh century, especially point
to the diligence with which the Monks devoted themselves

---

[3] Mart. Voy. Litt. (1724) 149.   [4] Ibid. 264.

to the copying of the Scriptures, and of religious works in general, as one of the principal causes of the deficiency of books of a secular character ; " the tenth century," they remark, " had not sufficed to repair the losses which literature had sustained in France, in the destruction of books which resulted from the ravages of the Saracens, the Normans, the Hungarians, and the Bulgarians ; although great efforts had been made to repair these injuries, books were still very rare, and this rarity threw many obstacles in the way of the prosecution of study ; and the Monks, who were then almost the only copyists, began by transcribing those books which they deemed most essential ; the Scriptures, the Liturgies, the writings of the Fathers, and the canons of the Church engaged all their diligence, so that it was not until some time had elapsed, that they could begin to multiply the poets, the orators, and the historians."[5] The records of monastic history afford us many proofs of the zeal with which the Monks, persevering as they were in copying books in general, devoted themselves with special energy to the transcription of the Scriptures, and present innumerable illustrations of the importance which they attached to this department of their admirable labours. Thus, when Olbert was sent from Lobbes to Gembloux, for the purpose of restoring the discipline of that Monastery, he began by setting the Monks to copying and meditating on the Scriptures, and himself wrote out the entire Bible ;[6] Abbot William of Hirschau, among the efforts which he made to sustain the character of his Monastery, and, through its instrumentality, to raise the order of St. Benedict in Germany to

[5] Hist. Litt. de France, vii. 3, n. 3. [6] Mabillon Act. SS Ord. S. Bened. viii. 531.

its ancient splendour, " knowing, as he had learned by laudable experience, that sacred reading is the necessary food of the mind, made twelve of his Monks very excellent writers, and committed to them the office of transcribing the Holy Scriptures ; besides whom there was an indefinite number of scribes who laboured with equal diligence in the copying of other books ;".[7] and it would be easy to multiply to any extent such incidental evidences of the diligence with which the Monks constantly toiled in the multiplication of the Sacred Writings. The utmost care, too, was taken to secure the accuracy of these copies of the Scriptures. We have already noted the exertions of Alcuin in correcting the punctuation, and restoring the text of the Bible, where these had been corrupted by the errors of copyists ; Alberic, Abbot of Citeaux, caused a Bible to be written in six volumes, and, with the assistance of learned Jews, collated it with Hebrew MSS ;[8] and the inscription in the great Bible at Clugni, written by the Monk Albert, attests the care which was exercised in the collation of MSS. of the Scriptures, and admirably displays the spirit in which such labours were undertaken. " This book was written by a certain Monk of Clugni, previously of Treves, named Albert, by the order and at the expense of the Lord Pontius, the venerable Abbot, Peter being also at that time Librarian, and providing, according to his office, all things necessary with joy and diligence. Moreover the aforesaid Monk, associating with himself a certain religious brother named Opizo, read through this book with great diligence, that he might improve it on the authority of other books, and twice he corrected it. Therefore the brother Albert, a sinner, prostrating himself at the

Chron. Hirsaug. i. 2   [8] Gallia Christiana, iv. 984.

feet of the seniors of Clugni, humbly entreats that they
supplicate God to grant to himself, and to his father, forgiveness of their sins."[9]   And it must be remarked that
we meet with frequent notices of individual labour in the
copying of the whole, or separate portions of the Bible,
which are generally spoken of in a manner which shows
that they were very far from being unusual, and from
which we derive a very striking view of the results which
must have been achieved by monastic diligence.   Thus
the anonymous Monk of Ratisbon tells us that, besides
being occupied in the task of instruction, he wrote out
with his own hand, not only two books of his own composition, but also three copies of the Gospels, two of the
Epistles and Gospels, and twenty Missals ;[1] a Monk of the
Abbey of Morigni says, " I have to the best of my ability
corrected and accentuated the entire Bible, from Genesis to
the last Epistle of St. Paul ;"[2] Gerhard, of Monte Sereno,
though suffering from a defect in his sight, wrote out six
Missals, a Plenarius, that is to say a volume containing the
whole of the Old and New Testaments,[3] and a Lectionary,
which contained the Epistles and Gospels for the year ;[4]
" Harduin, who lived in a remote cell of the Martyr Sa-
turninus, built by the blessed Wandregisilius, at Fontanelle, wrote with his own hand four volumes of the
Evangelists in Roman letters, one volume of St. Paul's
Epistles, one of readings from the Gospels, and one of

---

[9] Chron. Clun. ap. Bib. Clun. 1645.   [1] Mabillon Vet. Analect. 119.   [2] Chron. Maurin. ap. Duchesne. iv.   [3] This is
the signification assigned to the term *Plenarius*, in the life of Olbert
of Gembloux, as printed by Mabillon.   " Plenarium, vetus et novum
Testamentum continentem, in uno volumine transcripsit," Mabillon
Act. SS. Ord. S. Bened, viii. 531.   [4] Chron. Mont. Sereni.

the Psalms with the Ambrosian Hymns," in addition to many other books ;[5] Godfrey, of the Monastery of St. Martin, at Tournay, copied, among others, the Book of Proverbs, the whole of the Prophets, the Acts of the Apostles, the Canonical Epistles, and the four Gospels ;[6] Alufus, of the same Monastery, wrote out all the passages of the Old and New Testaments which had been expounded by St. Gregory ;[7] and a vast number of Monks were equally distinguished for the zeal with which they devoted themselves to the same pursuits. Some examples are especially remarkable, as that of the Monk Othlonus, of St. Emmeran, who copied, after he had entered that Monastery, seventy-six volumes, in addition to a multitude of Sermons, Tracts, and Epistles, and transcribed, among others, three copies of the four Gospels, two of the Epistles and Gospels for the year, four service books for Matins, and nineteen Missals ;[8] and the Nun Diemudis of Wessobrunn, who wrote out with her own hand two entire Bibles, one copy of the four Gospels, one of the Epistles, one of the Epistles and Gospels, and three Missals, each containing the Epistles and Gospels for the entire year, among the forty-three volumes which were produced by her indefatigable exertions.[9]

Still, it has been averred that, however much they may have read and studied, and copied the Scriptures for themselves, the Monks and Priests of the Middle Ages did not allow them to become accessible to the laity, or suffer the

---

[5] Chron. Fontan. ap. Dach. Spicileg. iii. [6] Heriman Narrat. Rest. Abb. S. Mart. Torn. § 76, ap. Dach. Spicileg. ii. 912.

[7] Heriman ap. Dach. Spicileg. ii. [8] Mabillon Annal. Ord. S. Bened. iv. 570. [9] Pez Diss. Isagog. ap. Martene Thes. Anecdot. Noviss. i. 20.

people to acquire a knowledge of their contents.   If this be true, it is indeed a grave imputation on their memory, and a grievous blot on the character of the Middle Ages ; it is essential, therefore, that we should inquire whether this assertion is sustained by the evidence of history.

Unquestionably, in those ages, Bibles, or portions of the Scriptures, were not found in the hands of the laity in the same profusion as at the present day ; but we need not have recourse to the supposition that the Church exercised Her influence to hinder the diffusion of the Scriptures, in order to account for a state of things, the existence of which it is not pretended for a moment to deny.   The circumstances of the age, the nature of the means by which books were multiplied, the comparative slowness with which they could be produced, and the absence of any cheap material, before the invention of paper, upon which they could be copied,[1] sufficiently account for this result, and preclude the necessity of seeking for any other explanation.   The Monks could not perform impossibilities ; zealous and indefatigable as they were, they could not confer upon their age the facilities which have resulted from the inventions of more modern days; the utmost that could rationally be expected of them is, that they should do all in their power to develope and employ the means actually within their reach for the diffusion of the Sacred Writings ; and if they did this, they deserve our earnest commendation.

To the assertion which has been constantly reiterated,

---

[1] The importance of this latter consideration is evident from the fact that of the £218 which a copy of the Catholic Canon of Scripture on parchment would cost at the present day, £85 would be the price of the parchment alone.

that the Church, in those ages, interposed obstacles to the free circulation of the Scriptures, and endeavoured, by the exercise of Her authority, to prevent the access of the laity to the Sacred Volume, the records of authentic history present the most emphatic contradiction. The annals of the Middle Ages exhibit not a single instance in which the word of God was treated by the Church, otherwise than with fervent and affectionate veneration ; while, on the other hand, they afford innumerable examples of the loving reverence with which She guarded and preserved that sacred treasure amid the convulsions of war, and snatched it from destruction in the crash of empires ; we seek in vain, in the records of mediæval centuries, for any act of the Church, in Her councils, tending, even indirectly, to prevent or impede the reading and diffusion of authentic versions of the unmutilated Scriptures ; but we cannot open a volume of the Chronicles in which the diligence of monastic historians has preserved the narrative of the deeds of our forefathers, without meeting with perpetual proofs of the reverence with which the Inspired Volume was regarded by our ancestors, and the scrupulous care which they exercised to preserve it from injury, and to indicate, by every external manifestation, their homage for this sacred gift of God to man. Those, indeed, who impute to the Church a contrary conduct, not only disregard entirely the truth of history, but charge Her with an inconsistency wholly inconceivable in its absurdity. If She had entertained this bitter enmity against the Bible—if She had so earnestly desired to prevent its contents from coming to the knowledge of the people—is it possible to imagine that She would have exerted herself as She did, in procuring the multiplication of copies of the Scriptures ?

that She would have compelled each member of Her Priest-hood to possess the most material portions of them for himself? that She would have inculcated upon them, in Her canons, as a sacred duty, the constant and diligent study of their contents ? that She would have given honour and dignity to those who peculiarly distinguished themselves by Scriptural knowledge ?_and that She would have manifested as She did, Her earnest desire to preserve the Bible [from injury, and to display Her deep and fervent reverence for the Sacred Volume ? For a long period the Scriptures lay entirely in Her power : by Her the several books of the New Testament were collected from their dispersion, and first united into a single volume; by Her the whole Bible was rendered from the original languages into the Latin, then the current tongue of Christendom. In later ages the inspired writings still remained subject to Her sole in-fluence : the Monks were the only copyists; in Monas-teries and Churches were almost the only libraries; the Priests and the Religious had in their hands the control of the multiplication, and the custody of a vast proportion of the existing copies of the Scriptures. If the Church had felt this strong desire, which has been imputed to Her by Her enemies, to bury the Bible in oblivion, and to seclude it from the knowledge of mankind, would She have pre-served it with such careful reverence, and thrust it, as it were, into the hands of all who were to minister Her sacred ordinances ? Would Her services have been filled with passages from the Scriptures ? the homilies of Her divines crowded with Scriptural quotations? the lives of Her Saints engaged in Scriptural commentary ? the schools in Her Monasteries renowned for their Scripture lectures ? and the days and nights of Her Monks occupied in reading and studying the Bible, and meditating on the words of Scripture ?   All these things, attested as they are by the evidence of history, are wholly inconsistent with a desire to conceal the Bible from mankind.

It is not denied that in later ages the Church saw fit to entrust a supervisory authority to Her Priesthood, empowering them to restrict the perusal, by the laity, of versions of the Scriptures in the vulgar tongues, when they deemed that such a step was rendered imperative by a regard for their spiritual welfare ; but it is to be observed that this measure was never adopted until after the growth of circumstances which appeared to indicate the necessity of stringent action ; for it was not until versions of the Bible, held by the Church to be mutilated and spurious, had issued from the press and become disseminated among the people, and false teachers, perverting the sense of Holy Writ, had sought to mislead the simple, by the citation of corrupted texts of their defective Scriptures in maintenance of their new opinions, that the Church put forth the strong arm of Her authority for the protection of Her children, and the preservation of the pure Faith which She had received as Her rich inheritance, to be conserved for the benefit of mankind.   That it was simply for the protection of the ignorant that this prerogative was committed to Her pastors, is sufficiently evident from the consideration that it was to the unlettered only, that the contemplated prohibition could ever by possibility apply.   To every man of education, the Latin is, and ever has been, a familiar tongue ; to such, the Vulgate is no sealed book by reason of its language ; and upon the free perusal by the laity of the Latin Scriptures there has never been, in any age or in any country, even the shadow of a restriction imposed by the authority of the Church. If She had been actuated by the fear which is imputed to Her by Her enemies, that the reading of the Bible would lead to the subversion of Her authority, by bringing to the knowledge of men truths fatal to the maintenance of Her dominion, surely Her precautions would have been directed against the educated rather than the unlettered ; if She could be content to see the scholar freely perusing every syllable of God's word, and felt the while no fear of the overthrow of Her power, it is scarcely probable that She would dread from the simple what She feared not from the learned, or deem that the ignorant peasant would detect the fatal flaw which had escaped the penetration of the philosopher. The fact that the reading of the Scriptures in Latin, still the learned language of the world, has never been subjected to the smallest limitation, affords the best illustration of the motives which actuated the Church when, in the sixteenth century, She empowered her Pastors to guard the unlettered from perversion, by restraining them, under special circumstances, from the perusal of the Scriptures in the vulgar tongues ; but in the centuries embraced within the limits of our inquiry, such restrictions had no existence, simply because the evils which made them necessary invaded not the peace of the mediæval world. True, the enemy of mankind was never wholly idle ; a few scattered heresiarchs troubled, from time to time, the well-being of society ; but it was not until a later age that the malady, hitherto confined to isolated districts, swelled into an epidemic, and desolated entire nations with its fearful scourge.

Ample evidence remains to us of the zeal with which

the Church in the Middle Ages sought to increase the facilities for the access of the laity to the Scriptures. Even in the earliest periods we meet with notices of translations of numerous portions of the Inspired Writings into the various modern languages; and many copies of these different versions still remain in preservation. In 807, Charlemagne caused the whole Bible to be translated into FRENCH;[2] in 820, Otfrid, a Benedictine Monk, composed in the same language a harmony of the Four Gospels;[3] in the same century, a version of the Psalms in French was made by order of Louis le Debonnaire;[4] in the twelfth century, translations of the Four Gospels, the Epistles of St. Paul, the Psalms, the Book of Job, and some other portions of the Bible, were made in the diocese of Metz;[5] in the fourteenth century, Jean de Vignay translated the Epistles and Gospels in the Missal, at the request of Jeanne de Bourgogne, Queen of Philip of France; and at a shortly subsequent period, Raoul de Praelles, at the command of Charles V. of France, made a French version of a portion of the Bible, from the commencement of Genesis to the end of the Book of Proverbs, a copy of which is preserved among the Lansdowne MSS. in the British Museum.[6] In the Bibliotheque du Roi, at Paris, are several old French versions of the Scriptures; of the twelfth century, three copies of the Psalms, and of the thirteenth and fourteenth centuries, nearly sixty different versions, comprising translations of the entire Bible, of the New Testament, of the Four Gospels, of the Epistles of St. Paul,

[2] Usserius. De Script. et. sacr. vernac. 111.   [3] Mabillon Annal. Ord. S. Bened. iii. 128. Hist. Lit. de Fr. vi. 73.   [4] Duchesne Receuil des Historiens de France, ii. 226.   [5] Hist. Lit. de Fr.— Epist. Innoc. III. ii. 432. 435.   [6] Lansd. MSS. 1175.

of the Apocalypse, of the Psalms, and of the Books of
Chronicles, Job, Esdras, and the greater and lesser Prophets ;[7] among the Cotton. MSS. in the British Museum,
we find a copy of the Gospels in French verse,[8] and a
Harmony of the Gospels which belonged to Canute ;[9] and
among the Harleian MSS. in the same collection, are two
copies of a French translation of a portion of the Bible,
from Genesis to the end of the Psalms,[1] and five French
versions of the Psalms, two of which are accompanied by
English translations.[2] Versions in ANGLO SAXON were
made by various hands. King Alfred is said, by the author
of the Historia Eliensis, to have translated the whole Bible;
Aldhelm translated the Psalms ; Ælfric rendered the
first seven Books of the Old Testament, and part of Job ;
and Beda translated the whole of the Old and New Testament, having completed his task with the last verse of
the Gospel of St. John but a few moments before he
expired.[3] In addition to this, many other versions were
made, of which copies yet remain in preservation. Among
the Cotton. MSS. in the British Museum, we find a copy
of the Book of Proverbs in Latin, with an interlinear
Anglo-Saxon translation,[4] a copy of the Book of Genesis
in Anglo-Saxon, with extracts from the other books of
Moses, and from Joshua,[5] a book of Precepts extracted
from the Proverbs,[6] and a Harmony of the Four Gospels ;[7]
among the Harleian MSS. we find the Four Gospels in

[7] M. P. Paris.　Manuscrits de la Bibl. du Roi. Tom. i. and ii.

[8] Cott. MSS. Domitian, xi. 87.　　[9] Cott. MSS. Caligula, A. vii. 5.

[1] Harl. MSS. No. 110. 116.　　[2] Harl. MSS. No. 273. 1170.
1896. 4070. 4327.　　　　　　　　　[3] Smith's Beda, 793.

[4] Cott. MSS. Vespasian, D vi. 2.　[5] Cott. MSS. Claudius, B. iv.

[6] Cott. MSS. Tiberius, A. iii. 99.　[7] Cott.　MSS.　Vespasian, D.
xxiii. 29.

Anglo-Saxon ;[s] and copies of the Heptateuch, the Psalter, and the Gospels, in the same language abound in various repositories.[9]

According to the opinion of Dr. Johnson, the English language assumed a distinctive form about the middle of the twelfth century ; in the thirteenth century a version of the whole Bible was made in ENGLISH, of which copies now exist in the libraries of the Bodleian, of Christ Church, and of Queen's College, Oxford; in the fourteenth century, John de Trevisa translated anew the entire Bible into the same language. Among the Cotton. MSS. we find an English Bible of the fifteenth century ;[1] and among the Harleian MSS. are copies of the Books of Job and Tobias, in English, of the fourteenth century,[2] and in the same language two copies of the Psalms,[3] one of a portion of the Old Testament,[4] one of the Acts of the Apostles and the Canonical Epistles,[5] and seven copies of the New Testament.[6] At Milan, in the Bibliotheca Ambrosiana, are several GAELIC interlinear translations of various portions of Scripture, of which one of the most remarkable is a copy of the Psalms, with the Commentary of St. Jerome, of the seventh century. Ernesti states that the New Testament was translated into the GOTHIC language by Ulphilas, bishop of the Goths, in the fourth century ; and in the public library of the University of Upsal, is preserved a copy of the Gospels, written upon vellum, in Gothic characters of gold and silver, supposed to be at least a thousand years old. About 980, Notker Labeo

---

[s] Harl. MSS. No. 3449. MSS. 64. 67. 76. 98. 152. 211.   [9] Wanley Cat. of Anglo-Saxon   [1] Cott. MSS. Claudius, E. 2.

[2] Harl. MSS. No. 3903.   [3] Ibid. 1770. 1896.   [4] Ibid. 2249.

[5] Ibid. 327.   [6] Ibid. 272. 940. 1212. 4027. 4890. 5017. 6333.

translated the Book of Job and the Psalms into the GER-MAN.[7] In the eleventh century, William of Bamberg, a Monk of Fulda, made a version of the book of Canticles in Teutonic prose ;[8] and in the Imperial Library at Volks-garten, is a German Bible, in six volumes, translated for the emperor Wenceslaus, in the fourteenth century. In the library of the cathedral at Florence, is a MS. of forty-two leaves, containing the first twelve chapters of the Gospel of St. Luke, in the ancient ITALIAN version of the sixth century ; in the Japanese Palace, at Dresden, is a Bible in BOHEMIAN, of the fourteenth century ; and Erpe-nius published the ARABIC New Testament from a MS. written in the year 1342. The earliest ARMENIAN version of the Scriptures was made by Miesrob, in the fourth century; and when, in the thirteenth century, the Churches of the Lesser Armenia and Cilicia submitted to the autho-rity of the Holy See, and Haitho, the King, became a Franciscan Friar, his first act was to prepare a new translation of the entire Bible into the Armenian tongue. A version in SWEDISH was made under the direction of St. Bridget, in the fourteenth century ; one in ICELANDIC was produced in 1297; one in FLEMISH, by Jacobus Merland, in 1210 ; in the latter portion of the fourteenth century, St. Hedwiga, wife of Ladislaus IV., had a trans-lation made of the whole Bible in POLISH, and in the same century, a second version was made in the same language by Jassowitz ; and several translations were made into the RUSSIAN—one of the new Testament in the tenth century, others in the eleventh, twelfth, thirteenth, and fourteenth centuries, and one of the entire Bible in the fifteenth.

[7] Usserius. De Script. et Sacr. Vernac. 126.
[8] Vet. Scr. et Monum. Ampl. Coll. 501.

In the SPANISH there existed several versions of the whole Bible; three in the Catalonian dialect, one produced in the twelfth century, a copy of which is in the Bibliotheque du Roi, at Paris,[9] another nearly as ancient, a copy of which is in the Bibliotheque Colbert,[1] and a third, bearing date 1407, a copy of which is preserved in the same collection;[2] one in the Valencian dialect made in 1405, by Boniface Ferrier, assisted by his brother, St. Vincent Ferrier; and one in the Castilian dialect, prepared by order of Alfonso the Wise, who died in the latter part of the thirteenth century;[3] in addition to which, a translation of the Book of Job and the Canticles was made about the same epoch by Luis de Leon.[4]

It must not be imagined that this brief enumeration comprehends all the versions of the Scriptures in modern languages made in the Middle Ages; a few only have been noticed, the particulars of which have been gathered togther under circumstances most unfavourable to such research; but from the nature of the results thus attained, an estimate may be formed of the conclusions which would be arrived at by more extended investigations. We have here collected notices of translations of the Bible into sixteen modern languages, all made between the fourth and fifteenth centuries; and these must obviously have been made for the use of the laity, since the Scriptures were invariably read by the Monks and Clergy in the Latin, then the universal tongue of learned Christendom. Often, indeed, this purpose was openly avowed. Thus Ælfric avers that he made his translation of the first

---

[9] Bibl. du Roi, cod. 9831. [1] Bibl. Colb. cod. 3821.
[2] Ibid. 181. [3] Mariana l. xiv. c. 17. p. 693.
[4] Bouterweck, Hist. of Span. Lit. 253.

seven books of the Old Testament, and part of Job, into Anglo-Saxon, at the request of Ethelwerd the ealdorman;[5] in the general preface to his translations, he declares that he rendered the Scriptures into the vernacular " for the edification of the simple, who know only that language :"[6] and Otfrid composed his harmony of the Four Gospels in French, in the ninth century, to gratify the wish of a noble lady, who desired him to undertake this labour for the purpose of providing the common people with a manual of sacred reading, which might take the place of the profane songs which then constituted their principal recreation.[7]

But, in truth, they can possess very little knowledge of mediæval history, who are ignorant of the zeal with which the Church inculcated on the laity the prayerful reading of the Scriptures as the surest aid to spiritual perfection. Aldhelm, writing to one of his former pupils, says, " To Ethelwald, my most beloved son and disciple, Aldhelm, the last of the servants of God, greeting. When you were with me I used to admonish you in words ; now that you are absent, I advise you by letter, presuming on that paternal authority over you with which God hath invested me, for truly can I say, in the words of the apostle ' it is the charity of Christ that urgeth me.' Let not then, my beloved, young though you are, the vain pleasures of the world enslave you, such as the custom of daily banquetings, indulgence in long and immoderate entertainments, continued riding and racing, or the loathful pursuit of sensual gratifications. Bear always in mind the text, ' Youth and pleasure are vain ;' never suffer yourself to be made

[5] Turner, Hist. of Anglo-Saxons, iii. 400.　　　[6] MSS. Camb. Wanley, 153.　　　[7] Mabillon. Annal. Ord. S. Bened. iii. 128.

a slave to the love of money, or of secular glory, or of that vain ostentation which is so hateful to God, remembering always the words of Christ, 'what profiteth it a man if he gain the whole world, but lose his own soul? For the Son of Man will come in His glory and that of His angels, and will render to every man according to his works.' Rather, my beloved, devote your time to the reading of the Scriptures and to holy prayer; and if, in addition, you wish to acquire some knowledge of secular learning, do so, but only with this view, that, since the meaning of every, or of almost every part of the divine law dependeth on the rules of grammar, you may be the better able to dive into the deep and sacred signification of the text, by your more perfect acquaintance with the forms in which it is expressed;"[1] St. Jerome says, "Cultivate with diligent affection a knowledge of the Scriptures, and you will easily overcome the lusts of the flesh;"[2] "See to it," says Geoffrey, sub-prior of St. Barbara, in Normandy, "that in your armoury of defence, which is your Library, that which is the great defence of all the other defences, be not wanting. That defence is the Holy Bible, wherein is contained the right rule of life and manners. There each sex and every age finds what is profitable; there spiritual infancy finds that whereby it may grow, youth that which may strengthen it, age that which may support it; a blessed hand which ministers to all, whereby all may be saved;"[3] and the precepts of Alcuin are precisely similar, " write the Gospels in your heart;"[4] " read diligently, I beseech you, the Gospel of Christ;"[5] " be studious in

[1] Anglia Sacra. ii. 5.   [2] St. Hieron. Epist. ad Rustic.
[3] Mart. Thes. Nov. Anecdot. i. 509.   [4] Alcuin Op. 1635.
[5] Ibid. 1561.

D

reading the Sacred Scriptures ;"[6] " I wish the four Gospels, instead of the twelve Æneids, filled your breast ;"[7] " the reading of the Sacred Books is necessary ;"[8] " study Christ as foretold in the books of the Prophets, and as exhibited in the Gospels, and when you find Him do not lose Him, but introduce Him into the home of thy heart, and make Him the ruler of thy life.''[9] These were the precepts inculcated by him in his writings, and not by him alone, but by a vast number of the monastic writers of the Middle Ages.

Various means were employed to facilitate the observance of the advice thus strenuously enforced. Some of the Monks employed themselves in extracting from the Scriptures various passages applicable to particular circumstances, and thus forming manuals of prayer and meditation for the laity. When the Danes, in the reign of Ethelred, renewed their predatory excursions into England, Ælfric, who had already translated portions of the Scriptures, made a selection from Holy Writ of examples in which prayer and repentance had appeased the wrath of God, and stated, in the proem, that he had collected these together for the use of his countrymen, that they might be led to seek the aid of Heaven in their endeavours to resist their enemies ;[1] and John, Abbot of Fescamp, composed for the Empress Agnes a book of devotions, consisting of selections from the Sacred Writings appropriate to her condition in life, saying in the dedication, " Long since, imperial lady, you were pleased to signify your desire that I should select from the Holy Scriptures some short and plain discourses, from which you might learn, according to

---

[6] Alcuin Op. 1583.   [7] Ibid. 1549.   [9] Ibid. 1546.
[8] Ibid. 1637.   [1] Ælfric de Vet. Test. 22—23.

your order, a rule of good life ; for every rank, age, and sex has its own peculiar instruction for conduct in the Sacred Books, so that each' one, walking rightly in the vocation in which he is called, may arrive at the Kingdom in which there are many mansions. Receive therefore, O excellent soul, noble example of holy widowhood, accept with a watchful mind this little work which you desired, and which, by the grace of Christ, I have compiled, which you will find to contain sweet words of heavenly contemplation. These are to be reverently read and meditated on with due fear, lest, coming to them in a cold and undevout frame of mind, you be judged guilty of rashness. From this you will understand that this book is chiefly intended for the use of those who do not suffer their minds to be darkened with carnal desires and worldly lusts ; and when these things are read with tears and great devotion, then the meek reader tastes with the palate of his heart the inward sweetness which is hidden in them. If it be thus, or rather since it is thus, let not the proud and fastidious mind dare to meddle with the secret and sublime words of the divine oracles, lest it fall into error ; for with blind eyes it cannot see the light. Hence it is that many rush, through heresy, into the abyss of eternal damnation, drawing down others along with them to death ; for the mysteries of Holy Scripture, which are rooted in heaven, are not fully intelligible to any even of the perfect in this world ; but they who, being wise with the wisdom of God, bring forth the fruit of profound humility, understand so much as is revealed to them by the Holy Spirit. Therefore read these things often, and especially when you feel your mind inspired by heavenly desire, for right is it that you, whose practice in

active life is so good, should take the wings of contemplation, and, soaring upward, should drink of the fountain
of eternal sweetness, saying with the Prophet, ' With Thee
is the fountain of life, and in Thy light we shall see light;
my soul hath thirsted for God, the living fountain.   Lord,
I have loved the beauty of Thy house, and the place of
the habitation of Thy glory.' "[a]

The Psalms formed the general manual of private devotion.   Beda arranged a Psalter, consisting of verses the
meaning of which was obvious, or their application general,
or which were calculated to teach great truths, or generate
pious sentiments ;[4] Alcuin composed another, by collecting
together, in eight sub-divisions, all Psalms having a
similar application, prefixing to each a title explanatory
of its object, and adding prayers suited to different occasions ;[5] and copies are still in existence of a poem of four
hundred and eighty lines, written in the eleventh century,
which contained an abridgment of the historical portions
of the Old Testament, with the addition of moral reflections,
suggested by the various events which it recorded, for
laic edification.

But it must not be imagined that the laity were compelled to content themselves with reading such *excerpta*
from the Scriptures ; had this been so, useless indeed
would have been the labours so zealously and widely
undertaken to make translations of the entire Bible into
the vulgar tongues of all European nations From the
causes which have been already noted, the possession
of Bibles by laymen was of course not so usual then
as at the present day ; but it was evidently very far
from being uncommon in mediæval centuries.   Copies

[a] Mabillon Annal. Ord. St. Bened. i. 133.   [4] Alcuin Op. i. 169.
[5] Ibid. ii. 21.

of the Scriptures were frequently given by laymen to Churches and Monasteries ; the records of their history are filled with memorials of such donations ; and many of those who were thus munificent to the establishments of learning and religion, at the same time preserved copies of the Inspired Volume in their own families, following the example of Everhard, Count of Friuli, in the ninth century, who, having already during his life given a Bible to a Monastery which he had founded at Cisoing,[6] left to his children at his death a Bible and four copies of the Gospels, one of which was bound in silver, another in ivory, and a third in gold.[7] Those whose worldly position was least favourable to the acquisition of such treasures often succeeded in obtaining them ; of St. Edmund it is recorded, that while at College, where he was emphatically a poor scholar, being the son of very humble parents, he possessed a Psalter and a glossed copy of the Twelve Prophets ; and those who were less fortunate, found in the Monastic Libraries, which were freely accessible to all, abundant facilities for pursuing their study of the Scriptures.

There appears, too, to have been no deficiency of other Bibles, equally within the reach of the laity, the placing of which in public situations, for the use of the people, was regarded as a most meritorious work of charity. Thus Thomas de Farnylaw, Chancellor of the Church at York, bequeathed at his death, in 1378, a Bible and Concordance to the Church of St. Nicholas at Newcastle, " there to be chained for common use, for the benefit of his soul ;"[8] Ceolfrith, Abbot of Wearmouth, having caused three copies to be made of the entire Bible, sent one as a present to

[6] Dach. Spicileg. ii. 879.   [7] Ibid. 877.   [8] Register of Wills at York.

the Pope, and placed the others in two different Churches,
" to the end," says Beda, " that all who desired to read
any chapter in either Testament might be able at once to
find what they desired ;"⁹ and part of the penance which
St. Dunstan imposed upon King Edgar for his abduction
of Wulfrith from the Convent at Wilton, was, that he
should promulgate a code of laws for the more impartial
administration of justice, and that he should, at his own
expense, transmit to every county in his kingdom copies
of the Holy Scriptures, for the instruction of the people.¹

The Monks exerted themselves most actively to induce
the laity to read the Sacred Writings. At the Monasteries
of St. Pachomius, where both infants and adults were
educated, all who received instruction were obliged to
learn by heart at least the New Testament and the
Psalms ;² and other Monastic teachers exacted similar observances. Those who could not read for themselves, had
the Scriptures read for them by the Monks and Clergy.
The Canons of Ælfric ordain that " The Priest shall on
Sundays and Festivals explain the Gospel in English to the
people ;"³ among the questions the Bishop was to ask
throughout his diocese, with a view to ascertaining the
capacity of each Priest to discharge his duties, he was to
inquire " whether he could well expound the Epistles and
Gospels ?"⁴ and the Monks of all orders followed the example of the first disciples of St. Pachomius, who, in
the Church which they built for the use of the poor, every
week catechised them, and read to them the Scriptures.⁵

While these means were diligently employed for the

---

⁹ Vit. Ceolfr. in App. Bed. Op. Min. 325.   ¹ Osbern Vit. St.
Dunstan.   ² Reg. St. Pachom. c. 139, 140.   ³ Wilkins Conc.
i. 250.   ⁴ Regino Prumiensis.   ⁵ Vit. St. Pachom. 19.

benefit of the humble, who, from the nature of their
position, were obliged to content themselves with merely
reading the Bible, ample facilities were afforded to those
who desired to enter more deeply into the study of the
Sacred Writings. In the Monastic Schools, which existed
in such vast abundance, the Scriptures constituted invariably a prominent branch of study ; and the Universities were equally renowned for the zeal with which these
admirable pursuits were prosecuted within their walls.
Some Monasteries attained a high repute solely on account of the superior character of the expositions of
Holy Writ which were given by their teachers : thus the
school in the Convent at Chelle, near Paris, was resorted
to, in the time of the Merovignians, by hundreds of both
sexes, to listen to the Scriptural lectures of St. Bertilla ;
the Franciscan convent at Paris, where two hundred and
twenty-two youths were educated, and where there were
delivered two Lectures on Theology every morning, and two
on the Scriptures every afternoon,[6] was often resorted to
by as many as seven hundred students at a time, in addition
to those who received regular instruction within its walls ;[7]
and it was from the high renown of the Irish Monasteries
for the admirable perfection of their Scriptural teaching,
that learned men were induced to visit them from every
part of Europe.[8] In all, the study of the Scriptures was
regarded as of supreme importance. "The Monks," says
Trithemius, "taught and explained the whole Sacred
Scriptures and theolgy ; teaching with a certain spiritual
sweetness they delighted, and with delight they moved
and influenced the hearts of all their hearers ;"[9] and the

[6] Wadding. Annal. 1234.   [7] Duchesne. Antiq. des Villes de
France.   [8] Beda, Eccles. Hist. iii. 7.   [9] Trithemius.

history of their Schools amply manifests how diligently they laboured in the discharge of this division of their duty to mankind.

The fact, that the laity attended these Schools in very considerable numbers, is in itself a sufficient proof that they actually availed themselves of the facilities thus offered to them, and zealously engaged in the perusal and study of the Sacred Writings. But we have no lack of evidence of Bible reading among the laity, in the Middle Ages, independently of that which was pursued in the Schools ; and the incidental notices which abound in the annals of mediæval history, clearly show that the practice so urgently inculcated upon them in their youth, was not suffered in after-life to fall into decay. Alcuin, in his letters to Charlemagne, informs him, with expressions of the most intense satisfaction, that the high-born dames, the powerful nobles, and the chivalrous warriors of France, all came to him, that he might resolve for them the difficulties which they had encountered in their reading of the Scriptures; and under that renowned Emperor the study of the Bible became the universal pursuit of those who found favour at his court.[1] Asser relates of King Alfred, that " it was his habit attentively and solicitously to hear the Sacred Scriptures read by his own subjects, or by foreigners when they came to him from abroad," and in the narrative of that Monarch's exile, we find it recorded hat it was his custom, when alone, to be constantly studying the Scriptures ;[2] Odo of Clugni tells us of his father, that " at his table there was always the reading of the Scriptures ;"[3] of Aufridius, a learned layman of the tenth

[1] Alc. Epist. Lebeuf Diss. sur l'etat des Sciences sous Charlemagne. Asser 45.   Ingulf. 26.   Ethel. Abb. 353.
[3] Mabillon Act. SS. Ord. S. Bened. vii. 189.

century, we learn that his conversation was full of re-
ferences to the Sacred Writings ;[4] Beda, addressing King
Ceolwulph in the opening of his history, says, "I cannot
but commend the sincerity and zeal with which you
diligently give ear to hear the words of Holy Scripture ;"[5]
and in narrating the journies of St. Aidan, he informs us
that "all who accompanied him, whether they were Priests
or laymen, passed their time in religious meditation, in
reading the Scriptures, and in learning Psalms." "The
whole Bible," says Sir Thomas More, "was, long before
Wycklyffe's days, by virtuous and well learned men, translated into the English tongue, and by good and godly
people with devotion and soberness, well and reverently
read,"[6] and the assertion of the illustrious martyr is confirmed by the admission of one of the most eminent of
the champions of the Reformation; "It is not much above
one hundred years," says Cranmer, "since Scripture hath
not been accustomed to be read in the vulgar tongue within
this realm; many hundred years before that, it was translated and read in the Saxon's tongue, and when that
language waxed old and out of common usage, because
folks should not lack the fruit of reading it, it was translated
again into the newer language."[7]

The Reformation, vaunted as the agency which first
rendered the Bible accessible to the laity, crowned its
triumph in England by prohibiting the perusal of the
Scriptures by the people; the statute of 33 Hen. VIII. c.
12, enacted that "no women not of gentle or noble birth,
nor journeymen, artificers, or 'prentices, should read the

---

[4] Mabillon Act. SS. Ord. S. Bened. viii. 78.   [5] Beda Eccles.
Hist. i. 1.   [6] Sir T. More, Dialogue concerning Heresies
l. iii. c. 4.   [7] Strype's Cranmer, app. 242.

Bible or the New Testament in English, to themselves or others, openly or privately ;" and the act of 34 Hen. VIII. c. 1, forbade the reading of the Scriptures in public, confined the permission to read them aloud to private families, to those who were of the rank of lords or gentlemen, and limited the liberty of perusing them personally and in secret, to men who were householders, and to females of noble or gentle birth. Such restrictions had no existence under the dominion of the Church ; even Luther pays this just tribute to Her fame, in that remarkable passage in which he delcares that " it was an effect of God's power, that in the Papacy should have remained : in the first place, sacred baptism ; secondly, the text of the Holy Gospel, which it was the custom to read from the pulpit in the vernacular tongue of every nation; thirdly, the sacred forgiveness and absolution of sin, as well privately in confession as in public ; fourthly, the most holy sacrament of the Altar ;"[8] and the true character of Her action is amply illustrated by the evidence which has passed under our consideration.

Such was the state of things during a period in which books could be multiplied only by the slow and laborious process of manual transcription ; when the hand of the Monk was the only engine which could be employed for the production of two copies of the Bible, where but one had been previously in existence ; when, consequently, impediments, almost insurmountable, existed to the complete fulfilment of the pious desire of the Church, to make the Scriptures freely accessible to all classes of mankind. But about the middle of the fifteenth century, an invention arose which removed these ancient obstacles, which made

[8] Luther, de Missa Privata, tom. vi. ed. Jenen. fol 92.

it easy to multiply to any required extent books of all
descriptions, and which, consequently, presented an instrumentality by the agency of which copies of the Bible
might be brought within the reach of many who had previously been compelled to content themselves with using
such MSS. of the Scriptures as were placed in public
situations, for the general benefit of the people.   It is important that we should ascertain what was the action of
the Church under this new phase of circumstances, and
discover whether She manifested the sincerity of Her
desire for the general diffusion of the Sacred Writings by
at once availing Herself of the means which thus came
into existence, for the further promotion of the end which
She had hitherto, under the greatest disadvantages, zealously
and consistently pursued.   That She had, during the period
which we have already reviewed, done all that could have
been expected of Her by the most exacting, has been
clearly demonstrated by facts which admit of no other
possible conclusion; it remains for us to ascertain whether
She was as indefatigable in promoting the printing, as
in encouraging the copying of the Scriptures ; and to this
end we may glance briefly at the period which elapsed
between the invention of printing and the publication of
Luther's German version of the Bible, so often extolled as
the event which first made the Sacred Volume accessible
to mankind.

Directing our attention, in the first place, to editions in
the ancient languages, we find that these were produced
in considerable abundance.   Of editions in the HEBREW
of the entire Old Testament, one appeared in 1488 ; another at Naples, in 1490 ; another in 1494 ; another at
Cologne, before the end of the fifteenth century ; and eight

others between 1500 and 1536 : during the latter period there were also printed fifty editions of separate books of the Hebrew Scriptures. Of editions in the GREEK, there were printed between 1500 and 1536, three of the Old Testament, twelve of the New Testament, three of the Psalms, and four of detached portions of the New Testament. Of editions in the LATIN of the entire Bible, there were printed at Mentz two without dates, as was frequently the case with the earliest printed books, one in 1455, two in 1462, and one in 1472 ; at Strasburg three without dates, and two in 1466 ; at Nuremburg, two in 1475, one in 1477, two in 1478, one in 1479, and seven others before 1500 ; at Cologne, two without dates ; at Basle, one in 1475, another in 1477, and two others before 1500 ; at Paris, one in 1475 ; at Placenza, one in 1475 ; at Vicenza, one in 1476 ; at Naples, one in 1476 ; at Venice, one in 1475, two in 1476, one in 1479, and another in 1487 ; at Ulm, one before 1500 ; at Rome one in 1471 ; at Florence, one before 1500 ; and one hundred and six others between 1500 and 1536 : during the latter period there were also printed in the Latin, sixty-two editions of the New Testament, and one hundred and thirty-three editions of separate portions of the Scriptures.

Turning now to the consideration of the editions which were published of translations of the Bible into various modern languages, the results which reward our investigations are yet more remarkable in their character. Of the entire Bible in the ITALIAN version of Malermi, there was published at Rome an edition in 1471, which appeared under the special patronage of Pope Paul II., and with the sanction of the Inquisition ; at Venice, one in 1471, one in 1475, two in 1477, one in 1481, one in 1484, and one in 1494; and twelve others appeared between 1500 and 1536 : during this latter period there were also issued in Italian, twenty-eight editions of various detached portions of the Sacred Writings.[9] Of the entire Bible in FRENCH, there was published an edition of the version of Guiars de Moulins, in 1478 ; one of the version of Menand in 1484; one of the version of Rely, after- wards Bishop of Angers, in 1487, of which twelve editions appeared at Paris, and four at Lyons, before 1536 ; one of the version of F. Julian Macho and P. Ferget, before the close of the fifteenth century ; and one of the version of Jacques le Fevre, revised by the divines of Louvain, in 1512, of which five editions were printed before 1530. Of the FLEMISH version, made in the thirteenth century, by Jacobus Merland, there appeared, of editions of the entire Bible, one at Cologne, in 1475 ; two at Delft, in 1477 ; one at Goude, in 1479 ; and fifteen others between 1500 and 1536 : during this latter period there were also printed in the Flemish, sixty-four editions of various sepa- rate portions of the Scriptures. In the SPANISH, an edition of the version of the entire Bible in the Valencian dialect, by Ferrier, appeared at Valencia in 1478, under the auspices and supervision of the Inquisition, and was again reprinted in 1515 ; an edition of the Epistles and Gospels in the Castilian dialect, by Ambrose de Montesina, was published in 1512 ; and in addition to these, Le Long

[9] Since the publication of Luther's German Bible, three Italian versions of the Scriptures have appeared: that of Bruccioli, published at Venice in 1532, and nine times reprinted within twenty years ; that of Maruoc- chini, which was produced at Venice in 1538, and was often reprinted ; and that of Martini, Archbishop of Florence, which appeared in 1769, with the express sanction of Pope Pius VII., and has passed through very many editions.

asserts, that almost every province of Spain had a version in its own dialect.[1]   Of the BOHEMIAN version, an edition of the entire Bible was printed at Prague, in 1478, another in 1488, and another in 1489 ; at Cutna, one in 1498 ; at Venice, one in 1506, and another in 1511.   Of the SCLAVONIC version, an edition of the whole Bible appeared at Cracow about the commencement of the sixteenth century.   Of the HUNGARIAN version, an edition of the Four Gospels was printed before 1536.   Of the GERMAN version of the entire Bible, there appeared at Mentz, one edition in 1462, another in 1466, another without note of place, but supposed to have been there printed in

[1] Le Long, Bibl. Sacr. i. 362.   If the publication of the Scriptures in the vernacular was not carried on in Spain at this early period, with as much energy as in other Catholic countries, the Spanish clergy in later times have amply atoned for this by a signal and admirable activity.   The Gospels and Epistles by Ambrose de Montesina were reprinted at Antwerp in 1544, at Barcelona in 1601 and 1608, and at Madrid in 1603 and 1615 ; the Bible, in Castilian, was printed at Ferrara, in 1553, from a version which, as the preface assures us, " Romanæ curiæ placuit plurimum ;" and another version in the same dialect appeared in 1567.   In addition to these, versions of the Scriptures in Spanish were published in 1569 by Cassiodoro di Regna ; in 1602 by Cipriano di Valera ; in 1793 by Don Felipe de St. Miguel ; and in 1794 by Padre Scio, afterwards Bishop of Segovia.   Finally, versions of the New and Old Testament, by Don Francisco Torreo Amat, afterwards Bishop of Barcelona, were issued respectively in 1823 and 1824, the learned translator declaring in his preface that he undertook the preparation of the version by the advice, and at the earnest solicitation of the whole government, ecclesiastical and civil, and that he published it " to promote the splendour of religion, purity of life, and the spiritual good of all the faithful," and the list of subscribers to his version, which received the special approval of the Pope, including seven Archbishops, sixteen Bishops, and a vast multitude of Clergy.   These, it must be observed, were all *separate versions ;* of each version there were printed very many editions.

1467, another in 1470, and another of the version of John Dietemberg, which was issued under the auspices of the Archbishop and Elector of Mentz, in 1534; at Augsburg, two in 1470, one in 1472, another in 1473, two in 1477, one in 1480, another in 1483, another in 1487, another in 1490, another in 1494, another in 1507, another in 1510, another in 1518, and another in 1524; at Wittenburg, one in 1470, another in 1483, and another in 1490; at Nuremburg, one in 1477, another in 1480, another in 1483, another in 1488, another in 1490, and another in 1518; and at Strasburg, one in 1485. This summary of German editions comprehends only those of the entire Bible; of editions of separate portions of the Scriptures, we have not the precise details, though they were produced in Germany in the same abundance as elsewhere. Nor should we omit to notice the splendid edition of the POLYGLOTT Bible of Cardinal Ximenes, which was commenced in 1503, the New Testament being completed in 1514, and the Old Testament in 1517, and the whole printed in 1522, with a dedication to Pope Leo X.; three copies being printed on vellum, and six hundred on paper, and the price of the latter fixed at two and a half crowns of gold, equivalent to £4 : 5s. of present value.[2] Of this edition but four copies yet remain in existence; and seeing that an edition in every respect so remarkable, and possessing so high a value, has

---

[2] According to M. Leber, the gold crown was worth in 1529, 42f. 50c. of modern value. Leber, Appreciation de la Fortune Privee au Moyen Age, 143. A copy of the Polyglott Bible of Cardinal Ximenes, on vellum, was bought at the Pinelli Sale, by Count McCarthy, for £483; the same copy was sold at the Count's Sale, in 1817, for £644.

almost entirely disappeared, we have certainly good reason to believe that many editions of the Bible, not presenting any special features, have perished in the lapse of years, and that those which we have noted are by no means the only ones which were then produced.

Confining ourselves, however, to the editions which nave been enumerated, we perceive that, in what might be strictly denominated ancient languages, there appeared during this period eighty-four editions of the Scriptures, sixty-two in Hebrew, of which twelve were of the Old Testament entire, and fifty of detached portions; and twenty-two in Greek, of which three were of the Old Testament, twelve of the New Testament, and seven of separate portions of the Scriptures. In the Latin, which occupied an intermediate position, as being the universal language of the Priesthood, and a familiar tongue to all learned men in the Christian world, there were published three hundred and forty-three editions, of which one hundred and forty-eight were of the entire Bible, sixty-two of the New Testament, and one hundred and thirty-three of separate books of the Sacred Writings. In the modern languages, the dialects of the humblest and poorest among the people, there were issued one hundred and ninety-eight editions; of which one hundred and four were of the entire Bible, comprising twenty in Italian, twenty-six in French, nineteen in Flemish, two in Spanish, six in Bohemian, one in Sclavonic, and thirty in German; and ninety-four of single portions of Holy Writ, consisting chiefly of copies of the New Testament and the Psalms. In all, including the Polyglott, six hundred and twenty-six editions of the Bible and portions of the Bible, of which one hundred and ninety-eight were in the languages of the laity, had issued from the press with the sanction and at the instance of the Church, in the countries where She reigned supreme, before the first Protestant version of the Scriptures was sent forth into the world.[3]

It is evident, therefore, that as the Church had, during all previous centuries, avowed in Her language and evinced in Her actions the most earnest desire to render the Scriptures accessible to all classes of men, so She lost not a moment in availing Herself of the facilities afforded by the invention of printing for the complete attainment of the object, the pursuit of which had ever engaged Her untiring energy, the placing of the Word of God within the reach of all who sought, in a spirit of pious humility, to gather comfort and instruction from the Sacred Volume.

By all classes of our mediæval forefathers the most profound and fervent reverence was manifested for the Scriptures. Even in the lavish munificence with which they were wont to devote gold, and silver, and ivory, and precious gems, to the adornment of the volumes which contained the records of inspiration, we trace an utterance of the loving veneration for the Bible which filled their inmost hearts, and found voice in the jealous care with which they sought to secure it from injury, and to shrine this priceless treasure in a gorgeous tabernacle, the splendour of which should worthily typify the fervency of their devotion. But the same feeling found expression through many other channels. Thus when the Emperor Henry II. had an interview with King Robert of France, on the banks of the Meuse, in the eleventh century, of all the rich presents

[3] Panzer. Annal. Typ. Brunet. Man. du Lib. Le Long Bibl. Sacr. &c.

offered him by that monarch : gold and silver and jewels, horses and knight's armour: he would accept only a copy of Gospels ;[4] and Duke Federigo, at the taking of Volterra in 1472, reserved only a Hebrew Bible for his own share of the spoils.   At the burial of a deceased Christian the Cross and the Book of the Gospels were laid upon his bier ;[5] and when the tomb of St. Cuthbert, at Durham, was opened in 1104, a copy of the Gospels was found on the lid of the inner coffin in which the body of the Saint reposed.[6]   The biographers of Bishops, and Monks, and laymen seem to have known no higher praise with which to gild the memory of those whose acts they recorded than this, that they were learned in Holy Scripture, and skilled in the knowledge of the word of God.   " Bishop Acca," says Beda, " was most learned in Holy Writ ;"[7] Adamnan was " a good and wise man, learned in Holy Scripture ;"[8] St. Ludiger, in the eighth century, was " deeply learned in the Scriptures, as is proved by the works which he composed.   He did not fail to instruct his disciples daily, and whatever he found to be inculcated in the Holy Books that he immediately endeavoured to per- form, and to lead others to observe ;"[9] Arnulf, a French Bishop, " came to Adamnan, who, finding him to be learned in the Scriptures, and acquainted with the holy places, en- tertained him zealously ;"[1] St. Dunstan devoted all the time he could spare from public duties, to religious exer- cises, and especially to " reading the divine Scriptures,

---

[4] Glab. Rod. ap. Baron. iii.
[5] Wulstan Vit. S. Ethel. ap. Mabillon Act. SS. Ord. S. Bened. Sæc. v. 623.   [6] Transl. S. Cuth. ap. Mabillon Act. SS. Ord. S. Bened. Sæc. iv. ii. 294.   [7] Beda Eccles. Hist. v. 20.   [8] Ibid. 15.
[9] Leib. Scr. Br. i. 93.   [1] Beda Eccles. Hist. v. 15.

and correcting copies of them;"[2] Anselm, Bishop of Lucca in the eleventh century, "knew almost all the Holy Scriptures by heart;"[3] Arnold, Bishop of Soissons in the same century, "spoke not a word to any human being for three years and six months, continuing rigidly silent, and delighting in heavenly contemplation, and unceasing meditation on the Scriptures;"[4] Thierry, Abbot of St. Hubert, "was so assiduous in the reading of the Sacred Scriptures, that he held them all in his memory;"[5] of Lambert, Abbot of Lobbes, in the eleventh century, "much might be said well worthy of note, concerning his love for the Word of God, and his acquaintance with the Scriptures, to the study of which he devoted himself at every possible opportunity;"[6] Oswy "sent a holy man, of modest behaviour, well learned in Holy Scripture, and diligently practising those things which he had learned therein, to be ordained Bishop in the Church at York;"[7] Egbert was "most learned in the Scriptures, and renowned for long perfection of life;"[8] Oftfor, "having applied himself to the reading and study of the Scriptures, in both the Monasteries of Hilda, at length, being desirous of attaining to greater perfection, went into Kent, to Archbishop Theodore of blessed memory;"[9] Alcuin, addressing Ethelhard, Archbishop of Canterbury, says, "through your pious care the reading of the Holy Scriptures is encouraged throughout your province;"[1] Beda, addressing King Ceolwulph, says, "I cannot but commend the sincerity and zeal with which you diligently give ear to hear the words

---

[2] Mabillon Act. SS. Ord. S. Bened. vii. 663.   [3] Ibid. ix. 480.
[4] Mabillon Act. SS. Ord. S. Bened. ix. 514.   [5] Ibid. 565.
[6] Dach. Spicileg. ii. 753.   [7] Beda Eccles. Hist. iii. 28.
[8] Ibid. 4.   [9] Ibid. iv. 23.   [1] Guil. Malms. Gest. Pont. Angl. i. 199.

of Holy Scripture ;"² Pope Gregory the Great especially commends Augustine to King Ethelbert, as " a holy Bishop full of the knowledge of the Sacred Scriptures ;"³ and it would be easy to fill a volume with citations of similar praises of holy men, for the extent and profundity of their Scriptural learning. The fact that the mediæval biographers invariably made this the key-note of their commendations, shows that they well knew that no other qualification was so highly esteemed by their contemporaries, or would so certainly secure the homage and affection of mankind.

Unquestionably in all these manifestations of reverence for the Scriptures, the laity did but imitate the examples set to them by their monastic teachers ; for the life of the Monks was one unceasing act of homage to the Word of God ; a deep and fervent veneration for the Bible breathed in all their actions. In the Rules which were framed for their government, the Sacred Volume was pointed to as the unerring guide of human conduct ;⁴ themselves had resigned the allurements of wealth, of pleasure, and of honorable ambition, that they might the more perfectly obey the precept of their Divine Master, by devoting themselves, in holy poverty, to ministering to the necessities of the poor and promoting the salvation of immortal souls ;⁵ and the same lessons which they had received for their own direction they promulgated for the instruction of mankind. But they were not content with simply inculcating these admirable precepts ; all the best energies of

---

² Beda Eccles. Hist. i. 1.   ³ Ibid. 32.
⁴ Reg. S. Bened. c. 73.   S. Athanas. Vit. S. Anton. c. 15.
⁵ " What is it to say, ' Give all thou hast to the poor, and follow me,' but to say, ' Become a Monk ?' " Pet. Clun. Epist. i. 28.

their minds were consecrated to the glorious task of rendering accessible to their brethren the sacred fount of eternal wisdom, whose streams had irrigated their own souls; in secluded poverty they devoted themselves to the severe manual labour of copying the Bible, and engaged with eagerness in the noble toil of translating it into the vulgar tongues of various nations, that the unlearned might become readers of the Word of God; in the Cloister they read and studied the Scriptures, that the sense of the Sacred Text might be yet farther elucidated by their careful commentaries; in their Schools they taught their pupils to understand correctly the Inspired Writings; in the Universities Scriptural Lectures embodied the results of their zealous studies and prayerful meditations; in their Libraries the Bible lay ever open to the search of all who sought to scan the sacred record; in their Churches, Bibles were placed for the use of the Laity, and Concordances attached to facilitate their researches; when they mounted the Pulpit, it was to inculcate upon their hearers the duty of reading and meditating on the Bible, and to preach those noble sermons, many of which yet remain to us, which are gemmed with Scriptural quotations, and in which the language and imagery of Scripture breathes in every line; and no sooner had human skill devised a means of book-multiplication, whose rapidity of action surpassed the boldest dreams of the ancient copyists, than they engaged at once its co-operation in the diffusion of the Scriptures, and caused the Bible to issue in vast abundance from the press, rendered into almost every tongue spoken in the Christian world.

Such was the Bible in the Middle Ages; a precious

treasure, guarded by the Church with jealous care and ceaseless vigilance, but guarded by Her only that it might be preserved in its integrity for the use and benefit of man ; shrined in Monastic Libraries, which were to the poor man as free of access as to the lordly baron, where the threadbare scholar was as welcome as the heritor of princely revenues ; chained in the open Churches that the humble might gather solace in his woe, and the penitent gain hope in his contrition, from the holy words which were traced upon the sacred page ; treasured by pious laymen, and handed down by them as a precious heirloom to their children ; cherished among the few books ranged on the single shelf in the poor scholar's lowly dwelling as the rich storehouse of all earthly and celestial wisdom ; the Vade Mecum of the Monk in his pilgrimages, of the Bishop in his journeyings, of the Student in his rambles, of the Priest in his mission of mercy into savage wilds ; the solace of the mourner, the hope of the afflicted, the joy of the poor, the manual of the Statesman, the text-book of the Philosopher, the central source of glory, whence issued the rays of light and beauty which made the loveliness of the mediæval world. Nobly, indeed, in this, as in all other respects, did the Church fulfil the sublime duties of Her sacred mission : by Her pious care the written moiety of God's Law was preserved from destruction amid the crash of empires ; copied by patient and indefatigable toils which vanquished the most tremendous obstacles ; disseminated throughout Europe, until it was within the reach of the humblest layman ; expounded in all lands from Her Altars for the guidance of the simple and the instruction of the devout ;

pointed out to Her children as the faithful monitor, whose inspired declarations were the foundation of Her authority, whose precepts were the unerring rules of Christian life; multiplied by printing presses in an abundance far transcending that of any other volume; and, by the zealous employment of every human means, conserved and perpetuated and diffused for the enlightenment and salvation of mankind.

THE MONASTIC LIFE

IN

THE MIDDLE AGES.

E

THE MONASTIC LIFE

IN

THE MIDDLE AGES.

WE cannot open a volume of the annals of mediæval history without discovering evidence of the vast and all-pervading influence which the Monastic Orders swayed in those ages over the destinies of mankind. The Monasteries were emphatically the nurseries of Heroes; not a great man, Priest, Poet, Warrior, or Statesman, whose budding intellect failed to receive from a Monastic hand the efficient nurture which matured it into vigorous development; not a great thought but had its germ beneath a cowl; not a great deed but owed its being to the promptings of a mighty heart throbbing beneath the mantle of religion. Half the high achievements of those illustrious times were wrought by men who had consecrated their lives to God; and when a layman was the favoured instrument of Providence in working out noble aims, it was to the seed implanted in his mind by Monastic teachers that he owed the birth of the sublime impulses which led him on to glory. As from central sources of all benignant influences, did fertilizing streams well forth from the Monasteries to bless and fructify the world; and the heavenly light which radiated from these holy sanctuaries shed its vivifying beams upon

E 2

the humblest and most desolate of mankind.   From the
one common fount came relief to the Body, instruction to
the Mind, and enlightenment to the Soul; the sacred symbol
of salvation crowned the roof which covered the asylum
of the destitute, the school of the ignorant, and the refuge
of the contrite sinner ; Sin, Ignorance, and Want, the three
giant monsters whose ravages devastate the world, found
there a fortress, manned by a sturdy garrison, sworn to do
battle against these triune enemies of mankind.

Yet very evilly have these holy labours of our Monastic
forefathers been repaid by the ungrateful children whose
chief blessings have sprung from their unwearying toils.
The zealous energy which struggled so heroically to increase
the sum of human happiness is rewarded with a howl of
bigoted execration, or, at the best, with a supercilious sneer
of self-satisfied contempt ; and for their sole visible guerdon
the hatred of some, the ridicule of others, and the in-
difference even of many of those who are reaping the
richest harvest from their exertions, is now accorded to
them by the world.   Well is it for them that their glorious
deeds need no human recompense, that the goal of their
toilsome pilgrimage was fixed, not in the temple of earthly
fame, but in the world beyond the grave.

It is, in great measure, our own fault that our minds
have become imbued with these grossly erroneous ideas
with regard to the Religious of mediæval centuries.   To
learn the character of Christian heroes we have sat at the
feet of infidel historians ; from the poisoned lips of Gibbon
we have drunk in honied lies, by which the arch-sophist
has defamed the mighty spirits of the Christian world; the
unbelieving Hume has been suffered to daub over with
unnatural pigments the memory of the men who lived and

struggled when England was the pride of Christendom ; and so, from the teachers who hated and despised the religion which was the mainspring of mediæval life, who deemed Christianity a fraud, Christ an imposter, and the Bible a bundle of romances, we have been content to draw a large portion of our knowledge of the history of the Christian world. What greater delight to them than to paint a Saint a hypocrite ? what higher glory than to depict the Monks as cunning dissemblers, practising on the credulity of mankind, or besotted sensualists, rioting in voluptuous excess ? what dearer object than to show that the hated faith has owned for its champions none but fanatics and fools ? But the infidels couched their lies in pleasant words, and wreathed their slanders into flowery sentences, and we have been content to swallow the poison because it is concealed in sugar-plums.

Other historians there have been whose writings have found favour with mankind, free indeed from the taint of infidelity, but animated by a spirit to the full as destructive of their trust-worthiness as guides to the comprehension of Catholic antiquity. From writers to whom the very name of the ancient Church is a scorn, who would look for true portraitures of the men who reared and sustained the mighty fabric of Her yet unconquered Empire ? There can be no hope of a fair trial when the prosecutor sits in judgement, no prospect of impartial history when the gall of sectarian hatred flows in the inkhorn of the historian ; the Monks have as little chance of receiving justice from a Robertson or a Warton, as from a Hume, a Gibbon, or a Voltaire. Each one of these writers has reasoned on a foregone conclusion ; hating the Monks, he has sought to discover : or failing this, to invent : some justification for his animosity. In an avowed partizan this would be of little moment; the other side would then remain for hearing, and in the free contest of conflicting opinions truth would achieve its wonted victory.   But with the vast majority of men the other side has never had a hearing ; the revilers of the olden time, veiling their true lineaments beneath a mask of pretended impartiality, have succeeded in imposing their denunciations upon the multitude as the judgements of unbiassed wisdom, and the many, deluded by their specious semblances, have adandoned themselves to their guidance, and accepted their philippics as faithful delineations of the character of our ancestors.

In order that we may attain to more accurate conceptions of the true condition of men in these by-gone centuries, it is but needful that we should open our eyes and examine for ourselves the evidence which remains to us of the spirit of our forefathers.   Of this there is no lack, if we will employ our faculties in its investigation. Our errors spring, not from a drought at the founts of History, but from our own indolence, which hinders us from carrying our pitchers to the well, and induces us to content ourselves with the muddy turbid waters which are conveyed to our own doors by uncleanly conduits.   At the fountain head all is clear, and sparkling, and wholesome ; but foul water-courses will corrupt the most limpid streams, and the channels through which we have received our historical knowledge have wofully defiled the pure current which has bubbled through them from the springs of antiquity.

An intimate acquaintance with the spirit of the Monastic Life is indispensable to the formation of a just conception of the tone of the mediæval mind and the character of mediæval society.   Viewing the Monastic Orders simply as an integral element of the antique social organisation, the number of those who embraced the religious life renders it needful that we should investigate the nature of the motives which impelled them to assume the habit, and the obligations which were imposed upon them by its reception. The histories of the Monasteries of France, contained in the Gallia Christiana, occupy thirteen volumes, comprising more than fifteen thousand folio pages ; in England, at the epoch of the Reformation, there were Six hundred and thirteen Monasteries, in addition to ninety Colleges and One hundred and ten Hospitals under the care of the Religious ;[1] and in every other Christian land these holy institutions existed in proportionate abundance. Each community generally consisted of a large number of individuals. Thus, for example, the Monastery of St. Finnian, in Ireland, contained at one time three thousand Monks ; the Abbey of St. Sylvester at Nonantula had, in the tenth Century, more than a thousand ; the Abbey of Jumiege, soon after its foundation, had nine hundred; the Abbey of Fulda had three hundred and seventy; the Abbey of Bangor in Ireland, established in the sixth century by St. Comgal, contained, before the death of its founder, four thousand; at Bangor in Wales there were eight divisions, each consisting of three hundred Monks ; at Clugni, in the twelfth Century, there were four hundred, and in the same Monastery Abbot Hugo, during the sixty-four years of his rule, received the vows of more than ten thousand postulants. Undoubtedly the number of inmates varied considerably in different Monasteries, but, while those which had acquired high renown for peculiar sanctity often contained vast multitudes of Religious, few, even among the least important communities, numbered less than a hundred

[1] Tanner. Notit. Monast.

brethren.   Each class of society had its representatives in
these pious sanctuaries ; not only the poor and the humble,
but men of highest rank and opulence, abandoned the
world to assume the habit of religion.   Elfgar, son of Earl
Godwin and brother to the Saxon Harold, was a Monk at
Rheims ;[2] Walter Mauclerc, Chancellor of England in the
reign of Henry III., resigning his earthly dignities, made
profession in the Order of St. Dominic and entered a
Monastery at Oxford ;[3] in the Abbey of St. Medard at
Soissons, the Kings Eude and Raoul were Abbots ; in the
eighth Century the Irish King Flaithertach, abdicating his
throne after a peaceful reign of seven years' duration, retired to end his days in a Monastery at Armagh, and his
example was followed by his successor Nial II., who, under
similar circumstances, and after the same length of rule,
embraced the religous life in the Monastery of Iona ; in
England more than thirty Anglo-Saxon Sovereigns resigned
their crowns that they might more freely struggle for eternal bliss in the peaceful solitude of Monastic cells.   St.
Carloman, the eldest son of Charles Martel, and uncle to the
illustrious Charlemagne, relinquishing to his son Drogo
the heritage of Austria, Suabia, and Thuringia, which had
been transmitted to him by his father, retired to the Monastery of Mount Soracte, but, his humility being wounded
by the honour which was there paid to him on account of
his contempt of earthly greatness, he fled in the night to
the Abbey of Monte Cassino, where he presented himself
as a poor Frank who wished to devote himself to a life of
penance ; and being received he lived there for a long time
unknown, and displayed such sublime humility that the

[2] Oderic Vital. iii.   [3] Tournon. Hist. des Hommes Illust.
de l'Ordre de St. Dominique.

leading of a few sheep to pasture was his daily appointed toil ;[4] and in the same Monastery Rachiz King of the Lango-bards, ended his life in the practice of the offices of religion.[5] The Emperor Lothaire, son of Louis le Debonnaire, took the habit in the Abbey of Prum ; Henry, brother to King Louis VII., renouncing his high ecclesiastical dignities, became a Monk at Clairvaux ; Duke Gerold of Saxony, together with his two sons, made profession in the Abbey of Enseidlin ; at Clugni Duke Hugo of Burgundy ex-changed the coronet for the cowl ; and many of the most illustrious of the Venetian Doges brought their lives of earthly glory to a peaceful close within the shelter of Monastic walls.[6] In the single Order of St. Benedict, four Emperors, forty-six Kings, fifty-one Queens, fourteen hundred and six Princes, and more than two thousand four hundred of the higher orders of the nobility assumed the habit of religion ; and the histories of the more renowned Monasteries present innumerable examples of the aban-donment of the luxuries of wealth, the delights of power, and the allurements of ambition by nobles and by knights, who renounced the world and its fleeting joys that they might more securely tread the narrow path to heaven. The vast number of the Monks, and the importance of a body which attracted to itself so many of the most eminent among men, and induced them to relinquish freely all that is dearest to the fallen nature of humanity, in order that they might be admitted to a participation in its privileges, would constitute alone a sufficient reason for investigating carefully the spirit of the Monastic Life and the nature of

[4] Annal. Sax. ap. Eccard. Corp. Hist. Med. Ævi. Chron. Mon. Casin. c. vii.   [5] Chron. Mon. Casini. c. viii..
[6] Martene Thes. Antiq. Ital. V.

the duties which devolved upon those who wore the habit of religion ; yet this is by no means the most powerful among the considerations which dictate the necessity of such an inquiry, as essential to the comprehension of mediæval history.   The Monastic Life was the realization of the ideal of the mediæval mind ; its aims were the objects dearest to the mediæval heart; its practical observances were the embodiments of the convictions of Christian antiquity with regard to the duties of man, and the means by which he could best achieve the fulfilment of his earthly vocation ; in its organization we behold an image of the spirit of those vanished centuries, a faithful reflex of the sentiments which in those days pervaded the Christian world.   In the ideas which found development in Monasticism resided the soul of the Past ; in the provisions of Monastic Rules and the lives of the Monastic brethren we contemplate the vivid portraiture of the antique mind ; and it is by the examination of the nature of those ideas, the character of those provisions, and the prominent features of the lives which were modelled in obedience to their monitions, that we can most readily arrive at a just appreciation of the spirit of our forefathers.

When St. Bernard was about to establish the Monastery of Villiers in Brabant, looking down upon the valley in which it was to be built, he said,   " In this place will many souls be saved."[7]   This was the fundamental aim of Monasticism, the culture of personal holiness, the purgation of humanity from its corruptions, the advancement of the immortal nature on its march to Paradise.   "The object of the Monastic discipline," says St. Anselm " is purity of heart, and its end everlasting life." " As no one,"

[7] Hist. Monast. Villarens. ap Mart. Thes. Anecdot. iii.

[8] Tractat. Ascet. St. Anselmi, ap Dacher. Spicileg. iii.

says Salvian, " does anything unless for the sake of safety
and advantage, so we undertake this mode of life because
we think it profitable, reflecting on the shortness of present
and the duration of future things, considering how little
are the former and how great the latter, remembering
that the judgment of sin will be tremendous and the life
with God and His Saints most blissful."[9]   It was pri-
marily to save their own souls that the Monks embraced
the religious life; each one among them would have echoed,
with a full acquiescence in their truth, those admirable
words of St. Bernard, " It is well for us to be here, since
here man lives more purely, falls more rarely, rises more
quickly, walks more carefully, reposes more securely, dies
more happily, is purified more rapidly, is rewarded more
abundantly;" they believed with Peter of Blois, that "the
highest wisdom is, not to read Plato or disentangle the
subtleties of Aristotle, but to love Christ, to serve Christ,
and in this most grateful and fruitful service willingly,
efficaciously, faithfully and finally to remain;"[1] and it was
in obedience to this conviction that they renounced the
pursuit of the riches and pleasures of earth and sought
refuge in the retirement of the Cloister.   " The first especial cause of a Monastic Life," says a writer of the fifth
century, " is the desire to avoid the occasions of sin,
to wage war with the perverse world, and to be delivered
from the peril of its snares;"[2] " the solitude, silence, study,
prayers, and meditations of Monks," says Thomas of
Kempis, " are designed to promote purity of heart;"[3] and
the same writer expresses in few words the motive which
impelled such vast multitudes to assume the habit of religion,

[9] Salviani Timoth. l. ii.   [1] Petr. Bles. Serm. liii.
[2] Consultat. Zach. et Appolon. l. iii 3. 4. ap Dach. Spicileg. x.
[3] De Claustro Animæ.

when he declares that "a simple and obedient brother, without many arguments and learned discourses, can arrive at the kingdom of Heaven with a pure conscience, and escape the eternal torments of Hell."[4]　"O peaceful and celestial life," says the illustrious Petrarch, "O life better than all lives, where salvation is expected, and the sweet yoke of the Lord borne in silence and in rest ; life which restores the soul, repairs the affections, reconciles sinners to God, and saves inumerable men from ruin ; life favourable to genius, disdainful of the body, the mother of nobility, the nurse of virtue, the mountain of contemplation. And what shall I say, unless that thou art all things together ? A life most happy and proper for every good work, a life for philosophers, for poets, for saints, for prophets."[5]　"A congregation of Monks," says Hugo of St. Victor, "is a Paradise, having the tree of life in the midst of it, yielding shade and fruit, that is, Christ giving life ;"[6] the rule and life of the Friars Minor, says St. Francis, "consists in observing the Holy Gospel of our Lord Jesus Christ, living in obedience, without property, and in chastity ;" "our Order," says St. Bernard, "is humility, peace, and joy in the Holy Ghost, our Order is silence, fasting, prayer, labour, and above all, to hold the more excellent way which is charity ;"[7] and the tenor and provisions of the various Monastic Rules sufficiently demonstrate that the advancement in spiritual perfection of those whose lives were to be regulated by their prescriptions was the fundamental object of their institution.　Assuredly in this earnest care for their own eternal welfare the Monks were animated by no merely selfish sentiment ; in their philosophy the love

---

[4] Thomas á Kempis. Serm. i. 5.　　[5] Petrarc. de Vita Solitaria, l. ii. tr. ii. c. 9.　[6] Ex. Miscellan. l. iii. 60.　　[7] St. Bernard, Epist. cxlii.

of God and the love of man were held to be so intimately
allied that neither could maintain a separate existence ;
according to their ideas, there could be no true love for
man which was not based upon the love of God, no real
love for God which did not produce abundant fruits of
charity to man : and the lives which they consecrated to
the service of Heaven, were devoted to pious labours
which conferred inestimable benefits on the world. Nor
did they conceive that the adoption of their peculiar state
of life was essential to salvation, and that for them was
reserved the special heritage of the joys of Paradise.
" Are the continent and the married to condemn each
other," says St. Bernard, " because they converse in the
Church according to their respective laws ? Are Monks
to blame Clerks, or are Monks of different orders to speak
disparagingly of one another ? How shall there then be
peace in the Church, in which there must be variety,
since it is impossible that one man should hold all Orders,
or one Order all men ? The Church is clothed in variety,
but all is peace. Each one, receiving his peculiar gifts,
ministers accordingly, one in this manner, another in that,
whether Cluniac or Cistercian Monks, or regular Clerks,
or faithful laics ; each order, each sex, each age, each condition, has its peculiar office, and exercises it in peace.
Each one has his particular vocation ; all things are not
expedient for all men, and different medicines are required
for different diseases."[8] " Each one," says the same holy
writer, " is to hold fast the good which he has, without
judging another holding other things, that whoso has received to be good may not envy those who are better, that
he who seems to himself to do better may not condemn

---

[8] S. Bernard, Apolog. ad Guil. c. iii. iv.

what is good in another, that he who can live most strictly may not despise those who cannot."[9]   Nothing was more earnestly inhibited in the Monks than harsh judgment of those who had not assumed the habit of religion; " when the brethren go forth from the Monastery," says the Rule of the Minims, " and see men clothed in soft raiment and feasting delicately, they must not despise or judge them, but let each one judge himself ;"[1] and this spirit of humility was a pervading element of the Monastic character. The Monks cherished no idea that the inmates of Cloisters were sole heirs to the bliss of Heaven ; knowing, that, to use the words of the Franciscan Antonio de Guevara, " once baptized, there is no order in the whole Church of God in which a good man may not be saved, and in which a bad man will not be condemned ;"[2] they recognised the truth which the same writer has admirably expressed, that " a perfect man makes the world a Monastery, and a profane man makes a Monastery the world ;"[3] and freely acknowledged, with Richard of St. Victor, that " even in the sterile and arid desert of the world the devout soul, while it labours for true joy, can fructify the barren soil, and bring forth even there something that will remain."[4] In every state of life they recognized its peculiar duties, the performances of which would be crowned with enduring rewards ; and, while electing for themselves that which Petrarch designates as " the quiet poverty, the sweet contemplation, the united fellowship, the celestial peace of the cloister ;"[5] not only as best suited to the necessities of their own souls, but also as most perfectly in

[9] S. Bernard de Præcept. et Dispensat.   [1] Reg. Min. c. xi.
[2] Ant. de Guev. Epist. ii.   [3] Ibid.   [4] Ric. S. Vict. in Cant. Cantic.   [5] Petrarc. Var. Epist. l. xix.

harmony with the evangelic counsels ; for " what is it," says Peter the Venerable, " to say, ' Give all thou hast to the poor and follow me,' but to say ' Become a Monk ?' "[6] they never dreamed that others might not ascend by other roads to the goal towards which they directed the steps of their earthly pilgrimage.

The Monastic Life being, as Dionysius the Carthusian observes, " a state in which the grace of God withdraws the soul from the tumult of external things to silent joys, that is, to the clearest splendour of supreme light, in which, free from the delusions of fleshly desires and unquiet phantoms, and wandering thoughts, it sweetly rests in love,"[7] and its highest aim being to secure the complete absorption of the soul in the contemplation of spiritual things, " living only in Christ and for Christ," as St. Bonaventura expresses it,[8] and the entire devotion of the energies of the mind to the pursuit of eternal beatitude, it necessarily presented many points of difference from the ordinary life of humanity, in the conditions by which it was surrounded, and the special duties which it imposed. The nature of these peculiar characteristics now remains for our consideration.

It was but natural that they who had renounced the riches, the honours, and the pleasures of earth, should retire from amidst the multitudes who still contended for these fleeting joys, and seclude themselves in the companionship of holy men, who had, like them, recognized the vanity of earthly things, and fixed their desires on the imperishable treasures of eternity. To this they were impelled by no cynical hatred of humanity ; they distin-

[6] Petr. Ven. Epist. i. 28.   [7] De Fonte Lucis.   [8] De Grad. Vit. Spirit. c. 82.

guished carefully, with Richard of St. Victor, between
" the world of which God is the Creator, of which it is
written ' mundus per ipsum factus est,' the world of which
God is the Saviour, of which we are told ' sic Deus dilexit
mundum ut Filium suum unigenitum dedit,' and the world
of which the Devil is the Prince, of which we read, ' nolite
diligere mundum ;' " [9] this last alone being the object of
their detestation.   " In this life," says Dionysius the Carthusian, " we see the beauty of God in all creatures, in
roses, and lilies, and other flowers, in herbs, in the shade of
groves, in the elegance of trees, in the loveliness of fields,
in the sublimity of mountains, in the lakes, rivers, and
streams, in the beauty of animals, and above all in that of
man," adding, in language which evinces how earnest was
the enjoyment of the Religious of those ages in the contemplation of these wonders of creative skill, and how
true the spirit in which they recognised and appreciated
their charms, " if God has chosen to place such beauty in
some material forms, that we seek with great desire to
behold them, and gaze upon them with such delight that
we can hardly be satiated or fatigued, or perceive the
lapse of time, how beautiful is God ;" [1] the Capuchin Friar
Lombez exclaims in the same strain, " If amid so many
wonders and beauties we are in a hard exile, as in truth
we are, the dignity of our souls must be very great, and
our true country wondrous fair, and the love of God for
us surpassing all conception, since He banishes us to such
an admirable world, a place so adorned with all kinds of
loveliness ;" [2] and St. Bonaventura teaches that, " turning
to creatures is no sin, if there be no turning away from

    [9] Ric. S. Vic sup. Apocalyps. l. iii. c. 8.   [1] De Venustate
Mundi, 22.   [2] Traité de la Joie de l'Ame, c. viii.

God, since we can be delighted in them innocently, when we are pleased with remarking their beauty, and we can be delighted in them meritoriously when that beauty is referred to God."[3] The Monks were neither gloomy misanthropists nor morose scorners of the loveliness of creation, but, filled with an earnest longing to attain to their celestial home, and feeling with St. Bernard, that " there are risks for innocence in delights, for humility in riches, for piety in business, for truth in loquacity, for charity in the companionship of this perverse world;"[4] and knowing, often from sad experience, the truth of the remark of Thomas à Kempis, that " the world knows so many modes of deceit and wickedness, contrives so many inventions, and has so many quarrels, that no one's peace can be safe, no one's faith firm, nor even can any one easily lead a pure life, unless he separate himself from the crowd of men, and seek Jesus Christ, to hear Him teach His Gospel in desert places,"[5] they deemed it expedient to withdraw themselves from the perils which, while dwelling among men, environed them on every hand, and to seek peace for their souls, and security from the assaults of temptation, by the abandonment of the pursuits which hurried so many to perdition. This was, in truth, like all other observances of the Religious, " less the cause than the consequence of the perfection which shone in them," as Mœhler well remarks, " for," he observes, " by means of divine grace the spiritual man predominates to such a degree in such privileged souls, and they are drawn with such force towards things unchangeable and holy, that the bonds which attach them to the things of this world are

[3] S. Bonav. Comp. Theol. Veritat. I. iii. c. 2.   [4] S. Bern. de Conversione, c. xxi.   [5] Dial. Novit.

scarcely felt; in them the spiritual almost wholly eclipses
the animal existence; they do not banish terrestrial thoughts
from their souls in order to find room for celestial thoughts,
but, all place being already occupied by these, it is impossible for the former to find access."[6] Still it must be noted
that the cloistered life was adopted by the Monks, not only
because their exalted spiritualism impelled them to retreat
from the scenes of worldly strife, that they might devote
themselves more uninterruptedly to divine meditation, but
also, because they were well convinced of the influence of
saintly intercourse, as an agency of advancement in perfection.   " Saul being among the prophets," says Father
Diego de Stella, " became a prophet and did prophesy,
but among fools he became a fool ; St. Peter being among
the Apostles, confessed Christ to be the Son of God, but
afterwards in Caiaphas' house, where he was with the
wicked, he did deny him.   It seemeth hereby that a great
alteration was made in the man by reason of the company
he was with.   If thou puttest dead among quick burning coals, they will soon be set on fire ;   draw thou near
then unto the burning coals, which are the virtues of
good men, for though thou be never so much wasted and
consumed by thine own evil life, yet good men with their
virtues will revive and quicken thee again."[7]   Their
highest aim being to realize in themselves the ideal of the
poor in spirit, who, according to Peter of Blois, is " he
who, distrustful of himself and denying himself for Christ,
has nothing in his thoughts or memory, nothing in delec-
tation or desire, but Christ ;"[8] they naturally conceived
that to attain this end it was needful that they should re-

---

[6] Mœhler. ap. Mor. Cath. l. x. c. 2.   [7] On the Contempt of
the World.   [8] Petr. Bles. Serm. xlii.

move themselves from the influence of all that could generate other thoughts, and give birth to less sublime aspirations ; and being well aware that, as one among them says,
" experience proves that the soul, dissipated by the curi-
osity of secular things, can with difficulty recollect itself,
and return to the meditation of celestial things ;"[9] and
that, as Cardinal Bona remarks, " the abundance of cares
and solicitudes which must belong to all who mix much
with the world, is an obstacle to that devout contemplation in which they wished to pass their lives ;"[1] they
deemed that it was only in the Cloister that they could
hope to arrive at that state of entire absorption in the
consideration of the mysteries of eternity, which would
enable them truly to reply to their questioners, as Abbot
Stephen to the old man who sought his counsel, " all I
have I will show to you, for day and night I behold nothing
but our Lord Jesus Christ hanging from the wood."[2]   " In
a community," says Thomas à Kempis, " man lives more
securely, and if sometimes he is troubled by one, on the
other hand he is consoled by another.   There he is ex-
cited to good by example, and warned from evil.   There
he finds persons he can love ; the censure on another is
an admonition to himself ; there each one guards the other.
There are diverse offices and one spirit of charity.   There
a man has many to pray for him, and at his last moments
to sustain him in his struggles against his temptations of
the devil ; there he has as many helpmates as he has com-
panions.   There he happily sleeps in the Lord, and has
many intercessors to implore his speedy deliverance from
purgatory ; there at his death he leaves heirs who will be

<hr>

[9] Joan. à Jesu. Instruct. Magist. Novit.   [1] De Divin. Psalmod.
502.   [2] Sophron. Prat. Spir. c. lxiv.

mindful of him; there his labour and good conversation
will not be forgotten, but will profit many in future times
for an example.   There he participates in the merits of
all; there he lives for a time with those with whom he will
hereafter rejoice for everlasting ages."[3]   In the adoption
of the cænobitic life, the Monks sought, not only to environ
their souls with a bulwark against the assaults of temptation, by alienating from themselves all the ordinary instrumentalities which Satan employs to allure frail humanity to destruction, and closing entirely the channels
through which his wiles find readiest access to the heart,
but at the same time to secure a constant stimulus to holy
resolution, in the force of mutual encouragement and example, which, potent in the world for evil, became in these
holy brotherhoods an unfailing source of highest edification.   " When man withdraws himself," says Abbot Ælred
of Rievaux, " from external tumults, and enters into the
recesses of his own mind,—when he perceives nothing
unquiet, nothing out of order, and feels nothing of ill-
will, nothing of remorse,—when he finds that all things
are cheerful, all harmonious, all peaceful and calm,—when,
like the father of a well-ordered family, he sees smiles on
all his thoughts, and words, and works,—there arises
within himself an unspeakable serenity ; from that serenity
springs delight; and, that delight rising into rapture, he
parises God the more fervently in proportion, as he sees
traces of the divine image within his own breast."[4]   Such
was the ideal of Monastic bliss ; and as this earnest longing after the ineffable joys which are born into the heart
that is at peace with God, found natural utterance in the
abandonment of all the glittering prizes which have exist-

[3] Serm. i. 2.   [4] Spec. Char.

ence only on this side of the grave, and each one of which sheathes beneath its beauteous form a venomed sting, and the election of the companionship of sympathetic souls, alike vowed to the undivided struggle for salvation, so this mode of life became, in its turn, the food of the holy aspirations which had given it rise, and fortified against all assaults the hearts of those whose wise? perception of the vanity of earthly things had impelled them to make consecration of their lives to Heaven.

The renunciation of the world obviously implied the observance of poverty and continence, since wealth and the delights of sense are the chief ends of the world's deserving, the objects whose attainment constitutes the aim of unregenerated existence. Thus, escaping from the snares which the lust of the flesh and the concupiscence of the eyes spread around the path of man, the pride of the heart yet remained to be vanquished by the entire subjugation of the individual will, for " from obedience," says St. John Climachus, " springs humility, and from humility a placid tranquillity of mind,"[5] and the inscription which Lydgate read in his youth beneath a crucifix in a cloister, " beholde my mekenes, chylde, and leave thy pride," was a brief summary of the lesson which meditation on that Divine example had imprinted in each Monastic heart.

This phase of the mediæval mind is perhaps that which appears to men of modern days the most mysterious and incomprehensible, for the deification of the individual will is in the nineteenth century the basis of Political Philosophy and the spirit of daily life ; to nothing is humanity now less prone than to the sacrifice of its own volition at the

[5] Grad. iv.

shrine of authority; and the idea of obedience as a Christian duty has become well nigh extinct among mankind. Certainly among the Monks it received no mere lip-service, but was an unvarying rule of action; and its source was in no servile prostration of intellect, but in a firm and well-grounded conviction of the necessity of humility in those who sought to be the true followers of Christ, and a just perception of the impossibility of attaining to perfect humility otherwise than by the entire abnegation of self-will. There were no exceptions to this discipline, " for," says Peter of Blois, " neither superior nor subject may lawfully follow his own will : for the legislator of Monks prescribed, as if by a general edict, that all should follow the Rule as their master, and from this law neither the Prior nor the Abbot is excepted ;"[6] but the submission thus demanded was held to be worthy only in so far as its motive was divine, since, as the writer last cited remarks elsewhere, " no affection, even pious, is meritorious to salvation unless it proceeds from the love of Christ, for when you hear something read concerning our Lord you may be moved to tears, in the same manner as you weep when you hear certain fabulous histories, but your tears are lost if you do not love God, if your tears do not flow from the fountains of the Saviour, from faith, hope, and charity ;"[7] and the Monks were well aware that their obedience was pleasing to God only when it sprung from perfect humility of heart, and had its root in a sense of their own nothingness, and an earnest desire to conform in all things to the will of the Almighty. In this age of self-deification, when every man would be his own King, and every man his own Priest, and we are fast hastening to the

[6] Petr. Bles. Epist. cxxxi.   [7] Petr. Bles. de Confessione.

grand climacteric, heralded in the revived Paganism of Fourier, of every man his own God, mankind are apt to deem that all who bow before authority must be slaves; the Sceptre and the Crosier have become, to their pride-clouded vision, mere symbols of despotism; but such ideas could find no dwelling-place in hearts in which Christian meekness had made its home. These true disciples of their Master knew that all sin springs from the preference of the individual will to the will of God; and in the mortification of this potent instrument of woe, they recognised an efficient mode of disarming the spiritual enemy of their souls, and removing one of the most fatal stumbling blocks from the path which led to the celestial goal.

The Monastic Life was a life of bodily mortification; one of the fundamental ideas which found embodiment in its organization was the conviction which reigned in the mind of the Religious, of the efficacy of penitential exercises, not only as an expiation, deriving its value from the merits of Christ, of their own offences, but also as a propitiatory sacrifice, rendered acceptable by its union with the Great Atonement, in behalf of the repentant sinners who had been reconciled to God and rescued from the perils of Hell by the worthy reception of the Sacrament of Penance, but to whom there yet remained due from Divine justice an infliction of temporal chastisement, to be undergone either in this world or in the next, before they could enter into possession of the joys of Paradise. But the penance of the Monks was far from consisting solely, or even principally, in external observances; they knew well that the most rigorous austerities are worthless if the heart remain impure, and their corporal mortifications were but adjuncts to the rigid discipline to which they subjected their souls. "The chief things of the Rule," says St. Bernard, " are its spiritual institutions. Better is humility robed in furs than pride in destitution. Better is a little meat for use than much vegetables for satiety. Wine in moderation, as St. Paul prescribes, is better than water and avidity. Nor should you glory in the labour of your hands, since Martha who served was reproved, and Mary who sat still was praised; for the true labour is that which is spiritual."[8]   St. Columbanus places the same truth as forcibly before his disciples : "Do not suppose," he says, "that it is enough to fatigue the dust of our bodies with fasts and watchings, if we do not also reform our manners. To macerate the flesh, if the soul does not fructify, is to till the ground without ceasing, and never to reap fruit from it. What signifies it to carry on a distant war, if the interior be a prey to ruin? The suffering of the body alone is vain; the care which man takes of his exterior is vain, if he do not also watch and preserve his soul. True piety consists in humility, not of the body, but of the heart."[9]   Nevertheless, while recognising, with Fulbert of Chartres, that " abstinence from meat does not avail with the Lord without the mortification of vices,"[1] they believed with St. Augustine, that " it is not sufficient to change our manners for the better, and to depart from evil, unless we satisfy God, by penance, for the things which we have done ;"[2] and being convinced that, as the same holy Father remarks, " if a man wishes to punish himself God will spare him,"[3] they joyfully embraced a life of voluntary endurance, in order that, thus discharging

[8] St. Bern. de Præcept. et Dispensat. v. 6.   [9] S. Instit. ii. ap. Bibl. Patr. xii. c. 10.   [1] Fulb. Car. Epist. xxxvi.   [2] St. Aug. Serm. cccli.   [3] Ibid. cclxxviii.

in this world a portion of the debt of suffering due to divine justice for their sins, they might pass the more rapidly through the purgatorial fires which lie between the grave and the gates of Paradise.

A large number of Monasteries owed their foundation to the remorse awakened by religion in the minds of great men, who, having been engaged during their early lives in deeds of blood and violence, sought, by devoting their entire wealth to the establishment of Religious Houses, and consecrating their remaining years to God in these pious retirements, to render their souls more fit for heaven ; and in every Cloister were found many, who, debarred from performing such distinguished acts of atonement by the absence of worldly means, offered a no less acceptable sacrifice by relinquishing, for themselves, the allurements of the world, and sanctifying, by penitential observances and labours of charity, the closing days of their existence. In many instances, too, those whose domestic ties disabled them from assuming the habit endeavoured to bear their share in the good work by giving realization to the pious desires of others, and either endowing new Monasteries, or adding to the possessions of those which owed to others their foundation. Many were the grants made by royal and noble donors to swell the revenues of these pious sanctuaries ; and many a holy fane which was to the world a source of priceless benefits, not only by the expiatory sacrifices which were constantly offered within its walls, in atonement for the sins of frail and feeble humanity, but also by the direct influence which it exercised in promoting the physical comfort, the intellectual advancement, and the spiritual elevation of the people, owed its existence to the benevolent care of pious laymen, who devoted a

F

large share of the rich inheritance of which God had made them stewards to the promotion of the ends ever dearest to the Christian heart. Thus was it that those princely domains, which were the pride of ancient Abbeys, and which enabled their inmates to provide so admirably for the most important behests of society, grew to full maturity; the penitent devotion of a conscience-stricken noble first consecrated to the service of Religion the broad lands which he had inherited from his ancestors, and, as years rolled on, the pious Prince, the saintly Bishop, the devout Baron, added their gifts to swell the wealth of the Brotherhood, whose existence was the life of civilization, of learning, and of religion.

So much calumny has been heaped upon our forefathers for this pious custom, which prevailed among them, of laying their rich gifts upon the Altar, and setting aside their most precious treasures for the service of religion, that it is due to their memory that we should endeavour to exculpate them from the grave charges with which mendacious bigotry has striven to deface this noble and truly Christian element in their character. It is true that the evil principles which are falsely attributed to our Catholic ancestors are precisely identical with those which are falsely imputed to their Catholic posterity : the same faith in the efficacy of external acts as substitutes for penitence, the same belief in the acceptableness before God of a rich gift, offered in place of a contrite heart : and we have therefore no reason to wonder that those who are silly enough to credit such absurd and baseless fabrications, promulgated with regard to men who live in the same day with themselves, should be credulous enough to be deluded by similar false statements, propounded with regard to their forefathers who flourished in bygone centuries. But the voice of the Church, proclaiming in all ages of Her history Her unvarying doctrine, presents an unanswerable refutation of these calumnies of Her defamers ; and the unanimous expression of the sentiments of Her children amply demonstrates how deeply Her holy precepts were graven in the hearts of Christendom. "The man," says the Synod of Cloveshoe, " who indulges his passions in the confidence that his charities will procure his salvation, instead of making an acceptable sacrifice to God, throws himself into the arms of Satan ;"[4] " repentance is then only of avail," says the Council of Calcuith, "when it impels the sinner to lament his past offences and restrains him from committing them again ;"[5] "no offering, though made to a Monastery," says Beda, " can be acceptable to God, if it proceed from an impure heart ;"[6] and the same views find utterance alike in the Canons of Councils and in the writings of the humblest members of the Monastic Brotherhood. The Monks, indeed, fully manifested their sense of the worthlessness before God of all such donations when they were not prompted by the pure intention and accompanied by the virtuous life which could alone make them acceptable to the Almighty, by the censures with which they visited the memory of those who, beneficent to the Church from interested motives, had failed to exhibit in their conduct the qualities which distinguish the Christian character. Of Clotaire III. the Monks of St. Denis say, " Of this king we have more of evil than of good to relate ; he was, indeed, generous to the Churches of the Saints, but nevertheless he had so many vices that they extinguished

<hr>

[4] Wilk. Conc. 98. xxvi. [5] Ibid. 181. [6] Bed. Epist. ad Egb. 312.

his virtues, if there were any in him.   He was a despiser
of women, and history does not record of him that his
life was worthy of praise or memory."[7]   Brunehaut, who
was a munificent donor to Churches and Monasteries,
receives a similar condemnation;[8] of Dagobert, who enriched and endowed their own Abbey, they declare that
" his virtues and graces were converted into vices by his
misconduct;"[9] Wadding the Franciscan visits with the
same reprobation Sigismund Malatesta, who was the
founder of the splendid Franciscan Monastery at Rimini;[1]
and innumerable similar examples might be cited, in which
the Monastic Annalists demonstrate as clearly their entire
appreciation of the doctrine of the Church that the merit
of a good deed resides, not in the act itself, but in the
motive which dictates it, and present an anticipatory refutation of the calumnious imputations with which their
enemies have sought to blacken their memory, attributing
to them the doctrine that a passport to Heaven could be
purchased by the largesses of impenitent iniquity.   The
circumstances under which such gifts were made, frequently
afforded the best illustration of the spirit in which they
were bestowed.   Often did the fervent preaching of a holy
man stimulate the devotion of the laity to acts of pious
munificence, as was the case when St. Francis preached
at Monte Feltro, and so moved the Count of Chiusi, that
he made voluntary proffer of the entire mountain of
Alvernia for the foundation of a Monastery;[2] and indeed
it was but rarely that the preaching of this illustrious Saint
failed to excite similar manifestations of holy zeal among

[7] Chron. St. Denis. v. 23.   [8] Ibid. iv. 21.   [9] Ibid.
v. 9.   [1] Wadding Annal. Minor. v. 1292.   [2] Les Chron.
des FF. Min. l. ii. c. 37.

his auditors. But these noble offerings were but the natural sequence of the richer gift which had preceded them ; the heritor of broad acres, who emptied his coffers into the treasury of the poor, gave but a secondary manifestation, in these donations of perishable wealth, of the strength of the divine impulse which had already inspired him to consecrate his heart to God, and to offer the evil passions of his corrupt humanity as an acceptable sacrifice to Heaven. The noble of the olden time, who laid his oblations upon the Altar, needed not to be told that his munificence was vain if it sprung not from a sanctified and contrite soul, for from his earliest years the unvarying teaching of the Church, breathing the same holy spirit in all ages of Her existence, and piloting through the troubled waters of the stream of Time the sacred bark which She had freighted with precious treasures at the sources of eternal Truth, had imprinted this lesson indelibly in his memory ; but, unhappily, in our own day few beyond the pale of Her communion look to Her own teachers for the exposition of Her doctrines ; the minds of the many are yet poisoned with the absurd lie that She will remit sin for the gift of lands, and pardon iniquity for gold ; and it behoves us, therefore, to exhibit the evidences of a truth which to the Catholic student needs not a syllable of demonstration.

Regarding the sufferings, the self-denial, and the holy deeds of the ancient cænobites simply as atonements for their own misdeeds, rendered acceptable in the sight of God by their union with that mighty Sacrifice from which alone such human expiations derive their value before the Almighty, the pious struggles of these devoted warriors wear an aspect glorious and divine, and the

mighty victories over human frailty which each day saw
achieved beneath the humble cowl and consummated in
the retirement of the lonely cell, present themselves as
immortal trophies of the omnipotence of Faith, thus over-
powering in the hearts of feeble mortals the potent wiles
of the enemy who is ever seeking to lure humanity to perdition.   Yet this is but one side of the picture ; contemplating thus the mortifications of the Monks, we regard
them in their least sublime aspect ; viewed in another
light, these triumphs over the flesh are yet more worthy
of our reverent admiration.   If the self-inflicted penances
of the Religious strike us as wondrous tokens of the
vigorous energy of their souls, when undertaken solely
to promote their own salvation, how much more illustrious
do they appear when achieved by men whose souls were
at peace with God, and who offered their vigils, their fasts,
their disciplines, their mortifications, and their prayers, as
expiatory sacrifices in atonement for the sins of an erring
world ; to the eye of Faith how lovely appears the spec-
tacle of these venerable heroes : more truly worthy of the
hero's fame than many a laurelled victor on ensanguined
plains, around whose brows the world has wreathed the
chaplet of renown : withdrawing themselves from the
allurements of earth, that they might become mediators
for mankind ; marshalling themselves into a spiritual
legion, aiding with pious arm the wayfarers who were yet
struggling against temptation ; a holy escort, guarding the
caravan of pilgrims across the desert of life, and warding
off from the feeble the perils which environ every heritor
of the frailties of humanity.   Viewed in this light, one
Monastery was more precious than a hundred fortresses,
one community of Monks more potent than a legion of

warriors ; for who shall say how much the arm of flesh was strengthened by the arm of the spirit ? who shall declare how many repented sins, still deserving the temporal chastisement with which Divine justice visits the iniquities of man, were expiated by the merits of the Religious ? who shall judge how large a share of national happiness and prosperity was conceded by an all-merciful God to the prayers of the pious recluses in Monastic cells ? The abnegation of self is the highest triumph of the purified soul over the frailties of humanity ; and truly no self-abnegation could be more complete than that which stimulated these holy men to abandon the pursuit of earthly joys, that they might, as the vanguard of the world, lay siege to the gates of Heaven, and smooth the road, over which others might journey to Paradise. In this, indeed, they transcended the Divine precept, for they loved their neighbour so much better than themselves that they ever sought to bear some share of the temporal punishment merited by his sins, that they might release him from the expiatory fires of the purifying world beyond the grave, and make him earlier a partner of their own beatitude.

But it was not alone by such purely spiritual agencies that the Monks sought to promote the well-being of humanity ; deeply impressed with the conviction that a faith barren of good works bears upon its front the index of its own unreality, and inspired by that tender affection for the whole family of mankind, which was but the natural offspring of the fervent love of God which filled their souls, they strove to multiply and diffuse on every hand the agencies of temporal solace, of intellectual advancement, and of spiritual elevation ; their lives were devoted,

not only to penance and prayer, but also to the performance of deeds of charity and mercy, which they deemed
to be instrumental to their own salvation, as inevitable
utterances of those human sympathies which their Great
Master had ennobled by juxtaposition with the adoration of
the Divine perfections, in the sublime precept in which
He summed up the duties of those who sought to render
themselves acceptable to the Almighty.

That the Monks laboured at all, is a fact apparently not
recognized by many among their adversaries.   No calumny
has been more frequently reiterated than this, that the
Religious of the olden time were slothful voluptuaries,
who assumed the habit from a love of luxury and ease,
and stupified their energies by sensual excess ; yet, assuredly they who urge against them such accusations, must
close their eyes to the evidence which is presented by every
page of the records which remain to us of the tenor of
their daily lives.   "In a Monastery," says Thomas à
Kempis, "it is permitted to no one to be idle, but to every
one is appointed a measure of appropriate work."[3]   "Different arts," says Duns Scotus, "are multiplied on account
of their limitation in respect to different capacities, or
divers agencies in form in respect to divers effects in
species."[4]   "In the Carthusian life," says the historian
of that Order, "there are so many occupations, that even
the unlearned can scarcely find time for all that is to be
done ;"[5] a still greater demand being made, of course,
upon the energies of those who devoted themselves to
study, or engaged in the work of instruction, in addition
to the manual labour which the Rule prescribed.   "In the

[3] Serm. i. 2.   [4] De Rer. Princip. i. 1.   [5] Petr. Sutor. de
Vit. Carthus. L ii. t. ii. c. 4.

fifth and sixth centuries," says Staudenmaier, " the Monks, when not engaged in teaching, tilled the ground and converted deserts into fruitful fields, and where there had been only wastes and barbarous Pagans, men saw gardens, meadows, and corn lands, as if a new created world;"[6] and Dunham avows that " we cannot shut our eyes to the fact that, for improvement in agriculture, the Germanic Empire was indebted to the Monks, for in whatever place these extraordinary men were located they soon showed what could be effected by willing minds still further influenced by the sacred obligations of duty, and from incontestable evidence we know that luxuriant meadows were soon made to start up from the fens, and ample harvests to wave on the black mountain or the sandy plain."[7] " On arriving at the Monastery of St. Æquitius," says Julian, who had been dispatched thither on a mission by the Supreme Pontiff, " I found some old men writing, and when I asked, ' Where is your Abbot?' they replied, ' He is cutting grass in the valley beneath the Monastery ;' " and William of Jumiege says of Herluin, the founder of the Abbey of Bec, and his Monks, " You would have seen them, after the first office of the Church, going into the fields to spend the day in agricultural labours ; the Abbot carrying the seeds on his head, and holding tools in his hands ; some clearing the ground, others carrying manure on their shoulders, and spreading it on the earth ; no one eating his bread in idleness, and all returning to the Church at the hour of the Divine office, and then sitting down to a meal of oaten bread and herbs and water."[8] In one mode or another the Monks

[6] Johan. Scotus und die Wissenschaft Seiner Zeit. i 73.
[7] Dunham, Hist. of Germ. Emp. ii. 78.   [8] Guil. Jum. l. iv. c. 9.

laboured unceasingly throughout their lives; the culture of the fields, the copying of books, the acquisition of learning, the dissemination of knowledge, the multiplication of the Scriptures, the relief of the destitute, the instruction of sinners, and the preaching of the Gospel, engaged their unwearying energy, and from the hour in which he first assumed the habit of religion to that in which he exchanged it for the shroud, the Monk was a ceaseless toiler for the benefit of mankind. Glance but at the Monastic Rules; from their tenor it will be seen that it was impossible that the Monks who obeyed their injunctions should be idle, since every hour had its appointed duty, incumbent upon all: trace the records of Monastic Life in contemporaneous Chronicles, or contemplate the monuments which remain to us of the pauseless toils of the Religious; these suffice to show how rigidly these obligations were fulfilled by those who had devoted their lives to the special service of the Almighty. And, for the imputation of luxury and sensuality, let the same evidence illustrate the truth of history. It needs but to open the volumes penned by their contemporaries, whether within or without the Cloister, to perceive how vast a body of testimony remains to us to avouch the purity of their lives. "Who," says the illustrious layman Odelirius, in the eleventh century, "can worthily relate all their vigils, hymns, psalmody, prayers, alms, and sacrifices? What denial of their own will for the love of our Lord Jesus Christ! What shall I say of the chastity of Monks, of their silence, of their modesty, of their obedience? Such an abundance of virtues confounds my astonished intelligence, and I confess that my tongue fails me to express it. From my tender youth I have long been admitted to the secrets of Monks, and by familiar relations I have learned thoroughly what were their manners. In consequence, when I consider the conduct of all mortals who inhabit the earth, I see that they are all, in their lives, inferior to Monks who live in obedience to their Rule."[9] " I see in Cloisters," says Peter of Blois, who was himself a secular Priest, " celestial men, or rather earthly angels, whose conversation is in Heaven, who with a noble pride despise the honours and riches of the world ;"[1] and of the Cistercian Order, the same writer remarks, " There is a most approved school of religion, there one finds the practice of the utmost modesty, regularity of manners, fraternal affection, peace of mind, community of possessions, the love of obedience, vigour of discipline, the bond of charity, the subjection of the flesh, the exercise of hospitality, liberty of study, the order of vigils, the calm of meditation, the devotion of psalmody."[2] " In all congregations of Monks," says St. Bernard, " you can behold men that are filled with consolation, abounding in joy, always cheerful and agreeable, fervent in spirit, meditating day and night on the Law of God, frequently looking up to Heaven and lifting up pure hands in prayer, careful observers of their conscience, and devout followers of good works ; to whom discipline is lovely, fasting sweet, the vigils short, manual labour pleasant, and the whole austerity of their conversation refreshing."[3] " It is the voice of all men," says Richard, Archbishop of Canterbury in the reign of Henry II., " that the professors of the Cistercian Order keep the footsteps of apostolical religion in moderation of food and raiment, in watching, in con-

[9] Oderic Vital. l. v.　　[1] Petr. Bles. Epist. cii.　　[2] Ibid. lxxxvi.
[3] St. Bern. In Ascens. Dom. Serm. vi.

fessions, in discipline, in psalmody, in humility, in hospitality, in obedience, and in all other fruits of love;"[4]
and Vincent of Beauvais describes Monks as " glorious
men, rich in virtue, studious of beauty, living at peace in
their domains, and obtaining reverence in the generations of
their nation."[5]   " If there be any perfection in this
world," says Hugo of St. Victor, " it can be found in the
cloister;"[6] and he denotes the source of the spiritual elevation of the Religious, by declaring that " the inhabitants
of Cloisters investigate the judgments of the Lord, not
secular judgments ; they keep the Law of the Lord by
living, meditating, and loving ; in which Law there are
two witnesses heard, life and conscience, two judges, meditation and science, two counsellors, the love of our
neighbour and the love of God."[7]   " What shall I say ?"
writes an Italian author of the fifteenth century, " of
Monks, of whom the number of most holy and learned
seems almost infinite ? We cannot deny that, both now
and formerly, there have been some bad men in that
habit; but who could number the good and illustrious ?
Who so mad as to think that, if men wished to be evil,
they would choose such a life as this ?   Truly, long since
all devotion of Christians, and nearly all religion, would
have perished, if these holy men had not, by their doctrine and example of life, protected the faith of Christ,
contending for it, as the Apostle says, through evil and
good report."   Undoubtedly there were occasionally found
in the Cloister evil men, strangers to the pious spirit to
which the Monastic Life owed its original institution ;
" in all the Religious Orders," as John of Salisbury re-

[4] Petr. Bles. Epist. lxxxii.   [5] Spec. Mor. i. 4.   [6] De
Claustro Animæ, l. ii. c. 17.   [7] Ibid.

marks, " there are found some of the faithful and some of the reprobate, yet the truth of religion and the sanctity of profession is not on that account obscured, for what profession is there, or what society has ever been read of, into which some blot did not penetrate ?"[8] and the abuses which sometimes crept into these holy communities were denounced by the Monks themselves, in language which evinces their cordial acquiescence in the sentiment that " though to enter a Monastery is the beginning of the utmost perfection, to live not perfectly in a Monastery is the utmost damnation ;"[9] and shows that they addressed their brethren on this topic with the confidence which animated St. Bernard, when he said, " In exposing abuses, I do not fear that I shall give trouble to those who love the Order, but I feel assured that they will look gratefully on those who attack what they themselves detest."[1] Abuses undoubtedly arose, which awakened the pious zeal of fervent brethren for their removal, and which no sooner sprung into life, than they gave birth to searching and vigorous reforms ; but we should guard ourselves against attaching an exaggerated importance to the complaints which find utterance in the writings of these austere cæno-bites, for in this age the mere mention of abuse in a Mo-nastery gives rise to imaginings of all conceivable cor-ruption, and generates the idea that each Cloister thus stigmatized was a hot-bed of sensualism and depravity. With our decayed spiritualism, the decadence which shocked the ascetics of former days would scarcely be deemed worthy of consideration, for if we examine their vehement denunciations of the enfeebled piety of certain

[8] De Nugis Curial. c. 21. [9] Nuremb. Doct. Ascet. i. iv. 36.
; [1] St. Bern. Apolog. ad Guilielm. c. 7.

isolated communities, we shall find that the gravest charges
urged are the shortening of vigils, the diminution of fasts,
the partial cessation of manual labour, and the decrease
of bodily mortifications ; the atrocious crimes which the
carnal fancy of modern fanaticism is wont to connect with
the idea of Monastic corruption were things undreamed
of by these holy men, who would have sighed if they
could have foreseen the advent of a day, when the decline
of antique piety, and the consequent lessened estimation
of the gravity of the evils which seemed to them so
weighty, should cause their language to receive a signification so far removed from their design. Yet even these
examples were exceptional ; the voice of those who best
knew their true character accords with the language of
Albertus Sartinuensis, who says of the Monks of his day,
with whom he had lived in relations of the closest intimacy, " They are men who, in my opinion, do all things
well ; who are grateful to their friends, pacific to their
enemies, solicitous for the dangers of others, and not neg-
ligent of their own ; who, casting off the pollutions of the
world, condemn what they once were, and love what they
are to be in the future life ; make themselves judges of
their own wanderings, exult in having escaped from the
disquietudes and tempests of the world, and, with minds
far above it, superior to all earthly power, devote themselves to virtue and justice, forgetting what is behind and
stretching forwards to what is before, thinking life tedious
and death most happy ; whose care it is never to yield to
vice, but to subdue it ; who deplore the passions of the
profligate, having by discipline restrained their own ; who,
through evil report and good report, in cold and poverty,
pursue their steady way, rejoicing more than the foolish

multitude in its vanities; and, what is above all, who so
completely subject and humiliate and neglect themselves
for Christ, that they bring into captivity every thought to
the obedience of Christ, and fear not to be counted fools
for his sake, saying with the Apostle, ' If any one seem
to be wise in this world, let him become a fool that he
may be wise :' lo! this is what I think of these men ;
such I know to be the pure and excellent lives of many of
them, such, at least, the innocuous character of the rest."²
Such testimonies are innumerable ; but the visible fruits
of the labours of the Monks, are alone sufficient to indicate to us the character of their lives. On the shelves of
many Libraries lie, neglected and uncared for, the volumes
which record the whisperings of their meditative souls,
and from which many a modern sage, who affects to despise the Monkish scribe, has stolen the ideas which he
has fashioned into the foundation of his own renown, and
often marred most vilely in the fashioning ; venerable in
their antique grandeur stand the majestic fanes which
they consecrated to the worship of the Most High, and
within whose sacred walls they gathered together the
richest treasures of the earth and sea, as thank-offerings
to Him who made the loveliness of the world. Themselves
have vanished from the living throng ; as mere specks in the
shadowy distance seem their venerable forms, moving amid
the scenes of an age so unlike our own, that we might
almost doubt whether it were peopled by sharers of the
same humanity ; but in the death of their bodies their
Thoughts remained immortal, and in these monuments of
their untiring zeal we see reflected the purity of their
souls. Such gigantic works as they achieved never owed

² Wadding, x.

their conception to men rioting in feasting and debauchery; such holy thoughts as were embalmed by their pens had never their birth in brains muddled with the fumes of wine or stupified by excess of gluttony. Not from the chamber of the wine-bibber, or the home of the sensualist, is heard the sweet chorus of pious Psalmody which daily rose from the Monastic Cell to Heaven; the Matin Bell wakens no toper from his heavy slumbers, to sing the praise of God at the first breaking of the early dawn; not to licentious revellers is accorded the loving veneration with which the Monks were regarded, by all who came within the sphere of their benignant influence. The oaten bread and herbs and water, which was the food of the Monks of Bec, served for the diet of many a pious brotherhood; and while the table of the guests was spread with generous profusion, the hosts contented themselves with the humble fare which best accorded with the spirit of penance and self-mortification which had impelled them to assume the habit of religion.

The Monks, then, were neither idlers nor voluptuaries; their lives were occupied in incessant exertions to promote the welfare of mankind; works of piety, of charity, and of mercy engrossed the entire energies of their souls, and the labours to which they devoted themselves were such, that, but for them, the world would have been a wilderness and society a mere savage horde, without civilization, without learning, and almost without religion. Often did they plant their homes amid uncultivated wilds, that they might reclaim them from their native barrenness for the use and benefit of man, and many a verdant plain is now radiant in the plenitude of rural beauty which their stout arms redeemed from waste, and converted from a trackless wilderness into an expanse of fertile meadows; many a time did they locate their dwelling-places in spots where no pious voices had yet awakened the echoes with the praise of God, that nations might be redeemed from heathen darkness, and new children be gathered into the fold of Christ.

In every Monastery was a School, in which the brethren gave instruction to all who sought intellectual cultivation; the children of the poor flocked to them for tuition, and their sublime piety made the Monastic School the favourite resort of those who needed not their bounty. With the learning which they imparted they mingled ever the teaching of Religion; well assured that Knowledge without Faith is a bark without a rudder launched on the billows of a stormy sea, they were no disciples of that modern Philosophy which would separate the culture of the mind from the training of the soul; impressed with a profound sense of the true destinies of humanity, they deemed that intellectual advancement is valuable only as an auxiliary to progress in spiritual perfection, and the lore of science then alone desirable when it aids the pilgrim in his march towards Heaven. A portion of their time was given to the copying of Books; but for them the literature which is most precious to us would have long since passed into oblivion; in the retired Scriptorium, the Bible, the writings of the Fathers, the Annals of ancient History, the speculations of antique Philosophy, were perpetuated and multiplied by their labours; the Scriptures, especially, were by them preserved and rendered accessible to mankind.

Often in Monastic Cells might be found criminals expiating, by years of penance, the offences for which the

State would have exacted the forfeit of their lives; for the Church, inspired ever by the spirit of Her Divine Master, sought rather the conversion than the destruction of the sinner, and the Monks constantly desired that offenders might be consigned to their tender care, to the end that by penitence they might become worthy of happiness in eternity. "At the time when King Otho went to Rome to be crowned Emperor," says Cæsar of Heisterbach, "leaving the government of the Moselle to his brother, Henry Palatine, a certain noble was condemned to death for pillaging— Daniel, Abbot of Sconavia, obtained pardon for him by his prayers, on condition that he would satisfy God for his sins in the Cistercian Order. Thus did he escape death and final perdition; and I have heard of many who similarly obtained deliverance by the intercession of our order."[3] Such incidents were of frequent occurrence in mediæval centuries. "The Monasteries," says Neander, "became often, for criminals, asylums of penitence and reformation; sequestered in these pious retreats, they were not only prevented from doing farther injury to society, but, by unremitting care and constant exhortation, they were aroused to serious and profitable reflection; and the Monks obtained without difficulty the demission into their hands of offenders condemned to death, that they might send them to end their days in the retirement of the Cloister. It may suffice, for an example of this, to relate an incident in the life of St. Bernard. On his way to visit Count Thibaut de Champagne, he encountered on the road a criminal, whom the officers of justice were conducting to the scaffold. Seizing the cord which bound the male-

[3] Illust. Mirac. l. i. c. 31.

factor, he presented himself, thus accompanied, before the
Count, who came forth to receive him with demonstrations
of the most profound respect. 'What are you dreaming
of, venerable father,' he said, 'that you desire to save a
man who has shown himself to be a very devil?' But
the Abbot of Clairvaux replied, 'I have no wish that so
great a criminal should be suffered to escape unpunished.
You propose to make him suffer the momentary pain of
death; but I will crucify him during many years, and
compel him to undergo throughout his life a perpetual and
unremitting chastisement.' The Count de Champagne
knew not how to reply, and the Saint, having divested
himself of his habit, clothed the criminal with it, and received him into his Monastery, where he lived for thirty
years."[4]

In their Hospitals the sick were ever received and tended
with loving care; no fee or reward remunerated the pious
assiduity of these zealous guardians; in the consciousness
that they were serving God by ministering to the afflicted
they found the most enduring recompense for their exertions, and the visitations in which they beheld the temporal chastisement of the sins of the sufferer, were made
by them conducive to his eternal welfare by the spiritual
instruction with which they accompanied the alleviation of
his physical infirmities. And, above all, the Poor found
in them the zealous servants of Heaven, who regarded the
rich possessions with which they were endowed by pious
benefactors, as a trust of which they were stewards for
the benefit of the destitute; to each one who sought relief
the ready alms was freely given, with a blessing and of
prayer; for the wayfarer there was a home, for the starving

[4] Neander Hist. de St. Bern. 2.   Herbert de Mirac. l. ii. c. 15.

their bounty provided all that was needful for the relief of his necessities. The solace of the physical woes of the indigent was a prominent object of the founders of Monasteries, and was frequently expressed in their charters ; thus Duke William of Aquitaine, the founder of the Abbey of Clugni, in the ninth century, says, "We prescribe especially that this our donation may be for a perpetual refuge to the poor who leave the world, bringing with them nothing but a good will, that so our provision may be made their abundance ; we desire also, that, as opportunity and power may be afforded, there may be, from this time forth, daily exhibited works of mercy to all the poor, to strangers and to travellers ;"[5] the Count of Montecava, in a diploma to the Cistercian Monastery of St. Maria Roccæmatoris, near Messina, in the twelfth century, says, "The Creator of all the world inspiring, I have considered that temporal goods have been committed to me in this life, as to every other mortal man, in order that by them, charitably and discreetly dispensed in divine worship, and in assisting the servants of God and the Poor, and in salutary works of mercy, I might acquire eternal possessions and the joys of celestial life, prepared for the faithful of Christ from the beginning of the world by the providence of His goodness : moved by this consideration, I have founded, to the honour of the eternal God and under the name of the most glorious Virgin Mary, an honourable mansion of the Cistercian order, with the intention that lauds, sacrifices, and pious ecclesiastical exercises may be for ever offered to Jesus Christ, son of the living God, night and day, and that it may conduce to the support and comfort of his servants, of Pilgrims, of sick and weary people, and of all

[5] Bibl. Clun. 2.

the miserable;"[6] and numerous other Charters contain similar expressions. King Alfonso, having built a splendid Cistercian Monastery in the vicinity of Burgos, erected near it a Hospice, which he so munificently endowed, that all travellers on applying there, at any hour of the day, had their wants supplied, and every night all who desired might lodge there, and the sick were retained and carefully tended until their recovery or death;[7] and such an establishment was invariably attached to every Cistercian Abbey.[8] In the twelfth century, the Monastery of St. Martin-le-Champs, at Paris, " was regarded as a kind of common asylum, above all those of France, for Bishops, Abbots, lay noblemen, Monks, Clerks, and poor people; the house was always full, and every one was received with a smiling countenance, which no importunity of the crowds could ever alter;"[9] at the Abbey of Tron there were two houses of the poor, one for their lodging in summer, and the other, with fire places, to serve the same purpose in winter;[1] and at Clugni the gate stood open from morning until night, and all who chose might enter, and found a hospitable welcome.[2] " I cannot speak in sufficient detail," says Oderic Vitalis, " of the hospitality of the Monks of Bec. Let any one ask the Burgundians, Spaniards, and other persons who come from far and near, and they will answer, and say truly, with what benignity they were received by the religious. The gate of Bec is open to all travellers, and no one there is ever refused bread. What shall I add? May He who has begun and who entertains the

---

[6] Sicilia Sacra. ii. 1287. [7] Ruder. Toletan. de Reb. Hispan. l. vii. c. 34. [8] Notit. Abbat. Ord. Cisterc. l. vii. 37.

[9] Bibl. Clun. 554. [1] Chron. Abbat. St. Trudon. liv. 10. ap Dacher. Spicileg. vii. [2] Petr. Ven. Epist. i. 28.

good which shines in them, maintain it until their arrival
at the port of salvation."[3]

Such unbounded hospitality was not confined to any one
Religious Order, or to a few peculiarly distinguished Monasteries; wherever they fixed their home, the Monks made
the solace of the needy a principal object of their exertions.
"We cannot but perceive," says Neander, "how necessary
the wealth of the Monasteries was to the happiness of
mankind, for the Monks well knew how best to employ
their riches for the common benefit, and we see that in
seasons of famine they afforded sustenance to hundreds
of the destitute.   A famine having arisen in Burgundy,
the poor flocked in vast numbers to Clairvaux; the Superior,
perceiving that it was impossible to furnish entire support
to all, chose two thousand out of their number, whom he
could recognize by means of a particular sign, and promised to afford to each of these the same measure of
assistance ; to the rest he gave less abundant alms.   The
Abbey of Prémontré, founded by Norbert, charged itself,
during a famine which occurred in his absence, with the
support of five hundred poor ; and under similar circumstances, the venerable Bishop Hugh of Grenoble sold all
the precious vessels of his Church, that he might be able
to afford ample nourishment to the destitute."[4]   Many
munificent donations were made to Monasteries, especially
on account of the charitable aid which they afforded to
the indigent ; in the eleventh century the Abbot Wulke-
tulus gave to the Abbey of Croyland the Chapel of St.
Mary at Spaldyng, with all the buildings belonging to it, to
defray the expenses of hospitality to the multitudes who

---

[3] Oderic Vital. l. iv.   [4] Neander, Hist. de St. Bern. 13.

were accustomed to resort thither ;[5] the Church of Hesel
was assigned by Pope Innocent III. to the Prior of Gis-
borne and his brethren, " because they give to all who
ask their aid, and apply their goods to hospitality with
such zeal, that no one departs from them empty handed ;"[6]
and multitudes of similar examples are furnished by Monastic Chroniclers.   The histories of Religious Houses
amply demonstrate the zeal with which the Monks applied
themselves to the discharge of the sacred trust thus committed to them by their pious benefactors, and their admirable beneficence was rewarded by the love and benediction of those who received such abounding benefits
from their charitable ministrations ; their bitterest enemies
are constrained to admit that the suppression or destruction
of Monasteries was ever followed by the lamentations of
the commonalty—a natural result, since they were to the
Poor an asylum in adversity, and a source of priceless
benefits in their days of highest weal.   To the Religious
it was truly a labour of love to become .the dispensers of
the bounty of the opulent ; many touching examples are
recorded of their joyful alacrity in the exercise of this
noble function, such as that of a Monk of Melrose Abbey,
in the thirteenth century, who was wont, during every day,
to sit with his Psalter at the door of the Church, holding
a basket of bread for the use of those who sought for
alms, or that of the illustrious Notker, who, when dying,
desired that the poor might receive their dinner beside his
bed, that his last glances might rest on the scene of their
enjoyment ; and the same feeling found utterance in the
high estimation which was accorded to the office of Porter,

---

[5] Hist. Ingulf. 66.   [6] Epist. Innoc. III. l. xiii. 208.

whose privilege it was to be the first to greet the indigent who sought relief. Who will say that such labours, prompted by love of God and charity to man, shall not have their reward in Heaven?

Thus briefly have we glanced at the spirit of the Monastic Life, and noted the prominent ideas which found development in its practical organization. The facts which have passed under our notice render it unnecessary to dwell upon the false views with regard to the Religious of the olden time which have been freely promulgated by some writers, and eagerly adopted by the prejudiced multitude; knowing what the Monks really were, we need no other proof that they deserve not the denunciations which have been levelled against them by adversaries who have striven to strike through them a blow at the Church which reigned supreme in the affections of the antique world, and whose teaching gave birth to the convictions which impelled them to adopt the habit of religion; comprehending the motives which induced them to embrace the cloistral life, and recognizing the zeal with which they devoted themselves to the promotion of the bodily and spiritual welfare of humanity, we require no other demonstration of the beneficent influence which they exercised upon the tone of society, and the powerful agency which they exerted in advancing the happiness of mankind. " Who is there," says Mabillon, " that has a just sense of Christian piety, and who examines the matter before God, but must esteem those men very useful to the Church who endeavoured to conform assiduously to the life of Christ; who celebrated the worship of God with all the devotion of which they were capable, offering their body and soul as a constant sacrifice of praise; who retained the ancient vestiges and example of Christian penitence in the Church; who opened public schools of virtue; who by their labour transmitted the monuments of ancient literature to posterity; who gave example to clerks to institute laudable societies; who erected as many Hospitals for the poor, as Monasteries in which diseases of the soul were cured, in which baptismal innocence was preserved inviolate, or restored when lost, and in which the wants of all the needy were supplied? Monasteries are hostels, in which not alone the cloistral flock, but, as Leodegavius testifies, the whole world is delivered from the corruptions of the age. Finally, who can say that they were useless to the civil and Christian republic, who covered with towns and villages so many provinces before uninhabited and desert, adorned them with edifices, enriched them with letters, and, by giving episcopal and pastoral institutions, brought so many millions of Pagans to the faith of Christ?"[7] It was not only by their actual labours, fruitful as these were of surpassing benefits, but also by the spirit of their general example, that these holy men were an incalculable blessing to the world; for what sinner could gaze upon the cowled Monk or barefoot Friar, knowing that he had resigned the world for the love of Heaven, without receiving a lesson more potent and enduring than the teaching of unnumbered homilies? what listener to a Monastic preacher could fail to be more deeply impressed by his monitions, from the knowledge that he who adjured him to relinquish all things for Christ had himself trodden the path which he pointed out to others? what man could fail to derive a high conception of the loveliness of Religion from beholding the calm and tranquil happiness of these pious cænobites, who,

---

[7] Mabillon Act. SS. Ord. S. Bened. Sæc. vi. Præf.

abstaining from all the pleasures of the world, had found in the bosom of Holy Church a felicity which cast into the shade all earthly joys, yet waited for its full consummation in the bliss of Heaven? Each Monastery was a commentary on the precepts of the Gospel, carved in stone; and if it be truly said that the life of one good man is more efficient by its example for the conversion of sinners than the lessons of many preachers, how vast an agency of good must have resided within the peaceful walls which each pious brotherhood made eloquent with the echoes of its songs of praise. Many a time must the deep tones of the Matin Bell have struck upon the ear of some sleepless worldling, giving him intimation that in that silent hour the community had gathered together in the Church for prayer; and who shall tell what sanctifying thoughts the force of such example may have awakened in the sinner's heart, winning his soul to contention for the joys of Heaven? The Monk, treading in his garb of homely serge the streets of the crowded city, was, in one respect, as the skeleton which the ancients placed at their banquets, a perpetual monitor of the common destiny of humanity; but the grisly guest of the antique festival was to man only an intimation that he must die, while the life of the Monk was to all a silent example of the practices by which they might make the grave the avenue of entrance into the glories of a beatified eternity. About the religion of our Monastic forefathers hung no gloomy doubt or shadowy uncertainty; before them, in distinct and visible reality, lay the road to Paradise; and in the pious labours of charity and religion they found a foretaste of the joys which awaited them in immortality. To make some spot upon God's earth more fruitful, more pleasant, more teeming with joy and usefulness to man ; to alleviate in some desolate dwelling the woes of physical misery and destitution ; to arouse in some uncultivated mind a love of learning, and lead it by the paths of knowledge into the ways of virtue ; to kindle in some unregenerate soul the vital spark of true contrition, and convert the sinner into the heir of an eternal crown ; these were the aims which inspired all their exertions and gave direction to all their labours. From the retirement of their peaceful sanctuaries their prayers and penances were ever offered up to God in behalf of a sinful world—sweet incense before the throne of Heaven ; and while they thus implored the mercy of the Almighty upon their erring fellow-creatures, they did not fail to strive unceasingly to win back the sinner to the ways of justice, and to awaken in the world-worn heart the true vitality which Faith breathes into the soul. All that was most admirable in the Middle Ages may be traced to its source in the influence which the Church exercised upon mankind ; and it was through the agency of the Monasteries that She was enabled to confer the most substantial and enduring benefits upon the world, promoting the spread of true civilization, encouraging the cultivation of knowledge, solacing the woes of poverty, and training the hearts of Her children in the love of God and the practice of the sublime duties of the Christian life.

Looking back upon all that we have learned with regard to the character of the Monks of the Middle Ages, can we hesitate for a moment to confess that such men—so humble, so zealous, so patient, so benevolent, so indefatigable, so devout—are well-worthy to receive the loving reverence of our hearts, and to be cherished as examples for the regulation of our lives ? Truly we could not propose to

ourselves nobler objects for our fervent veneration, our
humble but diligent imitation; look at them when we will,
their lives still wear the same high and heavenly aspect,
still manifest in every action the glorious spirit by which
they were animated to labour and to endure.   Glance at
them when, fixing their calm retreat in some uncultivated
wild, they toiled with unremitting energy until they had
made the grateful earth yield forth rich increase to the
labourer's hand; regard them when, in the retired Scriptorium, they devoted months of patient industry to the
production of another copy of the Sacred Scriptures, or
to the multiplication of the noblest works of ancient
Literature ; behold them when, ministering as the consecrated servants of the Most High, they poured upon the
amazed ears of listening Heathens the joyful tidings of
the Gospel, until the Pagan heart was melted by the
warm recital of God's eternal mercies, and a rich harvest
of regenerated souls was gathered into the garner of the
Church ; watch them at the gate of their holy and peaceful home, dealing out to the grateful multitude the ready
alms bestowed on every child of Him who called the
Poor especially His own ; contemplate them in the solitude of their cells lifting up pure hands in prayer, and
offering to God their vigils, their fasts, and their mortifications, as a propitiatory sacrifice in behalf of a sinful
world ; see them in their thickly scattered schools, training in virtue and piety the youthful soul, which, carrying
with it through life the lessons it had there received,
reaped in a better world their precious fruits, when the
germ which Monastic hands had nurtured in its budding
growth blossomed into an Angel within the gates of Paradise ; wherever we gaze upon them, we see one motive

animating all their actions—the desire to promote the glory of God, and to augment the happiness of man.   In prosperity and in affliction they remained unchanged; overwhelmed by adversity, or wending their holy way in tranquil joy, they were ever the humble, self-denying servants of Heaven, seeking refuge from the strife and temptations of the world beneath the habit of religion, only that they might become ministering Angels of love and charity to their fellow-men, and illustrating in their lives the noble truth which was graven indelibly in their hearts: **Laborare est Orare**:   "To toil to make God's creatures happy, is the noblest way of praising God."

BOOKS, LIBRARIES, AND SCHOOLS

IN

THE MIDDLE AGES.

BOOKS, LIBRARIES, AND SCHOOLS

IN

THE MIDDLE AGES

THE intellectual darkness of mediæval centuries has been long a favourite theme for popular declamation ; and assuredly, if we are to accept as a faithful delineation of the veritable aspects of the past the picture which some historians have drawn of the condition of our forefathers, the men of the Middle Ages well merit our grave commiseration. In the sketches which such writers, supplying by the vigour of their fancy the deficiency resulting from the poverty of their erudition, have presented for our contemplation, books figure as the golden apples in the gardens of the Hesperides, few, precious, and inaccessible ; and the masses of Europe are pourtrayed in their narratives as steeped in the most profound ignorance, and deprived of access to all means of mental cultivation. According to such annalists, the student who, in those days, sought to add a few volumes to his library, was compelled to repair to the scribe with the title deeds of a hundred acres in his pocket, as a fund wherewith to secure this modest accession to his literary possessions, since, if we are to credit their averments, a flock of sheep was a small equivalent to offer in barter for a saintly homily or a volume of an

old historian, and a knight's fee scarcely sufficed to purchase an illuminated missal or a copy of the Sacred Scriptures
Upon their showing, schools for the laity were, in those
ages, things unheard-of and unknown, and the humble
wended his way from the cradle to the tomb through the
gloom of an intellectual night, which no kindly hand sought
to irradiate with the light of learning.

The examination of the truth of these allegations
possesses an interest and importance even beyond that
which attaches to it as a simple historical investigation.
Foremost among the chosen weapons of the controversialists
who have waged war against the ancient Church, has ever
figured the assertion that in the ages of Her highest power
She displayed Herself the foe of knowledge, and strove to
strengthen Her influence by the debasement of the intellect
of man ; and many among the multitudes who have derived
their ideas of the history of bygone centuries from the
representations of Her foes, yet believe that She has uniformly
endeavoured to crush the intelligence of humanity, and to
load with heavy fetters the minds of Her children as the
surest means of securing their subjugation to Her sway.
To demonstrate that She has, in all ages, contended nobly
against ignorance, and developed with unwearying zeal
the means at Her command for the enlightenment of the
people ; to prove that the epoch of Her highest might was an
era of libraries and schools, especially characterised by the
assiduity with which the agencies of instruction were
multiplied for the peculiar benefit of the humble ; to show
that, if ignorance existed in those ages among the masses, it
was not because She did not place abundantly within their
reach the most extended facilities for the acquirement of
knowledge ; will be to vindicate Her fame from one of the

foulest of the aspersions which have been cast upon it by the sectaries of later times ; and for the attainment of this end it needs but that we should interrogate the witnesses who lived in antique days, and learn from the testimony of mediæval writers the true nature of the advantages which were enjoyed by our forefathers.

Every enquiry into the intellectual condition of the Middle Ages necessarily resolves itself into an investigation of the agencies employed by the Church for the mental elevation of humanity; in this noble work She was the only labourer; whether we consider the extent of book-multiplication or the diffusion of educational institutions, the results which reward our search are invariably the records of the triumphs achieved by men who had dedicated their lives to God and wore the habit of religion. In the Monasteries dwelt the Scribes who multiplied by transcription the treasures of antique wisdom, the Scholars who added new wealth to the stores of literature, and the Teachers who laboured in the cultivation of the youthful mind; the Monks were at once the copyists, the authors, and the schoolmasters of the mediæval world, and from the Cloister the lights of Faith and Learning shed their mingled beams upon mankind.

In estimating the claims of any age to our admiration, we are to consider, not the nature and extent of the advantages which it enjoyed, but the use which it made of those actually in its possession; if the then existing facilities for social and intellectual advancement were carefully developed and faithfully employed, their paucity constitutes no valid reason for withholding the meed of our approbation. Thus we are not to look for an abundance of books in an age of manual transcription at all comparable to that which

belongs to an age of printing-presses ; all we are entitled
to expect is an abundance commensurate with the means
which were possessed for their multiplication.   Whether
such really existed in the Middle Ages is the question
which now remains for our consideration.

From the provisions of Monastic Rules, which prescribe
the devotion to study of a specified portion of the time of
the Religious, and contain minute directions for the custody
and periodical distribution of the books belonging to the
community,[1] it is evident that a library constituted at all
times an essential adjunct to a Monastery ; it appears, indeed, to have been generally one of the first things thought
of in the formation of such an establishment, and the
Monks devoted themselves with zealous energy to the
preservation and augmentation of their literary possessions.

In the narrative of the foundation of a Monastery by
St. Eligius, Bishop of Noyon, in the seventh century, we
find it recorded that he transported thither waggons heavily
laden with vessels for all purposes, both of wood and
brass, bedding, table linen, a great number of religious
books, and all other things necessary for a Monastery ;[2]
Guibert of Nogent, speaking of the first disciples of St.
Bruno, says, " choosing to live in the utmost poverty, they
nevertheless collect a most rich library;"[3] in the Annals of
Corby, in Saxony, we are told that in 1097 Machwartus
made a law that every novice should on the day of his
profession give a useful and valuable book to the library,
and that every Superior of a Monastery subject to his own
should compose a chronicle of his house and send it to

---

[1] Reg. St. Bened. c. 48. 55. Reg. St. Pachom. Reg. St. Isid. Martene de Antiq. Monach. Rit. I. c. 7.   [2] Vit. S. Elig. ap Dacher.
Spicileg. ii. 76.   [3] De Vitâ Suâ. i. 10.

him to be a memorial to future ages;[4] and the renown which the Monasteries had acquired for literary wealth in the thirteenth century is evidenced by the Bull issued by Pope Innocent IV. in 1246, in which, calling attention to the poverty of the churches of Prussia and Livonia, which, being infant, were unprovided with the necessary books, he especially invited Monks to send some to them out of their abundance.[5] Many Abbeys, by reason of the magnificence of their collections, attained to pre-eminent renown; world-wide was the fame of the libraries of Fulda, of Corby, of St. Gall, of Gemblours, of Lobbes, of Hirschau, of Lorsch, of St. Emmeran at Ratisbon, of Tegernsee, of St. Martin at Spanheim, of Einseidlin, of St. Remi at Rheims, of Clugni, of Gembloux, of St. Benedict sur Loire, of St. Victor and St. Germains at Paris, of St. Medard at Soissons, of St. Martin at Tours, of Alvelda, of St. Benedict at Sahagun, of St. Paul at Barcelona, of St. Vincent at Oveido, of Alcobaca, of St. John in Verdara and of the Augustinian Hermits at Padua, of Bobbio, of SS. John and Paul at Venice, of La Chiusa, of Monte Cassino, of Nonantula, of Camaldoli, of Squillace, of St. Maria Maddalena at Florence, of the Franciscans at Cesena, of St. Maria Novella, of Santa Croce, of Pomposa, of Piscara, and of St. Saviour at Messina; but while these and others which might be named were especially distin-guished, every Monastery contained its store of intellectual treasures, which underwent constant augmentation. The most eminent laymen vied with each other in adding to the opulence of Monastic libraries. St. Louis left his books to be divided between the Franciscan and Dominican Orders; Cassiodorus presented to the Monks of Squillace

---

[4] Annal Corb.   [5] Voigt. Gesschichte Preuss. ii. 49.

a large collection of MSS. which he had gathered together
for them at Rome, and to which he made many subsequent
additions, and gave his own extensive library to the Monastery of Monte Cassino; Cosmo de Medicis enriched
with noble libraries the Monasteries of St. Francesco, of
St. George at Venice, and of St. Bartholomew near Fiesole;
Malalesta Novello of Rimini bestowed a splendid collection of books on the Franciscans of Cesena; the Archduke
Henry III. of Bavaria gave a rich library to the Abbey of
Tegernsee, in which he was wont to pass much time in devout meditation; and records of such gifts abound in
Monastic Chronicles. These donations afford proof that
large collections of books sometimes existed in the hands
of individuals, and examples of this, though necessarily
limited in number by the circumstances of the age, are by
no means of rare occurrence. The library of King
Charles V. of France contained nine hundred volumes;[6]
Frederick II. formed an excellent library;[7] King Robert
of Sicily, in the fourteenth century, possessed a large collection of books; of Richard of Bury, Bishop of Durham, in the thirteenth century, it is recorded that, besides
having libraries in all his palaces, the floor of his common
room used to be so strewn with books, that it was difficult to
approach him; Rotger, a German Bishop in the tenth
century, was accustomed to carry his library with him in
his journeyings;[8] Octavianus Præconius, Archbishop of
Palermo, not only possessed an amply furnished private
library, but had always an abundance of books 'placed in
the hall of his palace, that those who came to transact
business with him might not be idle while they waited.

[6] Boivin. Mem. Acad. des Inscript.   [7] Pet. de Vin. l. iii. Ep. 67.
[8] Mabillon Acta SS. Ord. S. Bened Sæc. v. Præf. §. 2.

but might have employment for their minds ;[9] when St. Boniface was attacked and despoiled by the Frieslanders, " on breaking open his chests they found not gold but books, and in the place of silver, which they had expected, they discovered only copies of the Sacred Writings ;"[1] when Odo, afterwards Abbot of Clugni, vacated his office of Precentor and Schoolmaster of the Cathedral Church of St. Martin at Tours, to enter the Priory of Beaume, he carried with him his library, amounting to a hundred volumes ;[2] among the various gifts which the Abbot Saba of St. Salvator de Scholari presented to a Church which he had built before embracing the religious life, we find enumerated " three hundred beautiful MSS. ;"[3] and the author of the *Mirouer du Monde* declares that in the Castle of Anthony de Guigius, at the foot of the Jura, was a library containing many beautiful and valuable volumes.[4] Unquestionably, however, the Monasteries possessed the greater portion of the books which existed in the Middle Ages ; and this, not only because the price of MSS., though far from being so elevated as has been supposed by some, was nevertheless sufficiently high to present a serious obstacle to their accumulation in any very considerable number by private individuals, but also because the eminently associative spirit of those ages generated the desire to place these literary stores in the position in which they would conduce most fully to the general utility ; men laboured in those days less for themselves than for society, and the wealthy nobles and powerful monarchs, whose opulence had enabled them to amass large collec-

---

[9] Sicilia Sacra, i. 203. [1] Vit S. Bonifac. ii. 177. [3] Mabillon Act. SS. Ord. S. Bened. vii. 126. [3] Sicilia Sacra, ii. 1004. [4] Gouget Bibliotheque Française, ix. 226.

tions of books, cheerfully ceded them to the Monasteries, in which their perpetual conservation was better assured than it could possibly be while they remained in private hands, and in which they were freely accessible to all who desired to profit by their contents.   For the Monastic Libraries were in the fullest sense of the term Public Libraries; the inscription in the Bibliotheca Marucelliana at Florence, " Publicæ et maxime pauperum utilitate"—for the use of the public and especially of the poor—embodies the idea which presided over the formation of such collections in mediæval centuries, when they were gathered together, not as objects of vanity or display, but as a practical means of rendering knowledge accessible to those whose poverty prevented them from possessing libraries of their own.   Not only were students permitted to read the books in the libraries, but they were also suffered to carry them to their own homes ; and when some Abbots had discontinued this practice, in consequence of the injury which the books occasionally sustained, the Council of Paris, in 1212, ordered the immediate resumption of the ancient custom, declaring that the lending of books may justly be reckoned among the most eminent of the works of mercy.[5]   The language of Richard of Bury, in the thirteenth century, admirably reflects the spirit of the Monks and their benefactors, and pourtrays the motives which actuated the establishment and augmentation of their literary collections.   "Moved," he says, " by Him who alone granteth and perfecteth a good will to man, I diligently enquired what among all the offices of piety would most please the Almighty and most profit the Church militant.   Then before the eye of my mind there

[5] Annales de Phil. Chr. xviii. 450.

came a flock of chosen scholars, in whom God the Artificer, and Nature his handmaiden, had planted the roots of the best manners and sciences, but whom penury so oppressed that these fruitful germs were dried up, since, in consequence of want, they were watered by no dew in the uncultivated soil of youth, so that their virtue lay hidden and buried, and the crop withered away, and the corn degenerated into tares, and they who might have grown up into strong columns of the Church by the capacity of their genius, were obliged to renounce the pursuit of learning. What can a pious man behold more deplorable ? What can more excite his compassion ? What can more easily dissolve into warm drops a congealed heart ? Therefore I considered how much it would profit the Christian republic to render assistance to the poor, and to nourish students, not with the delights of Sardanapalus, or the riches of Crœsus, but with the modest provision of scholars. How many have we seen conspicuous by no lustre of birth, and no hereditary succession, but assisted by the piety of good men, who have deserved apostolic chairs, in which they have served the faithful, subjected the proud, and procured the liberty of the Church ? Thus the result of my meditation was pity for this obscure race of men, who might render such service to the Church, and a resolution to assist them, not only with means for their subsistence, but also with books for their studies."⁶ The Monastic Libraries belonged, not to the Monks alone, but to the People, and the demonstration that a Library was an essential adjunct to every Monastery is a proof that, not only in large cities, but also in smaller towns, and even in villages, there existed in the Middle Ages

⁶ Ric. de Buri Philobiblion Proleg.

vast stores of Books, which were to every one as accessible as if they had been his own. It mattered little that the price of books was high, since from the Religious the scholar could obtain the loan of the most precious volume; and the simple fact that our ancestors declared their libraries to be for the benefit of the poor, and instituted regulations for the lending of books to those whose slender means prevented them from buying them for themselves, indicates an intellectual elevation in the humbler classes which forms no element of the picture which popular historians have sketched of the condition of mediæval society. These collections were of course greatly diversified in size; in early ages they were probably in general small, since we read that in the ninth century the Abbey of Croyland possessed between seven and eight hundred MSS.,[7] and that of Centule not much more than five hundred;[8] but at a later period of the mediæval epoch, many Monasteries contained libraries of considerable magnitude, as might indeed be inferred from the dimensions of the apartments destined to the conservation of their books, such as that in the Franciscan Monastery at London, which was one hundred and twenty-nine feet long and thirty-one feet broad, or that in the Abbey of Wells, which was lighted by twenty-five windows on each side.[1] In the Abbey of Novalise in Piedmont, there were, in the tenth century, six thousand volumes;[1] the library of Clugni is described as rivalling in magnificence that of the Emperors at Constantinople;[2] the extent of that of Fulda, in which the books were classified in forty-eight divisions,

[7] Ingulf. ap. Gale. Script. v. Spicileg. ii. 311. Sacr. Præf. xxviii.
[8] Chron. Cent. ap. Dacher.
[9] Leland.
[1] Eugen. de Levis Anecdot.
[2] Gervaise Vie d'Abeillard.

according to their subjects, may be judged from the fact, that from the era of its foundation in the time of the Carlovignians, twelve Monks were constantly employed in augmenting its contents ;[3] at Spanheim, two thousand volumes were added by Trithemius alone during the twenty-three years of his rule ;[4] the Abbey of Peterborough, in England, possessed at an early period seventeen hundred volumes ;[5] the Abbey of St. Benedict sur Loire, in France, contained five thousand volumes ; Gerbert affirms that in every town in Italy books were to be found in vast abundance ;[6] and an idea may be formed of the number of MSS. in the library of St. Salvator de Settimo from an incident recorded by Gaspar Jongellinus, who relates that when the Monastery had been on one occasion converted into a temporary fortress, in time of war, certain of the Florentine soldiers by whom it was occupied, who had sallied out against the enemy, were unable to return, the bridge which crossed the moat surrounding the Abbey having broken under their weight, but those who remained within the walls filled up the moat with books taken from the library, and thus made a causeway by which their comrades were enabled to regain their quarters in safety."[7] - No Monastery was deemed complete without a large store of books ; " a Monastery without a library," says Geoffrey, Sub-Prior of St. Barbara, in Normandy, in the twelfth century, " is like a Castle without an Armoury, for our library is our armoury, whence we bring forth the sentences of the divine law, like sharp

---

[3] Ziegelbauer Hist. Lit. Ord. S. Bened. i. 483.   Brower Antiq. Fuld. 45.   [4] Trithemius Nepiachus. ap. Eccard.   [5] Leland. Marsham. Preface to Dugdale's Monasticon.   [6] Tiraboschi, iii. 3.   [7] Notit. Abb. Ord. Cisterc. l. vii. 38.

of Lambert, Abbot of Lobbes,[4] and Halynard, Abbot of
St. Benign ;[5] and their tender love for books is amply
evidenced by the precautions which they prescribed for
their conservation. "With great care," says Thomas à
Kempis, "the library of sacred books is to be preserved
from all defilement of dust, from fire and from damp,
from thieves and from the perils of war, from the corro-
sion of worms and from all stain and rent of leaves. He
is not worthy to read a sacred book who knows not how to
take care of it, and who neglects to restore it to its proper
place. Thus must be preserved the treasury of the
Church, made and edited by holy doctors, written and collected by good writers, and provided by God for the consolation of many."[6] The Rule of St. Pachomius directed
that none should leave open the books which they had
been reading after they had done with them, and that all
books should be returned to the librarian every evening,
entering into minute provisions for their arrangement and
custody ;[7] the *Coutumier de Citeaux*, speaking of the in-
tervals of study, says "if it be necessary to go anywhere,

---

[4] "Concerning the assiduity and devotion of his prayers, the grace
of compunction which he evinced, the constancy of his reading, to
which he applied himself not only at home but even when travelling
on horseback or lodging on the road, the sparingness of his food and
clothing, the love which he cherished for the Word of God and for the
science of the Scriptures, to the study and collection of which he applied himself whenever he could find opportunity, the fervour of his
love for God and for his neighbour, which he manifested in worthy
works, it would be difficult to treat sufficiently." Fulcuin de Gest.
Abb. Lobiens. ap. Dacher. Spicileg. vi.   [5] "The Abbot Haly-
nardus was so fond of reading, that even on a journey he often carried
a little book in his hand, and refreshed his mind by perusing it on
horseback." Chron. S. Ben. ap. Dacher. Spicileg. ii. 392.

[6] Thomas à Kempis, Doctrinale Juvenum, c. 5.   [7] Reg. S.
Pachom.

let the person to whom the book was entrusted place it back on the shelf, or, if he wish to leave it on the desk, let him make a sign to the brother next to him to take care of it;"[8] the Rule of St. Isidore required that all the books should be returned to the librarian every evening;[9] the Rule of St. Benedict is copious and explicit in the directions which it gives for the classification and care of the books, and their protection from loss or damage;[1] and Beda relates that St. Benedict Biscop was most solicitous to provide before his death for the conservation of the splendid library which he had brought from Rome to England.[2] The Monks, indeed, universally displayed their sympathy with the ideas which Richard of Bury expresses with regard to the duty of keeping watchful guard over these monuments of intellectual exertion. " Not alone do we serve God," he remarks, " by preparing volumes of new books, but also by preserving and treating with great care those we have already. Truly, after the vestments and vessels dedicated to our Lord's body, sacred books deserve to be treated with the highest reverence. All negligence in regard to books is prohibited by the example of our Saviour, for we read that when He had read the book which was delivered to Him He did not return it to the minister until He had closed it again with His most sacred hands ; from which students ought to take example never to commit the least negligence with regard to books."[3]

But the Monks were not content with cherishing the books which were already in their possession ; a large

---

[8] Martene, de Antiq. Monach. Rit. i. c. 7.   [9] Reg. S. Isid.
[1] Reg. S. Bened.   [2] Beda, Vit. Abb. Wiremuth. 299.
[3] Ric. de Buri. Philobiblion, 17.

portion of their time was consecrated to their multiplication for the benefit of mankind.   Who that has directed any share of his attention to the history of Monasticism, has not heard of the Scriptorium, the peaceful retreat in which the pious cænobites laboured to perpetuate, for the use of succeeding generations, the noblest works of ancient learning, and the most precious monuments of the genius of the illustrious sages of the Church of Christ?   Who that feels delight in meditating on the priceless benefits which the humble toils of lowly labourers have conferred, under God's blessing, on the world, has not at some time striven to picture to his mind the state in which Christian literature would have been at the present day had it not been for their silent exertions, which have been repaid in later ages only with contumely and reproach?   While the rest of men busied themselves in eager struggles for wealth or power, these zealous artists were engaged in the nobler task of perpetuating and multiplying the means of human knowledge; often, amid the convulsions of empires, beholding the work of their hands, and the store of literary treasures which had been created by the industry of their predecessors, swept into annihilation by the ravages of war, but ever applying themselves again to their glorious toils, and endeavouring to obliterate the traces of the calamity, and to repair the destruction which had overtaken these treasured trophies of their patient zeal.   Truly the world can never too highly appreciate its debt of gratitude to the Scriptorium of the ancient Monastery, and the hooded scribes who pursued within its walls their tranquil toils.

It was by no means unusual for the benefactors of Monasteries to bestow liberal endowments on the Scriptorium, for the special encouragement of the labours which were therein pursued ; thus, to that of St. Edmundsbury was assigned the profit of two mills, to that of Ely the revenue of two Churches, to that of St. Swithin, at Winchester, the tithes of a valuable rectory; and such examples, which are of frequent occurrence, manifest the high importance which was attached to this branch of Monastic exertion. The copying of books was regarded as an eminent work of piety ; " when you are dead," says Thomas à Kempis, " those persons who read the volumes which were formerly written beautifully by you will pray for you, and if he who giveth a cup of cold water shall not lose his reward, much more he who gives the living water of wisdom shall not lose his recompense in Heaven ;"[4] and the inscriptions in many ancient MSS. afford evidence of the conviction which reigned in the minds of the Religious that their zealous toils for the augmentation of the stores of intellectual wealth were most acceptable in the sight of the Almighty. The labours undertaken in this pious spirit were pursued with unwearying assiduity. " One of the most usual labours of the Monks," says Mabillon, " was the copying of books. Cassiodorus recommended it to them above all others; Trithemius enforces the same view in his seventh Homily, as well as in one of his works especially devoted to that subject, and entitled ' *De Laude Scriptorum Manualium*.' We learn from the testimony of Palladius, that this was one of the chief occupations of the disciples of St. Pachomius ;[5] and St. Jerome enumerates it among the employments of solitaries. ' They copy books,' he says, ' that by the labour of their hands they may gain food, and at the same time promote the edifica-

---

[4] Thomas à Kempis, Doctrinale Juvenum, c. 4.
[5] Pallad. c. 39.

tion of their minds.'[6]   St. Ferreol in his Rule directs that those who do not labour in the tilling of the soil shall employ themselves in the copying of books;[7] St. Nil the younger had no other occupation; and St. Gregory of Tours, speaking of a holy recluse in his diocese, says that 'by this labour he extinguished all evil thoughts that might arise in his mind.' "[8]   The copying of books formed part of the constant employment of the Monks in the ancient Monasteries of Egypt,[9] and of the disciples of St. Martin;[1] and an ancient historian of Durham declares of the Religious, that they " were always virtuously occupied and never idle, but either writing of good and godly works, or studying the Holy Scriptures."[2]   In the ninth and tenth centuries the monks of St. Gall devoted themselves to this labour with the utmost diligence, bringing MSS. from France and Italy, in order to collate their copies and secure their critical accuracy, and entering into a widely extended correspondence, in order to obtain access to various libraries. An old Chronicler of the Monastery of St. Riquier, in the reign of Robert of France, towards the close of the tenth century, says, " Books of great science, excellent pearls, are now restored, while others are written out for the first time;"[3] Abbot William of Hirschau, in the eleventh century, set apart twelve of the brethren, whom he caused to devote themselves especially to the transcription of the Scriptures, and appointed one Monk of learning and experience as a superintendent over " the infinite number of

[6] St. Hieron. Epist. ad Rustic.   [7] " Paginam pingat digito qui terram non proscindit aratro."   Reg. S. Ferreol, c. 28.   [8] Greg. Tur. de Vit. PP.   Mabillon Tr. des Etudes Monast. 148.
[9] Cassian Inst. l. iv. c. 12.   [1] Supl. Sev. in Vit. S. Mart. vii. 473.   [2] The Ancient Rites of Durham.
[3] Chron. S. Riq.

others who laboured in the transcription of general books;"[4] Abbot Frederick, of the same Monastery, was so zealous in his devotion to this work, that he was accustomed to take his seat in the Scriptorium among the brethren and share their toils ;[5] and such was the importance attached to this branch of Monastic industry, that a Chapter of the Cistercian Order, held in 1134, made it the subject of a special Canon, ordaining that "in all Scriptoria, and wherever the Monks are, according to custom, engaged in writing, silence shall be kept as in the Cloister."[6] Special privileges were accorded to the Religious of various Monasteries, to facilitate the binding of the books which they produced. Although hunting had been strictly interdicted to ecclesiastics by the Council of Agde in 506, and the Council of Epon in 517, which prohibition was extended in the time of Charlemagne to all orders of Monks, and even to Knights Templars, yet under that Monarch permission was given to the Monks of St. Denis, and of St. Bertin at St. Omer, to hunt in their woods for the purpose of procuring skins for binding their books ;[7] leave was conceded to the Religious of the Abbey of Sithiu to employ their servants in a similar manner ;[8] and Geoffrey, Count of Anjou, in founding a Benedictine Monastery at Saintes, in the eleventh century, gave to it a tenth part of the deer on some lands in the island of Oleron, to supply covers for the volumes which were transcribed by the brethren. It may be fairly inferred from the concession of these facilities, that the Monks were in the habit of producing a great many books ; since it would hardly have occurred to their benefactors to

[4] Trithem. Chron. Hirsaug. i. 221.   [5] Ibid.   [6] Monast. Cisterc. i. 272.   [7] Chron. Monast. S. Bertin. l. x. ap. Mart. Thes. Anecdot. iii.   [8] Chron. Sith.

manifest their generosity, by placing within their reach the
means of procuring an abundance of skins for binding their
volumes, if the industry of the Religious in the copying of
MSS. had not been matter of general notoriety.   The
borrowing of books for the purpose of transcription was a
custom very prevalent in the Middle Ages; the correspondence of Mediæval Abbots presents innumerable
evidences of the zeal with which they sought, by a re-
ciprocal interchange of duplicates and the mutual loan of
books, in order that they might be copied in the Scriptoria
of their respective Monasteries, at once to augment their
own libraries and to extend to others the benefit of their
literary possessions.   Gerbert, Abbot of Bobbio, afterwards Pope Sylvester II., in a letter to the Monk Rainald,
says, " I entreat you to render me one service, which you
can do without danger or injury to yourself, and which will
bind me most closely to you.   You know with what zeal
I seek for copies of books from all quarters, and you know
how many writers there are both in the cities and in the
country parts of Italy; I entreat you then that you cause
transcripts to be made for me of these books," which he
then proceeds to enumerate.[9]   The same Abbot, in other
letters, writes to Thietmar of Mayence for a part of one
of the works of Boethius, which was wanting in his own
copy;[1] to the Abbot Giselbert, concerning some deficiencies
in his copy of treatises of Cicero and Demosthenes;[2] to
Airard, respecting the correction of a MS. of Pliny, and
the copying of some other works;[3] to the Archbishop of
Rheims, desiring him to borrow for him, from the Abbot
Azo, a copy of Cæsar, and promising in return to lend

<hr>

[9] Gerbert. Epist. 130.   [1] Ibid. 123.   [2] Ibid. 9.
[3] Ibid. 7.

him eight volumes of the works of Boethius;[4] and to Egbert,
Abbot of Tours, to whom he communicates the diligent
efforts he has been making to found a noble library, and
the extent to which he has employed transcribers in various
cities, not only in Italy, but also in Germany and Belgium,
and concludes by entreating him to aid him by procuring
copies to be made for him of certain books, of which he
appends a list, which were to be found in France, but were
not so easily accessible elsewhere.[5]   All these instances
are selected from the letters of a single Abbot; but the
Abbot Gerbert was by no means an unique example of
zeal in literary pursuits; the splendid libraries which adorned
the Monasteries of various countries of Europe attest the
frequent existence of Religious as ardent in their love of
learning, and as energetic in their efforts to give extension
to their collections; and the letters of mediæval Monks
present innumerable proofs of the practice, to the prevalence
of which was due the creation of many of those magnificent stores of MSS.   Lupus, Abbot of Ferrieres, writes
to Alstig, Abbot in the Church of York, desiring him to
lend him certain works to be transcribed, and promising
that they shall be faithfully returned,[6] and again to Pope
Benedict III., making a similar application;[7] in the eighth
century we find Pepin applying to Pope Paul III. for some
Greek books for the Abbey of St. Denis, which were sent
according to his request;[8] and it would be easy to fill many
pages with citations of similar examples.   Further, it is to
be noted as an evidence of the dignity which the Monks
were accustomed to attach to the labour of book-multipli-

[4] Gerbert. Epist. 8.   [5] Ibid. 44.   [6] Mabillon Annal. Ord.
S. Bened. ii. 684.   Lupus Epist. 2.   Bibl. Patr. ix.   [7] Muratori
Antiq. Ital. Med. Ævi. vii. 111, 835.   [8] Cenni Codex Carolin. i. 148.

cation, as well as of the diligence with which it was pursued, that we meet frequently with honourable mention of those brethren who had distinguished themselves by special assiduity in this department of Monastic exertion, and whose achievements are recorded as a glory to the community which numbered them among its members. In many Monasteries was observed the custom which prevailed at the Abbey of Tegernsee, in Bavaria, where the names of those who were most skilful in writing and illuminating were registered in the archives ;[9] and some of the instances of individual labour which are recorded in the annals of various Religious houses are most remarkable in their character. Thus Othlonus, a Monk of St. Emmeran, having written much during his early years, transcribed, after he entered that Monastery, three copies of the Four Gospels, nineteen Missals, two copies of the Epistles and Gospels read in the Mass during the year, four service books for Matins, and twenty-eight other volumes, not to enumerate the detached Sermons, Epistles, and Tracts, which he copied at various times for different individuals ;[1] Diemudis, a nun of Wessobrunn, in Bavaria, transcribed with her own hands forty-three volumes, among which we find enumerated two copies of the entire Bible, two copies of the Four Gospels, five Missals, and a copy of the Canonical Epistles ;[2] Harduin wrote out four copies of the Four Gospels, one copy of the Epistles of St. Paul, three volumes of Sacramentaria, one volume of readings from the Gospels, and eight other books, chiefly of large size ;[3] Gerhard of Monte Sereno, though impeded in his

---

[9] Jaeck Galerie der Klöster Deutschlands.   [1] Mabillon Annal. Ord. S. Bened. iv. 570.   [2] Martene Thes. Nov. Anecdot. i. 9.
[3] Chron. Fontanellens. ap. Dacher. Spicileg. iii.

labours by defective vision, transcribed six Missals, a Plenarius (that is to say, a volume containing the whole of the Old and New Testaments[4]), a Lectionary, and fifteen other volumes;[5] Godfrey, of the Monastery of St. Martin at Tournay, was "a very skilful scribe, and left many MSS. in the Church, namely, the Morals of St. Gregory on Job, in six volumes, an excellent collection of Books of Holy Scripture, which, commencing at the Book of Proverbs, contained the Prophets, the Acts of the Apostles, and the Canonical Epistles, a Missal from which Mass is said every day in the Monastery, a copy of the Four Gospels, the tract of St. Augustine, 'De Civitate Dei,' and his En- chiridion, and many other books;"[6] a Monk of Ratisbon wrote out, not only several works of his own composition, but also twenty Missals, three copies of the Four Gospels, two copies of the Epistles and Gospels for the entire year, and four books of Matins;[7] Maurus Lupi, a Florentine Monk of Camaldoli, while living nine years in the desert and more than forty in the Monastery of St. Matthias de Muriano, transcribed more than a thousand volumes;[8] and like examples of unwearying zeal are by no means rarely encountered in the records of Monastic History. These men are mentioned by the old Chroniclers, who commemorate their labours with a reverential admira- tion which evinces the high esteem in which they held such noble exertions; yet they differed from those who were less renowned only in the extent, and by no means in the nature of their toils. The copying of books was to the Monks a labour of love, to which they de- voted themselves with willing hearts; tedious and onerous

[4] Mabillon Act. Ord. S. Bened. viii. 531.

[5] Chronicon Montis Sereni.   [6] Hermann. ap. Dacher. Spicileg. i. 912.   [7] Mabillon Vet. Analect. 119.   [8] Annal Camaldul. 67.

is was the task, they found abundant compensation in the
consciousness of the blessings which their diligence conferred upon mankind. "Happy intention," says Cassiodorus, "praiseworthy assiduity, by the hand to preach to
men, with the fingers to open the lips, in silence to give
salvation to sinners, and with a pen to fight against the
unlawful suggestions of the devil ; for Satan receives as
many wounds as the writer puts down words of our Lord.
Resting in one place, he goes, by means of the dissemination of his work, through different provinces; his labour
is read in holy places ; the people learn from it how they
may be converted from an evil will to serve God with
a pure heart." Such was the spirit which breathed in
the heart of the mediæval Scribe, such the thought which
found living utterance in those illustrious exertions which
perpetuated for the world the most precious treasures of
antiquity.

In truth, the assiduity of the Monks needs no other demonstration than is afforded by the existence of the visible
trophies of their patient zeal which have passed uninjured
through the grasp of Time, and yet survive to bear witness
to the industry which gave them being. Although more
than thirteen hundred and fifty years have elapsed since
the commencement of the mediæval epoch, and more than
four hundred years have passed away since the pen of the
scribe was superseded by mechanical appliances, a vast
number of the MSS. produced by the Religious in the
Middle Ages still remain in preservation ; there is not a
Public Library in Europe which does not boast the possession of many of these memorials of antiquity, twenty-
four of the most noted of these containing together nearly
three hundred and eighty thousand MSS. ;[9] very few private

[9] The Libraries referred to are the Vatican Library, at Rome, which

collections of any importance are without some such relics of vanished centuries; such of the Continental Monasteries as yet survive, cherish in their libraries numerous fruits of the diligence of their inmates of the olden time ; and there can be little doubt that if all the mediæval MSS. the existence of which is known, could be gathered together, we should behold a collection of not far short of a million volumes. Bearing in mind the rarity of copies of early printed books—of which a striking but by no means singular example is presented by the celebrated Polyglot Bible of Cardinal Ximenes, of the edition of six hundred and three copies of which, printed in 1522, only four copies are now in being—and remembering that the oldest of these printed books is but as ancient as the most modern of the MSS. to which we are referring, we cannot resist the conclusion that the store must have been vast indeed of which so gigantic a fragment has survived the ravages of

contains 23,580 MSS., the Bibliotheca Ambrosiana at Milan 5500 MSS., the Bibliotheca Laurentiniana at Florence 9000 MSS., the Bibliotheca Riccardi at Florence 3000 MSS., the Library of the Grand Duke at Florence 1500 MSS., the Bibliotheca Magliabecchiana at Florence 12,000 MSS., the University Library at Bologna 4000 MSS., the University Library at Florence 6000 MSS., the Bodleian Library at Oxford 30,000 MSS., the Library of the British Museum 100,000 MSS., the Public Library at Stuttgart 1800 MSS., the Royal Library at Munich 18,000 MSS., the University Library at Munich 10,000 MSS., the Benedictine Library at Mölk 1500 MSS., the Library of the Seminary at Prague 3700 MSS., the Royal Library at Berlin 5000 MSS., the University Library at Gottingen 5000 MSS., the Library in the Japanese Palace at Dresden 2800 MSS., the Imperial Library at Vienna 16,076 MSS., the Imperial Library at St. Petersburgh 15,471 MSS., the Bibliotheque de Burgogne at Brussels 16000 MSS., the Bibliotheque de St. Genevieve at Paris 2000 MSS., the Bibliotheque de Monsieur at Paris 6000 MSS., and the Bibliotheque du Roi at Paris 80,000 MSS.

decay; and this impression will be strengthened by the consideration of the various active agencies which have tended to promote the annihilation of these fragile treasures, and which can be shown to have operated most extensively in their destruction. Foremost among these may be placed the incessant warfare which, in early ages, desolated the face of Europe, and in which the Monasteries naturally suffered, not only on account of the spoil to be obtained by their pillage, but also from their being frequently the shelter to which many fled for refuge on an unlooked-for incursion of the foe. In England fifty-three Monasteries were destroyed by the Danes,[1] and in addition to these we meet with mention of thirty-seven Religious Houses which were in existence previous to the Norman Conquest, but of which no traces can be discovered subsequent to that event,[2] and which, therefore, probably perished in the convulsions which accompanied it; in France we find recorded three hundred and seventy-eight instances of the destruction of Monasteries in war, of which one hundred and five are specified as having been wrought by the Normans, fifty-nine by the English, twenty by the Saracens, eight by the Hungarians, eight by the Danes, six by the Spaniards, six by the Vandals, five in Civil War, four by the Burgundians, four by the Huns, two by the Goths, one by the Wisigoths, one by the Lombards, one by the Flemish, and one by the Frieslanders, besides one hundred and forty-seven which the Gallia Christiana chronicles without special designation of the assailants;[3] and many were destroyed in the earlier periods of the

---

[1] Tanner Notitia Monastica. See note (A) at the end of the volume.
[2] Ibid. See note (B) at the end of the volume.   [3] Gallia Christiana. See note (C) at the end of the volume.

Middle Ages, of which not even the names survive.[4] The ravages of Fire aided in the work of devastation; in France alone, eighty-one examples are noted of the demolition of Monasteries by accidental conflagrations;[5] in England, though it is difficult to arrive at even an aproximative estimate of the actual extent of the injury arising from this source, we encounter frequent incidental mentions of the destruction of Religious Houses by such calamitous occurrences; and Ludewig remarks, " For my own part, I declare that I have never been in any archives in Germany, though I have visited them without number, in which the keepers have not attributed their present deficiencies to fires, which have destroyed the most valuable and important documents."[6] Finally, the disastrous apostasy of the sixteenth century consummated the overthrow of many Monasteries which had passed unscathed through other perils; in France one hundred and fifty-one of these establishments perished from the violence of the sectaries,[7] who, after having carried off everything of readily convertible value, generally completed their work of havoc by setting fire to the building, leaving the books to perish in the flames;[8] and in England six hundred and thirteen Monasteries were suppressed at the epoch of the Reformation,[9] in addition to ninety Colleges under the care of the Religious.[1] Thus, in two countries of Europe, War,

[4] Gallia Christiana, x. 1226. xi. 710. 910.   [5] Ibid.   See note (D) at the end of the volume.   [6] Ludewig. Reliq. Manuscr. Præf. lxxxiv.   [7] Gallia Christiana.   See note (E) at the end of the volume.   [8] For examples of this, cf. Martene Voy. Litt. (1717) i, 6. 14. 32. 37. 65. 184. 228. 252. ii. 5. 10. 16. 36. 43. 49. 52. 54. 64. 67. 112. (1724) 112.   Mabillon Iter. Burgund. 30.

[9] Tanner Notitia Monastica. See note (F) at the end of the volume.

[1] One hundred and ten Hospitals, and two thousand three hundred

Fire, and Heresy achieved the demolition of thirteen hundred and thirteen Monasteries; and as we have already seen that a library universally formed part of such establishments, it is easy to perceive how vastly these calamities must have diminished the store of MSS. accumulated by the diligence of mediæval scribes. But other lands were not exempt from similar visitations; War and Fire wrought their ravages in Spain, in Italy, and in Ireland, and in Germany Heresy added to these its desolating scourge; and although we have not the means of arriving at as precise details with regard to those countries as with respect to France and England, the facts which we have noted enable us to judge how immense must have been the destruction of Monasteries throughout the Christian world.

As regards the Religious Houses which were suppressed in England, it may perhaps be objected, that as their extinction was effected, not by warlike assaults, as in France, but by the calmer agency of executive authority, we are by no means justified in assuming that the destruction of their libraries accompanied their fall. That it was not the necessary accompaniment, is doubtless true; but that it did actually take place, is unhappily but too easily capable of demonstration. Wielding different weapons, and marching by diverse roads to their common goal, the sectaries of France and of England manifested one spirit in the unbridled fury with which they assailed the literary monuments of Christian antiquity, and, demolishing the annals and chronicles of bygone ages, destroyed at the same time the volumes which bore witness to the wisdom of their Philosophers and the piety of their Divines. It

and seventy-four Chantries shared the fate of the Monasteries. Lord Herbert, Life of Henry VIII.

seemed as if they desired to obliterate, if it were possible, even the memory of the Past, to engulf in oblivion the achievements of its Knights, the thoughts of its Students, and the unwearied labours of its Missionaries, and to blot out the remembrance of Christian antiquity, by entombing in one common and irretrievable destruction all that bore witness to the incidents of its history and the character of its people. The most earnest among the champions of the Reformation in England, are loudest in their denunciations of the dismal wreck which was achieved by the apostles of Anglicanism, and bewail with bitterness the reckless immolation of the monuments of ancient learning which signalised its victory.

" One among the misfortunes consequent upon the suppression of the Monasteries," says Dr. Collier, a Bishop of the Anglican sect, " was an ignorant destruction of a great many valuable books. Printing was then but a late invention, and had secured but a few books in comparison to the rest ; the main of learning lay in MSS., and the most considerable of these, both for number and quality, were in the Monks' possession. But the Abbeys at their dissolution falling oftentimes into hands who understood no farther than the estates, the libraries were miserably disposed of. The books, instead of being removed to royal libraries, to those of Cathedrals, or the Universities, were frequently thrown in to the grantees as things of small consideration. Now these men oftentimes proved a very ill protection for learning and for antiquity ; their avarice was oftentimes so mean, and their ignorance so undistinguishing, that when the covers were somewhat rich and would yield a little, they pulled them off, and threw away the books, or turned them to waste paper ; and thus many noble libraries were destroyed, to a great public scandal and an irreparable loss to learning."[2] "About the year 1550," observes the same writer, " the Council Book mentions the King's sending a letter for the purging of his library at Westminster. The persons are not named, but the business was to cull out all superstitious books, as Missals, Legends, and such like, and to deliver the garniture of the books, being either gold or silver, to Sir Anthony Aucher. These books were many of them plated with gold and silver, and curiously embossed, and this, as far as we can collect, was the superstition that destroyed them. Here avarice had a very thin disguise, and the courtiers discovered of what spirit they were, to a very remarkable degree. The Oxford Libraries had much the same quarter this year from the King's visitors as that at Westminster. To give some instances, Merton College had almost a cart-load of MSS. carried off and thrown away to the most scandalous uses. These books were upon Divinity, Astronomy, and Mathematics, by the most eminent of that society. Balliol, Exeter, Queen's, and Lincoln Colleges were purged of a great part of the Fathers and Schoolmen, and to show that the discretion of some people was much of the same size with their justice, and what antipathy they had to learned men, great heaps of these books were set on fire in the market-place. The Public Library, made up in a great measure of the books given by Angerville, Bishop of Durham, Cobham, Bishop of Worcester, and Humphrey, the good Duke of Gloster, underwent the same fate. The books marked with red were generally condemned at a venture for Popery, and where circles and mathematical figures were found, they

[2] Collier Eccles. Hist. ii. 1. iii. p. 166.

were looked upon as compositions of magic, and either torn or burnt. And thus an almost incredible collection, both for number and for value, was either seized by the visitors, turned into bonfires, or given to bookbinders and tailors for the use of their trades."[3] Other writers of the same sect amply confirm these melancholy details. "All arts and sciences," says Fuller, "fell under the common calamity. How many admirable MSS. of the Fathers, Schoolmen, and Commentators were destroyed by this means! What number of historians of all ages and countries! The Holy Scriptures themselves, much as these men pretended to regard them, underwent the fate of the rest. If a book had a cross on it, it was condemned for Popery, and those with lines and figures were interpreted the black art, and destroyed for conjuring. And thus divinity was profaned, mathematics suffered for corresponding with evil spirits, physic was maimed, and riot committed on the law itself."[4] "Whole libraries," says a writer in the Letters of Eminent Persons from the Bodleian, "were destroyed, or made waste paper of, or consumed for the vilest uses. The splendid Abbey of Malmesbury, which possessed some of the finest MSS. in the kingdom, was ransacked, and its treasures either burnt or sold to serve the commonest purposes of life. An antiquary, who travelled through that town many years after the dissolution, relates that he saw broken windows patched up with remnants of the most valuable MSS. on vellum, and that the bakers had not then consumed the stores they had accumulated in heating their ovens."[5] Of the Commissioners who remained in Oxford in 1550,

[3] Collier Eccles. Hist. ii. 1. iv. p. 306.   [4] Fuller Church Hist. 1. vi. p. 335.   [5] Letters of Eminent Persons from the Bodleian, i. 278.

after the visitation of 1549, Anthony Wood remarks, " The principal ornaments, and at the same time supports of the University, that is the Libraries, filled with innumerable works both native and foreign, they either permitted or directed to be despoiled. Hence a great multitude of MSS., having no mark of superstition about them, (unless it were to be found in the red letters on their titles) were adjudged to the flames or to the vilest purposes. Works of Scholastic Theology were sold off among those exercising the lowest description of arts, and those which contained circles or diagrams it was thought good to mutilate or burn, as containing certain proof of the magical nature of their contents."[6] And Bale, the Anglican Bishop of Ossory, in Ireland, and one of the bitterest among the foes of the ancient Church, observes, " Never had we been offended for the loss of our libraries, being so many in number and in so desolate places for the most part, if the chief monuments and most notable works of our most excellent writers had been reserved. If there had been in every shire of England but one solemn Library, for the preservation of those most noble works, and preferment of learning in our posterity, it had been somewhat. But to destroy all without consideration, is, and will be for ever unto England, a most horrible infamy among the grave seniors of other nations. A great number of them which purchased these superstitious mansions, reserved the books in their libraries, some to scour their candlesticks and some to rub their boots; some they sold to the grocers and soap-sellers; and some they sent over sea to the book-binders, not in small numbers, but at times whole ships full, to the wondering of foreign nations. Yea, the

[6] Ant. Wood. Hist. Univ. Oxon.

Universities of this realm are not all clear in this detestable fact. I know a merchantman, who shall at this time be nameless, that bought the contents of two noble libraries for forty-shillings price; a shame it is to be spoken. This stuff hath he used instead of grey paper, for the space of these ten years, and yet he hath store for as many years to come. I judge this to be a truth, and utter it with heaviness, that neither the Britons under the Romans and Saxons, nor yet the English people under the Danes and Normans, had ever such damage of their learned monuments as we have seen in our time. Our posterity may well curse this wicked fact of our age, this unreasonable spoil of England's most noble antiquities."[7]

Such avowals from the pens of Protestant writers, render needless the demonstration of the destruction of the libraries of the English Monasteries at their suppression, by the testimony of Catholic historians. We have therefore evidence of the demolition, in France and England alone, of fourteen hundred and three libraries, including those of the English Colleges; and presuming the causes which operated in Spain, in Italy, in Germany, and in Ireland to have caused a proportionate devastation, it appears evident that an enormous loss of the literary productions of mediæval centuries must have resulted from these accumulated calamities. Time also brought decay to these fragile treasures, and achieved the destruction of many which war and fire had spared; and, taking into account the influence of all these combined causes, it can scarcely be denied that the large number of mediæval MSS. yet surviving, affords alone a convincing proof that

[7] Bale, Declaration in Leland's Journal, 1549; Fuller, Church Hist. 1. vi. 335.

the store of books must have been indeed enormous, of
which so gigantic a debris remains to us from the wreck
which has been consummated during the lapse of centuries.   The evidence of the industry of the Monks in
transcription would alone have sufficed to give birth to
this conviction ; the visible tokens of their assiduity which
surround us, confirm the conclusions which have resulted
from the consideration of their labours, and place them
beyond the possibility of contradiction.

Since the Monastic Libraries, so thickly scattered
throughout Europe in the Middle Ages, were, in the fullest
sense of the term, Public Libraries, and placed their
volumes within the reach of all who sought to peruse
them, even at their own firesides, the price of books was
a matter of far less importance than it would have been,
had less extensive advantages been offered to those who
desired to consecrate their leisure hours to intellectual
pursuits ; the student could pursue his toils, at some dis-
advantage, truly, but without serious obstacle, without possessing a library of his own, when the volumes which
adorned the shelves of the Abbey were open to his access,
and might be carried to his home ; in the facility with
which he could obtain from the Monks the loan of valuable
works, the Scholar of those days enjoyed a privilege which
is sought in vain by him who treads in his footsteps in
the nineteenth century.   Still, it must not be imagined
that the enormous prices which some modern writers have
recorded as paid for individual books, present a fair view
of the actual cost of MSS. in the Middle Ages, and that
we are to conclude that those who desired to obtain a few
volumes were compelled to spend a fortune in their acquisition ; although the data in our possession with re-

gard to this interesting question are less complete than might be desired, we have yet ample ground for the conclusion that those who were content with simple and unadorned MSS., devoid of the rich illuminations and gorgeous paintings which decorated many of the volumes produced by mediæval scribes, could obtain them at much less expense than has been generally supposed. In a catalogue of the library of Charles V. of France, made in 1423, eight hundred and fifty-three of the volumes which it contained, were valued in the aggregate at two thousand three hundred and twenty-three livres, four sous, equal in present value to £4088 16s. 8d.;[8] but this estimate, which gives an average value of £4 15s. 3d. per volume, appears to be considerably below the real worth. M. Leber gives the price of a copy of the Four Gospels, in 1287, at four livres, ten sous, equal in present value to £20 10s.;[9] M. Petit Radel states, that "in the thirteenth century the average price of unilluminated books was from four to five hundred francs of present value,"[1] or from £16 to £20; and the data furnished by the tables of M. Leber show that this sum fairly represents the value of a volume of ordinary size, plainly transcribed, in the fourteenth century. Three elements went to make up the price of a MS. in those days; the cost of the parchment, the sum paid for copying, and the amount charged for the binding of the volume. The price of a skin of common parchment was six deniers, equal to about 2s. 4d. of modern value;[2] twenty livres tournois, equivalent to a little less

---

[8] Boivin Mem. Acad. des Inscript. la Fortune Privée au Moyen Age, 87.
les Bibliotheques.
[9] Leber Appreciation de
[1] Radel. Recherches sur
[2] Leber Fort. Priv. au Moyen Age, 74. The skin of vellum of the best quality cost ten deniers, equivalent to about 3s. 8d. of modern value. See note (G) at the end of the volume.

than £32 at the present day, is the sum recorded as having been paid, in 1395, to a Scribe at Paris for the transcription of the Homilies of St. Gregory, which, supposing the work referred to to have been the Forty Homilies of St. Gregory on the Gospels, as is most probable, would make the cost of copying about 5½*d.* per folio ;[3] and the cost of binding a quarto book without clasps, was about three sous, or nearly 7*s.* per volume.[4]

From these data it is easy to calculate what would have been the price, at that period, of any given volume.   The present work, for example, taking the text alone, without including the notes or appendix, forms about eleven hundred and twelve folios, the copying of which would have cost £25 9*s.* 8*d.* ; written in the small character generally employed in those days, it would have filled on both sides nineteen skins of parchment, the price of which would have been £2 4*s.* 4*d.* ; and this, with the addition of 7*s.* for the binding, would have made the entire cost £28 1*s.* The accuracy of these calculations appears to be confirmed by the price quoted as having been paid for a copy of the Gospels, which is stated to have been £20 10*s.* ; for the four Gospels contain, on a rough average, eight hundred and sixty-two folios, which would cost for transcription £19 15*s.* 1*d.*, filling on both sides fifteen skins of parch-

---

[3] Leber Fort. Priv. au Moyen Age, 182.   The Forty Homilies of St. Gregory on the Gospels contain about 1441 folios.   [4] Leber Fort. Priv. au Moyen Age, 183.   In this example, which refers to the year 1397, the sum of eleven livres, seven sous, and eight deniers is recorded to have been paid for the binding of sixty-two volumes : but to twenty-three of these a clasp was put, the price charged for the clasps being two sous each.   The cost of binding, with a clasp, was therefore five sous, or 11*s.* ; without the clasp, three sous, or 7*s.*

ment, costing £1 15*s*., making the price, with the binding, £21 17*s*. 1*d*.

It must be noted, however, that evidence exists to show that Books were frequently procurable in the Middle Ages at a smaller cost than these data would lead us to conclude. Thus, for example, the Catholic Bible, copied on parchment and bound in six volumes, would have cost about £320, supposing it to have been paid for at the rates upon which our calculations have been based ; but in the *Breve Recordationis* of the Abbot Bonus, detailing the history of the foundation of the Monastery of St. Michael at Pisa, mention is made of a Bible purchased by the community, towards the close of the eleventh century, for a sum equivalent to about £250 of modern value, which, deducting the cost of the parchment and binding, leaves only £223 4*s*. 8*d*., or about 4*d*. per folio, as the cost of transcription ; and even this is spoken of as if it were a large price. The inference resulting from this fact is still farther confirmed by the example already referred to of Odo, afterwards Abbot of Clugni, who, when he quitted his position of Precentor and Schoolmaster in the Cathedral Church of St. Martin at Tours, carried with him to the Priory of Beaume his private library, amounting to a hundred volumes ; since it is scarcely possible that one in so comparatively subordinate a position should have been able to accumulate books to the value of £2000, which would have been the worth of this collection, even supposing that none of the works it embraced exceeded in bulk a copy of the Gospels.

The explanation of this seeming discrepancy probably lies in the fact, that the sum quoted by Leber as having been paid for the transcription of the Homilies of St.

Gregory was given to a secular Scribe, who received a much larger remuneration than would have been accorded to a Monastic copyist ; but we may at least be certain that, in basing our calculations with regard to the price of any particular work on the data which we have here adopted, the results attained will never fall short of, though they may often exceed, the truth.

It must be remembered, however, that in those centuries many circumstances contributed to give a special value to individual copies of books, and to enhance their cost to an almost incalculable extent; and in the influence of these causes is to be found the explanation of the examples which have been recorded by many writers of enormous prices paid for single volumes during the Middle Ages. The worth of a MS. augmented in proportion to the excellence of its calligraphy and the minute fidelity of its transcription ; while in modern times the Printing Press makes every copy of a large edition of a book the perfect fac-simile of the rest, as elegant in execution and as accurate in its text, in those days each individual copy was an edition in itself, standing upon its own merits alone ; if rude in its penmanship or faulty in its text, then of small value, but if copied with scrupulous care by a skilful penman, and diligently collated with the original until it varied not from it in a single letter, then of far higher worth. But the difference in cost thus produced was but trifling as compared with that which resulted from the specific value as works of art which belonged to the most elaborate MSS. of mediæval centuries, and of which it is difficult to form even an approximative estimate ; the gorgeous illuminations and exquisite paintings which were lavished upon these precious volumes often surpassed a hundred-fold in intrinsic worth the text which they adorned, and the book which a common scribe had copied in a few weeks of time, often engaged the most accomplished artists of the age during many months in its embellishment. Taking into account the frequently quadrupled worth arising from the perfection of the text, and the altogether inestimable value of the elaborate ornaments which made each page a marvel of artistic skill, and bearing in mind the costly bindings—sheets of sculptured ivory, and plates of silver or of gold, resplendent with precious gems—in which MSS. were frequently encased, we shall find a ready explanation of many a tale of enormous prices paid for books which would otherwise lead us to form a very erroneous idea of their general value in the Middle Ages, since we should act as foolishly in judging of the cost of humbler but as useful volumes from that of these splendid specimens as would the future Antiquary, living in centuries yet to come, in estimating the usual price of the works of Shakspere in our days, from the record of the sum paid for a richly bound copy of Boydell's magnificent folio illustrated edition of his writings. Not many years have elapsed since the sale in London of Bowyer's folio Bible, filled with exquisite illustrations from the pencils of the first artists of the age, which was valued at £3000 ; such a fact might be recorded with great exultation by some future Robertson, writing many hundred years hence, as an irrefragable proof of the rarity and dearness of books, and especially of the Bible, in the nineteenth century, and his readers might never suspect that at the same epoch and in the same country some thousands of copies of the same book might have been bought for the sum paid for this one gorgeous exemplar. So it is with regard to the

books of the Middle Ages; the superb volumes, whose
beauty and costliness caused them to be commemorated
in the pages of antique chroniclers, bore a high price, because, independently of their delicate penmanship and
perfect accuracy, the fruit of prolonged and diligent labour,
and their magnificent binding, in itself sometimes worth
a fortune, they possessed a distinct value as works of art ;
but books not thus enriched bore, as we have already seen,
a price infinitely below that which has been attributed to
them by many historians.   They were of course far more
costly than at the present day ; the dearness of the only
then existing material upon which they could be copied,
the bulk which necessarily belonged to written volumes,
and the expenditure of time and toil involved in the process of manual transcription, had their inevitable influence
upon the price of literary productions ; but when these
were alone operative, and the books produced were not
further raised in value by the internal embellishments of
art and the profuse employment in their external adornment of materials of high intrinsic value, their cost was
as moderate as was compatible with the circumstances of
the age, and placed them within the reach of many beyond the limits of the opulent classes of society.   But, as
has been already noted, the price of books was of secondary
importance, when the humblest had free access to the
Monastic Libraries, profusely scattered throughout every
European land, and obtained readily from the Monks the
loan of the most precious volumes.

The fact that Libraries were in those ages established
avowedly for the benefit of the poor, necessarily gives rise
to the supposition that the masses in mediæval centuries were
by no means under the dominion of the general ignorance

which has been imputed to them by some historians. Assuredly, the lending of books would never have been so urgently prescribed, had there been none who were capable of availing themselves of the privilege thus conferred ; such pious benefactors as Baptist Goy, the first Curé of the Church of St. Magdalen, at Paris, who left a large portion of his library for the use of his indigent parish- ioners,[a] would never have dreamed of thus manifesting their bounty, had the intellectual condition of the lowly been such as debarred them from profiting by their perusal ; and the inscription on the Bibliotheca Marucelliana at Florence, "Publicæ et maxime pauperum utilitati," would never have been placed over the portal of that repository of learning, had the poor, for whose advantage the collec- tion was thus declared to be peculiarly designed, been im- mersed in the mental darkness which it has been the general custom to attribute to the humbler classes at that epoch of European history. Many circumstances tend to strengthen the impression to which such facts naturally give rise : the translation of the Scriptures into the vulgar idioms, pursued with energetic zeal during the Middle Ages, shows that there were many readers, for whose re- quirements it was necessary to provide, beyond the circle of the Scholars to whom the Latin was as familiar as their mother tongue ; and the character of some of the books which were rendered into the language of the commonalty, such as the work of Boethius, *De Consolatione Philosophiæ*, which was translated into Anglo-Saxon by King Alfred in the ninth century, into German by the monks of St. Gall in the eleventh century, into Flemish at an early period, as appears by a MS. of that version still preserved at Paris,

[a] Lebœuf. Hist. du Diocese de Paris, l. ii. c. 4.

I

and into other popular languages,[6] the various scientific treatises translated into the vernacular in the ninth century by Raban Maur,[7] and the *Satiricon* of Martianus Capella, which treated of Grammar, Logic, Rhetoric, Mathematics, Geometry, Music, and Astronomy, and of which MSS. are in existence of a German version of the eleventh Century,[8] would seem to indicate that the tastes of those for whose use such translations were designed, were not entirely devoid of cultivation.   That such should have been the case will appear by no means singular, after a brief review of the agencies which were in those centuries provided for the education of the people; it needs but to contemplate the schools of mediæval days to perceive that, if ignorance existed among the multitudes, it sprung not from a deficency of means of enlightenment, freely accessible to all, and to comprehend that Libraries · for the poor were but natural adjuncts to that vast and efficient machinery of popular instruction which spread its ramifications throughout Europe.

In this, as in every other good work, the Monks were the most active labourers ; to the zealous toils which they undertook for the preservation and multiplication of the literary treasures of antiquity were added unwearying exertions to disseminate the blessings of knowledge among mankind.   In the Monasteries established by St. Pachomius, the Patriarch of Monasticism, a principal feature of each was a School in which lessons were given daily to all

[6] Baehr, Gesschichte der Röm, Lit. im Karol. Zeit. Pauly, Real Encyclopädie der Classischen Alterthumswissenschaft.   [7] Mabillon, Annal. Ord. S. Bened. ii. l. xxvii. c. 12. 14.   Rudolf von Raumer, Die Einwirkung des Christenthums auf die Altochdeutsche Sprache, 228. Hist. Litt. de France. iv. 15.   [8] Baehr. Röm. Litt. ii. § 395.

who desired to receive them ;[9] and before the close of the eighth century two Schools were found in every Monastery, the one claustral, in which were pursued the studies of the Monks and aspirants for Holy Orders, the other public, which was open to all who sought instruction,[1] this last being again divided into the Major and Minor School, the former of which was designed for the cultivation of the higher branches of learning, while the latter was devoted to the imparting of the rudiments of knowledge. Wherever the Monks established themselves, their appearance heralded the advent of intellectual advancement. Dr. Collier avows that " when the Monks were settled in England, in the reign of Sigbert, they promoted a general improvement, and were very industrious in restoring learning ;"[2] when the Danes had destroyed a great number of English Monasteries, we read that King Alfred hastened to restore them, since he found that their overthrow, by depriving the people of the benefit of the Schools which they contained, had caused an immediate decay of learning ;[3] and in the seventh century the Irish Monasteries, of which the most famous were the Abbeys of Louth, of St. Ivar in the Island of Beg-Eri on the coast of Wexford, of Clonard in Eastmeath, of Rathene, of Lismore, of Ross, of Bangor, of St. Mary at Clonfert, of St. Ninnidius on the Island of Dam-Inis in the Lake of Erne, and of Immay on the coast of Galway,[4] had acquired such eminent renown, that men flocked thither from England in vast multitudes, to profit by the advantages of study within their

---

[9] Mabillon Tr. des Etudes Monast. 14.   [1] Mabillon Annal. Ord. S. Bened. ii. l. xxv. c. 64. Hist. Litt. de France, iv. l. 33. ix. 92. 132.   Baluz. Capit. Reg. Fr. i. 585. § 45.   Baehr. Röm. Lit. § 4. Mabillon Tr. des Etudes Monast. c. xi.   [2] Collier Eccles. Hist. ii. l. ii.   [3] Spelman Vit. Alf. Append. No. 3. p. 106.
[4] Monast. Hibernic. 410.

walls.[5]   But it is needless to adduce individual examples,
the full citation of which, in truth, would be the transcription of the annals of Monasticism ; the simple fact
that a Public School for the instruction of the laity formed
a part of every Monastery, is sufficient, when considered in
connection with the immense number of Religious Houses
in every part of Christendom, to convey an idea of the
abundant facilities for the acquisition of knowledge which
were thus rendered accessible to mankind.   In the Monastic Schools instruction was always gratuitously bestowed ; often, indeed, the Monks were not content with
teaching without fee, but carried yet farther their bounty,
as in the Irish Abbeys, where, in the seventh century, as
Beda tells us, all who repaired for study received from the
Religious daily food and the books of which they stood
in need,[6] in the Abbey of Jumiege, where the children of
the poor were nourished at the cost of the community,[7]
and in many other Monasteries whose wealth rendered
possible such munificence ; but, in all, the advancement of
the pupil was the sole reward which the teacher sought
for his labours, and the humblest could as freely participate
in the benefits of the school as the possessor of the richest
gifts of fortune.   The life of Pope Sylvester II. affords an
interesting example of the facilities which the Monastic
Schools afforded for the developement of lowly genius,
which would otherwise have remained inert in obscurity.
The son of a peasant dwelling among the mountains of
Auvergne, he was sent in early youth to the School in the
Abbey of St. Aurillac ; there his latent abilities quickly
manifested themselves to the Religious, who took him

[5] Beda Eccles. Hist. l. iii. c. 27.   [6] Ibid.   [7] Deshayes
Hist. de Jumiege.

thenceforth under their special protection, laboured diligently in his instruction, and, when he had completed the accustomed course of study, sent him to travel, in order that he might augment his stores of learning; visiting the most renowned Abbeys of France, and subsequently those of Spain and Italy, he found in all a cordial welcome, and, remaining some time in each, made great progress in erudition;[6] and at length this peasant boy, who in the nineteenth century might have whistled life-long at the plough, became the famed Abbot Gerbert of Bobbio, a generous patron of letters, and an earnest labourer for the intellectual elevation of his fellow-men, and passed ultimately from the dignity which he so nobly sustained to the elevation of the Supreme Pontificate. In like manner, our countryman Pope Adrian IV. was the son of a menial in the service of the Abbey of St. Albans; and, in truth, the majority of the renowned Churchmen of mediæval centuries were men of obscure origin, who would have remained through life in the lowly rank in which they had been placed by birth, had not the Monastic School opened to them its gates, and accorded to them, without fee, the instruction which gave development to their genius and enabled them to become illustrious benefactors of mankind. The Monks, too, displayed their zeal for the diffusion of learning by frequently establishing Schools apart from those within the walls of their Monasteries; thus Abbot Joffred, of Croyland, sent to the Manor of Cotenham some of the brethren, who used to walk to Cambridge daily to give lectures in a barn, where they speedily collected a vast number of pupils and instituted a regular course of studies, Brother Odo teaching Grammar early

[6] Hock. 61.

in the morning to the younger boys, Brother Terricus lecturing at Prime on the Logic of Aristotle, with the commentaries of Porphyry and Averroes, Brother William reading at Tierce the Rhetoric of Cicero and Quintilian, and Brother Giselbert expounding before Sext the text of the Sacred Scriptures, on which he also preached publicly to the people on all Sundays and Saints' days;[9] and the origin of many Universities may be traced to Schools of this description, which owed their foundation to Monastic zeal.

Next in importance were the Cathedral Schools, which were first established in Spain in the sixth century, it being provided by the Council of Toledo that all children offered by their parents should dwell under one roof, and be instructed under the superintendence of the Bishop.[1] The example thus presented was speedily imitated in other lands, and similar Schools were multiplied in all parts of Europe ; in the eighth century, the School in the Cathedral of Utrecht had acquired so wide a fame that scholars repaired thither from France, from England, from Saxony, from Sweden, from Bavaria, and from Friesland;[2] that of Rheims, under Hincmar, and Foulques, his successor, in the ninth century, attained an European celebrity;[3] that of Paderborn, under Bishop Meinwerc, in the tenth century, was renowned as a seat of learning ;[4] that of Lyons, in the eleventh century, was denominated the " Mother and Nurse of Philosophy;"[5] that of Tournay,

[9] Petr. Bles. Cont. ad Hist. Ingulf. ap. Rer. Angl, Scr. i.
[1] Conc. Tolet. ii. Can. i. iv.   [2] Buddingh. Geschiedenis van opvoeding en onderwys in de Nederlanden. 6. 8.   [3] Anquetil. Hist. de Rheims. i. 152.   [4] Vit. Meinw. ap. Leib. Coll. Scr. Brunsw. i. 523.   [5] Bibl. Clun. 282.

in the eleventh century, was frequented by students from Burgundy, from Italy, and from Saxony, as well as from other lands ;[6] that of Liege, under Wazo, in the eleventh century, had achieved a pre-eminence which secured for it the title of the " Fountain of Wisdom," and endowed it with universal renown ;[7] and the same might be said of many others which possessed equal fame. In the twelfth century, the establishment of such seminaries was made of general obligation ; the third Council of Lateran, in 1179, decreed " that, since the Church of God is bound, as a pious Mother, to provide that every opportunity for learning should be afforded to the poor, who are without help from patrimonial riches, in every Cathedral there should be a master to teach both Clerks and poor Scholars gratis ;" and Pope Innocent III. extended this injunction to other Churches, requiring that in each should be provided the means of gratuitous education. The Scholastics who presided over the Cathedral Schools were invested by the third Council of Lateran with power to superintend and license the schoolmasters in their respective dioceses, a function which they appear to have discharged even previous to this concession ; and it would seem that these were, at any rate in England, very widely distributed, since the Council of Westminster, in 1138, prohibited the Scholastics from accepting payment for the licenses which they granted to schoolmasters in towns and villages ;[8] whence it appears that, in addition to the Monastic Schools, other academies were to be found, even in the humbler hamlets, where, indeed, their foundation had

[6] Hist. Litt. de France, vii. 95. [7] Chapeauville. Anselmus, i. 281. 287. 292. 309. Mabillon Annal. Ord. St. Bened. iv. 413.

[8] Johan. Bromp. Chron. 1348.

been urgently recommended by the Council of Vaison, in 529.   In all these, instruction was given without charge ; Pope Alexander III. made this the subject of an epistle to the French Bishops, in which he charged them to take special care that the masters exacted no payment from their pupils, " lest knowledge should seem to be exposed for sale, which ought to be offered gratuitously to all."[9]

Parochial schools appear to have been in existence from a very early period.   In the eighth century, Theodulf, Bishop of Orleans, in a Capitulary addressed to his Clergy, says, " Let all Priests open Schools in the towns and country places, and if any among the faithful desire to confide to them their children to be instructed in learning, let them by no means refuse to receive and educate them, but, on the contrary, let them teach these little ones with perfect charity, remembering that it is written, ' They who shall have been learned shall be radiant as the brightness of Heaven, and they who shall have instructed many in the ways of righteousness, shall shine as stars throughout eternity.'   And for teaching these children they shall seek no payment, and shall receive nothing but what the parents may offer to them voluntarily and through affection."[1]   " Mass Priests," says an Anglo-Saxon Canon, " shall always have at their houses a school of learners, and, if any good man will trust his little ones to them for lore, they shall right gladly receive and kindly teach them, nor shall they for this demand anything of the parents, beside that which these may give of their own free will ;"[2] Charlemagne, in the Capitulary of 789, addressed to Priests, directs them to endeavour to collect and keep

[9] Martene. Vet. Scr. ii. 853.   [1] Launoi de Scholis Celebris, iii. p. 27. Labbe, vii. 1163.   [2] Thorpe, ii. 414.

under their care not only children of servile condition, but also the sons of freemen, and to be diligent in the establishment of Schools ;[3] Reculfus, Bishop of Soissons, in the tenth century, admonished his clergy to devote special attention to the supervision of their schools, and to be no less attentive to the cultivation of virtue in their pupils than to the enlightenment of their minds ;[4] and many similar proofs might be adduced of the important share which was borne by the Parochial Clergy in the work of popular education. While the Priests were charged with the instruction of such of the children of the commonalty as were not among the frequenters of the Monastic Schools, the Bishops discharged the same duty towards youths of high rank or pre-eminent ability, whose tuition was one of their customary occupations. In an old Anglo-Saxon Treatise on the obligations attached to various states and professions, the chapter on the daily work of a Bishop defines it to be, " in the first place, of right, his prayers, and then his book-work, writing, and studying, and teaching, and his Church hours in the right time, always in the manner that thereto belongeth, and the washing of the feet of the poor, and the dealing out of alms, and the ordering of work where it may be needful ;"[5] and the most eminent Ecclesiastics were most active in the pursuit of the labours of instruction thus comprehended among the duties appertaining to the office of the Episcopacy. Wilfrid, Archbishop of York, had always under his care many sons of great men, who were sent to him for education, whether they were designed for clerical

[3] Baluz. Capit. Reg. Fr. i. 257, § 70—714, § 68.   [4] Hist. Litt. de France, vi. 83, 84.   [5] Thorpe, ii. 311.

or laic pursuits ;[6] of Egbert, who occupied the same an-cient Metropolitan See, we are told by Alcuin that he loved to take under his care youths of good capacity, and, sup-porting them from his own purse, to guide them affection-ately in the paths of learning ;[7] and of the same illustrious Prelate, it is recorded that, as soon as he was at leisure in the morning, he was accustomed to send for some of the young clerks, and, sitting on his couch, to teach them successively until noon, at which time he entered his pri-vate chapel, and offered the Holy Sacrifice ; again, after dinner, summoning his pupils, and listening to them while they discussed literary questions in his presence, and, in the evening, reciting with them the office of Complin, and dismissing each one with his blessing ;[8] Archbishop Theo-dore had a great number of disciples, to whom he daily gave instruction in sacred and secular learning ;[9] of Ethel-wold, Bishop of Winchester, we are told that " he de-lighted to teach children and youth, and to encourage them to diligence and virtue by his pleasant admonitions;"[1] Notker, Bishop of Liege, in the tenth century, of whom it is recorded that he not only superintended the Scrip-tural studies of Clerks, but also instructed the young laics who had been confided to him for tuition in the arts ap-propriate to their several ranks of life,[2] was always ac-companied in his journeyings by some of his pupils, whom he watched over with paternal love, and to whose

---

[6] Guil. Malms. de Gest. Pont. Angl. iii.
[7] " Indolis egregiæ juvenes quoscunque videbat,
    Hos sibi conjunxit, docuit, nutrivit, amavit."
                        Alcuin, Pöema. de Pont. Eccles. Eborac.
[8] Mabillon Acta SS. Ord. St. Bened. Sæc. iv. 149.
[9] Beda. Eccles. Hist. l. iv. c. 2.   [1] Wolstan, Vit. Ethelw.
[2] Chapeauville. Anselmus, i. 218, 219.

education he devoted himself with untiring energy and
remarkable success;[3] Bishop Wazo, who occupied the same
See in the eleventh century, and by whom the students
who flocked to the Cathedral School of Liege from all parts
of Europe were welcomed with affectionate hospitality,
and provided with the means of subsistence when their
poverty rendered such bounty needful, was equally assiduous in the tuition of his numerous disciples;[4] and the
same might be said of a multitude of other Prelates, who,
in addition to their zealous labours in the superintendence
of the Cathedral Schools in which they directed the studies
and themselves instructed the more advanced students ;
distinguished themselves by the diligence which they displayed in the instruction of the youths who had been specially confided to them for tuition.

To the Monastic and Cathedral and Parochial Schools,
which were under the exclusive control of the Clergy,
must be added the Chaptral Schools, which appear to have
been generally submitted to a mixed jurisdiction. The
government of these institutions was very varied in its
character ; occasionally the Scholastic was appointed by
the Bishop, without reference to the temporal authority,
as at Courtray ;[5] sometimes the superintendence of the
Schools, claimed as a prerogative by the civil power, was
delegated in perpetuity to the Chapter, as at Turnhout ;[6] not
unfrequently the Scholastic was nominated by the Sovereign,
as at Brussels,[7] or by the feudal Lord, as at Namur, or by

---

[3] Mabillon Annal. Ord. St. Bened. iv. 201.   Chapeauville, Anselmus, i. 217.   [4] Ibid. 280.   [5] Miræi Opp. Dipl. i. 563,
ii. 837, 838.   [6] Ibid. iii. 437.   [7] Diploma of Jean I. 1273.
Ordonnance of Jean III. 1320.   Wauters Hist. de Brux. i. 88.

the Chapter subject to the approval of the Suzerain, as at
Ghent;[8] at other times the jurisdiction over the Schools
was exercised by the Chapter conjointly with the Municipal authorities, as at Ypres[9] and at Antwerp.[1]   In these
Schools the instruction was not always gratuitous ; in
some towns this was the case, as at Namur and at Antwerp ;[2] but in others a charge was made for education,
as at Brussels, where there were, in 1320, eleven such
establishments, one superior for each sex, four primary
for girls, and five primary for boys, in which the pupils
paid annually twelve sous,[3] equivalent to a little less than
£2,[4] and at Ypres, which possessed, in 1253, three great
Schools, in which the scholars were subjected to an annual
charge of ten sous,[5] equivalent to about £2 5s.,[6] for which,
however, they were to be supplied with parchment.   Other
Schools also existed, which, though generally directed by
the Monks or Clergy, were not immediately connected with
any of these organizations.   Such were the Schools
founded by the Counts of Raperschwil in the neighbour-
hood of St. Gall, which, though independent of the Abbey,
were protected and encouraged by the Monks ;[7] such were
the Schools which flourished in some parts of England in

[8] Warnkönig Flandrische Staats und Rechtsgeschichte, i. § 48.
[9] Ibid. i. 440, 443. ii. 170, 172, 179, 180.   [1] Diercxsens
Antverpia Christo Nascens, ii. 8, 9.   [2] Ibid. 8.   [3] Ordonnance of Jean III., 1320.   Wauters Hist. de Brux. i. 88.
    [4] In the first half of the fourteenth century the Livre was equivalent
to about 84fr. 50c., or £3 6s. of modern value.   Leber. Fort. Priv. au
Moyen Age, 103.   The sou was therefore worth about 3s. 3½d.
    [5] Warnkönig Fland. Staats und Rechtsgesch. i. 440.   [6] In the
latter half of the thirteenth century, the Livre was equivalent to about
113fr. 80c., or £4 11s. 4d. of modern value.   Leber. Fort. Priv. au
Moyen Age, 103.   The sou was therefore worth about 4s. 6¾d.
    [7] Ildefons von Arx.

the reign of Henry III., of which Fitz-Stephen makes mention of three established in London, and holding high repute for learning ;[8] such were probably the eight Schools which Lothaire I. founded in 823, in the principal towns of Italy ; such were the Schools for the poor which were frequently created by pious benefactors, as the Ecole des Bons Enfants, which existed at Rheims from the thirteenth century,[9] the establishment bearing the same name at Brussels, which was endowed by Pierre Van Huffele, Chaplain of St. Gudule, in 1358, with all his property, and farther enriched in 1377 by Jean T'Serclaes, Archdeacon of Cambray, who provided it with the means necessary for the lodging and nourishment of twelve poor scholars between the ages of nine and eighteen years,[1] and the many similar foundations which existed in other parts of Europe ; such also were the Schools of the Hieronymites, a pious confraternity bearing considerable resemblance to the Christian Brothers of modern days, and instituted by Gerard Groote in 1396, whose establishments were numerously diffused throughout Central Europe. In Holland, in addition to the Monastic and Cathedral and Chaptral Schools, arose in the thirteenth century the Communal Schools, which were under the sole jurisdiction of the temporal power, and appear to have been superintended by laic instructors. These were divided into Greater and Lesser Schools ; of the former, one of the most renowned was that of Zivolle, which in the fourteenth century numbered nearly a thousand stu-

[8] Guil. Stephanid. Descript. Civitat. Lond. 4. France, xvi. 39. Anquetil. Hist. de Rheims, l. iii. de Bourgogne, Cod. 16,575, fol. 3, 4.

[9] Hist. Litt. de
[1] MS. Bibl.

dents, many of whom had repaired thither from remote regions; the latter were dedicated to elementary tuition.[2]

In the latter portion of the mediæval epoch the Universities arose in considerable abundance; in Spain alone there were twenty-seven of these institutions, the three greater at Salamanca, Alcala, and Valladolid, and the most celebrated of the twenty-four lesser at Saragossa, Valencia, Seville, Grenada, Itruria, Cervera, Toledo, and Santiago; and not less than fifty-six were founded in Europe before the close of the fifteenth century. Many of these were frequented by vast multitudes of students; that of Bologna, which was specially famed for the study of Jurisprudence, and in which were counted seventeen nations of *citramontani*, and eighteen nations of *ultramontani*, numbered in the middle of the thirteenth century ten thousand students,[3] which rose in the fourteenth century to thirteen thousand;[4] that of Paris was so thronged, that its students constituted in the twelfth century half the population of the city,[5] and in 1453 they were twenty-five thousand in number;[6] that of Prague, at the commencement of the fifteenth century, contained forty thousand students; that of Oxford contained in the fourteenth century, three hundred Colleges and Halls,[7] and an immense number of students;[8] and those of Padua, Salamanca, Naples, Toulouse, Montpelier, Salerno, Perugia, and Cologne acquired a repute which attracted to them crowds of students from every part of Europe. In the Universities the poor were not forgotten; everywhere Colleges were founded for their

[2] Buddingh. Gesch. van opv. en onderw. 40.　　[3] Tiraboschi, iv. 47.　[4] Muratori. Script. Rer. Ital. xvi. 325.　　[5] Hist. Litt. de France, ix. 663.　　[6] Villaret. Hist. de France, xvi. 341.　　[7] Ant. Wood. Hist. Univ. Oxon. 265.　　[8] Ibid. 206.

special benefit by royal and noble donors, who provided, not only for the gratuitous education of the indigent, but also for their sustenance during the period of their studies, so that the lowliest were enabled to participate in the advantages afforded by these renowned seats of learning. Thus, for example, in the single University of Paris, there existed the College of Navarre, founded by Jeanne · de Navarre, wife of Philippe le Bel, in 1304, for seventy students, twenty in Grammar, each of whom received weekly four sous, about 13s. 3d.; thirty in Logic and Philosophy, who had each six sous, about 19s. 10d., and twenty in Theology, who were allowed each eight sous, about £1 6s. 6d. ; the College of Thirty-Three, established for thirty-three students in Theology, whose number was fixed to correspond with the years of the life of Christ ; the College of Montaign, founded in 1314 for eighty-four poor scholars, in commemoration of the twelve Apostles and the seventy-two Disciples of our Lord ; the College of Harcour, endowed in 1280 for poor Norman students ; the College of Boissi, whose founder, Etienne Vidé, declared that he designed it " for those who are not nobly born, but sprung from the ranks of the common people, and poor, as we are and as our forefathers were ;" the College of Cornouaille, founded in 1317, for indigent scholars from that diocese ; the College of Boncourt, established in 1357 for poor students ; and the Scotch and Italian Colleges, founded respectively in 1323 and 1333 for poor scholars of those nations ; and such foundations were numerous in every part of Europe.

The diffusion of knowledge among the people was an object of earnest solicitude to the Councils of the Church, whose Canons manifest the pious zeal for the spread of

popular enlightenment which animated the hearts of the
Ecclesiastics of mediæval days ; taking the ninth century
as an example, we find that the Council of Orleans, in 800,
urged upon the Parish Priests the duty of establishing
Schools in towns and villages, and giving gratuitous instruction to all children who might be confided to them by
their parents ; the Council of Mayence, in 813, directed the
Clergy to admonish their parishioners to send their children to the Monastic and Parochial Schools ; the Councils
of Arles, of Rheims, of Tours, and of Chalons-sur-Saône,
in 813, had for chief object the encouragement of education, and directed the establishment of Schools for the
culture of sacred and secular learning ; that of Rome, in
826, enforced the foundation throughout Christendom of
Episcopal Seminaries, of Parochial Schools in towns and
villages, and of others wherever opportunity existed ; the
fifth Council of Paris, in 829, besought Louis-le Debonnaire to establish at least three great Schools in fitting
localities, " that he might thereby secure to the Church of
God augmentation of glory and increase of utility, and to
himself a rich reward, and an undying memory ;" the
Council of Valence, in 855, urged the multiplication of
Schools for the study of divine and human sciences ; the
Council of Kiersey-sur-Oise, in 858, exhorted Charles-le
Chauve to labour for the encouragement of learning ; the
Council of Savonnières, in 859, invoked the co-operation of
Princes and Bishops in the foundation of Schools for the
study of the Sacred Scriptures and the cultivation of the
liberal arts ; the Council of Langres, in 859, impressed in
like manner upon temporal and ecclesiastical rulers the
necessity of augmenting the number of Schools for the
pursuit of divine and human learning ; and the same spirit

breathed in the decrees of Councils held at other periods during the Middle Ages. The most eminent Prelates distinguished themselves by the energy with which they laboured to promote the intellectual advancement of humanity; St. Dunstan, in manifesting himself, as William of Malmesbury says, " next to King Alfred, the greatest promoter of learning that ever appeared in Britain;"[9] Honorius, Archbishop of Canterbury, in encouraging Sigbert of East Anglia in the institution of Schools, and procuring the aid of learned men from France in the direction of the studies therein pursued;[1] Egbert, Archbishop of York, the disciple of the illustrious Beda, in superintending with assiduous zeal the School at York, in which Alcuin laid the foundation of his glorious career, and establishing there a noble Library for the farther promotion of learning;[2] Ethelwold, Bishop of Winchester, in delighting to surround himself with youthful disciples, labouring in their tuition and encouraging them to diligence and virtue;[3] Reculfus, Bishop of Soissons, in urging upon his Clergy the duty of devoting special attention to the superintendence of their Schools, and striving to make their pupils not less eminent for the purity of their lives than for the splendour of their erudition;[4] Leidrade, Archbishop of Lyons, in occupying himself diligently in the formation and regulation of Schools, in which the study of the Scriptures was cultivated with admirable success;[5] and Wazo, Bishop of Liege, in exercising a vigilant guardianship over the Schools, teaching in them himself, conversing

---

[9] Guil. Malms. l. ii. § 149. [1] Beda Eccles. Hist. l. iii. c. 18.
[2] Alcuin de Pont. et Sanct. Eccles. Eborac. ap. Gale, i. 730.
[3] Wolstan Vit. Ethelw. 617. [4] Hist. Litt. de France, vi. 83.
[5] Launoi de Schol. Celebr. c. vii. p. 39.

affectionately with the scholars concerning their studies, welcoming with hospitality the multitudes of students who came thither from foreign lands, and furnishing the means of subsistence to those who needed charitable aid,[6] were but the types of the Hierarchy of which they were illustrious members ; in all lands the Bishops of the Christian Church were the most active patrons of learning, founding and endowing Schools, making vigorous efforts to secure the aid of eminent Scholastics in the direction of the studies of their pupils, engaging personally in the work of instruction, and demonstrating, by their zealous exertions for the diffusion of knowledge, the fervour and sincerity of their desire for the enlightenment of mankind. " Persevere, O my most dear and amiable Prince," wrote Alcuin to Charlemagne, " in your most honourable course of making the improvement of your subjects in knowledge, virtue, and happiness, the great object of your pursuit, for this shall redound to your glory and your felicity in the great day of the Lord, and in the eternal society of His Saints. Such noble designs and glorious enterprises will not, you may rest assured, remain without reward ; for though the life of man is short, the goodness of God is infinite, and He will recompense your momentary toils with joys which shall never end."[7] Such were the thoughts which dominated the hearts and moulded the lives of the Ecclesiastics of mediæval centuries.

The subjects studied in the Schools of the Middle Ages of course varied according to the class for whose use they were especially designed. In the Chaptral and Parochial Schools, and the Minor Schools of the Monasteries, which

---

[6] Chapeauville Anselmus, i. 281.
Lect. Canisii. ii.

[7] Epist. Alc. ap. Antiq.

satisfied the requirements of the children of humble rank, whose education was but preparative to the active toils of a laborious existence, the instruction given appears to have comprehended the articles of Christian Faith, Morals, Grammar, Music, and Arithmetic ; beyond these limits it is not probable that it often extended, though we find that Logic was taught in the Chaptral School at Ypres,[8] and the fact that the director of that of St. Pharailde at Ghent was a Master of Arts,[9] would induce the supposition that some of the higher branches of knowledge formed part of the tuition there bestowed. But in the Major Schools of the Monasteries, as well as in the Cathedral Schools, the studies pursued embraced a far wider range ; in these were cultivated the Divine Sciences and the Liberal Arts, the former comprehending the study of the Scriptures, and Dogmatic and Moral Theology, the latter being sub-divided into the *Trivium* and *Quadrivium*, the *Trivium* including Grammar, Logic, and Rhetoric, and the *Quadrivium* comprising Mathematics, Geometry, Music, and Astronomy.[1] Occasionally a different classification

---

[8] Warnkönig Flandr. Staats und Rechtsgesch. i. 443.   [9] Ibid.

[1] Greg. Tur. l. x.   Aldhelm. MSS. Reg. 6, B. viii. fol. 30.   Alain de Lille Anti Claudianus. Diploma of Philip of Brabant to the Univ. of Louvain, 1428.   Ducauge Gloss. Cantu Hist. Univ. vii. 466. Œuvres de St. Foix, iii. 339.   Cramer Geschichte der Erziehung und des Unterrichts in den Niederlanden, 5.   Rud. von Raumer die Eniw. des Christ. 199.   The Seven Liberal Arts were enumerated in the barbarous distich :

`   GRAM. loquitur ; DIA. vera docet ; RHET. verba colorat ;
   MUS. canit ; AR. numerat ; GEO. ponderat ; AST. colit astra ;`

and the aim of each study in the lines :

`GRAMMATICA—Quidquid agunt artes ego semper prædico partes.
DIALECTICA—Me sine doctores frustra coluere sorores.
RHETORICA—Est mihi docendi ratio cum flore loquendi.`

was attempted; thus, for example, Alcuin, whose agency in the revival of letters in France, under Charlemagne, has secured to him so important a place in the intellectual history of Europe, in the course of education which he recommends, divides the Liberal Arts into *Physica, Logica,* and *Ethica; Physica* admitting of six sub-divisions into Mathematics, Geometry, Astronomy, Mechanics, Music, and Medicine; *Logica* comprising Dialectics and Rhetoric; and *Ethica* teaching the regulation of the conduct by the four virtues of Prudence, Justice, Fortitude, and Temperance;[2] but the division into the *Trivium* and *Quadrivium* prevailed in the Schools throughout the whole of the Middle Ages.   Among the General Text Books which were employed in the study of the Liberal Arts, may be enumerated the *Satiricon* of Martianus Capella, written at Rome about 470, which was divided into nine books, the first two being introductory, and each of the remaining seven being devoted to one of the sciences embraced in the *Trivium* and *Quadrivium;*[3] the Treatise *De artibus ac disciplinis liberalium artium,* composed by Cassiodorus in the sixth century;[4] the *Origines* of Isidore, Archbishop of Seville in the seventh century, a work which may be denominated encyclopædic, of which the first five books treat of Grammar, Rhetoric, Philosophy, Dialectics, Music, Mathematics, Mechanics, Astronomy, Jurisprudence, Chronology, and History, the sixth of the Holy Scriptures,

MUSICA—*Invenere locum per me modulamina vocum.*
GEOMETRIA—*Rerum mensuras et rerum signo figuras.*
ARITHMETICA—*Explico per numerum quid sit proportio rerum.*
ASTRONOMICA—*Astra viasque poli vindice mihi soli.*
    [2] Alcuin, ii. 332.   [3] Baehr Röm. Lit. ii. § 395.   Pauly Real Encyc. Greg. Tur. l. x.   The *Satiricon* was translated into German at an early period; of this version MSS. of the eleventh century are in existence   [4] Baehr Röm. Lit. ii. § 396.   Pauly Real Encyc.

the seventh and eighth of God and the Angels, the ninth of the different languages and nations of the earth, and the remaining books of Etymology ;[5] the Treatise of Alcuin on the Seven Liberal Arts ;[6] and the Commentaries on the *Satiricon* of Capella, produced in the tenth century by Remy d'Auxerre,[7] and Duncan of the Abbey of St. Remigius ;[8] but in addition to these, which may be regarded as Manuals of the entire course of secular studies, many separate works were constantly in use in the Schools, in the pursuit of each branch of learning. Thus, for Grammar, they employed the treatise of Donatus, who flourished at Rome in the fourth century, and numbered St. Jerome among his pupils, entitled *Ars, seu editio prima de literis, syllabis, pedibus, et tonis, editio secunda de octo partibus orationis, et de barbarismo, solæcismo, schematibus, et tropis ;*[9] the *Commentariorum grammaticorum libri xviii. ad Julianum* of Priscian, renowned at Constantinople in the time of Justinian, of which the first sixteen books treat at considerable length on the eight parts of speech, and the remaining two on syntax, and the minor Tracts by the same writer, *Partitiones versuum xii principalium : De accentibus ;* and *De declinatione nominorum ;*[1] the *Institutiones Grammaticæ* of Flavius Sospater Charisius, who taught at Rome in the fifth century ;[2] the two Treatises, *De arte grammaticâ* and *De Orthographiâ*, produced by Cassiodorus in the sixth century ;[3] the three books *De differentiis seu proprietate verborum*, written by Isidore, Archbishop of

[5] Baehr. Röm. Lit. ii. § 401.   [6] Ibid. 3er Suppl. 337. 338.
[7] Hist. Litt de France, vi. 120.   [8] Ibid. 549.   [9] Baehr. Röm. Lit. ii. 599.   Pauly. Real Encyc. Cramer Gesch. der Erz. in den Nieder, 257.   [1] Ibid. 258.   Hist. Lit. de France, xvi. 142, 144. Pauly. Real Encyc.   Baehr. Röm. Lit. ii. § 397.   [2] Pauly Real Encyc.   [3] Ibid.

Seville in the seventh century ;[4] the Grammatical Compendium of St. Boniface, Archbishop of Mayence ;[5] the four Treatises of Beda, entitled *Cunabula grammaticæ artis Donati restituta : De octo partibus orationis : De orthographia : and De metricâ ratione*,[6] and the writings of Alcuin, *De grammaticâ* and *De orthographiâ*,[7] composed in the eighth century ; the *Excerptio de arte grammaticâ Prisciani*, of Raban Maur, Archbishop of Mayence,[8] and the Commentaries of Sedulius on Donatus, Priscian, and Eutychius,[9] and of Bishop Erchambert,[1] and Abbot Smaragde,[2] on Donatus, produced in the ninth century ; the Grammars of Hilperic,[3] Gunzon,[4] and Abbon de Fleury,[5] and the Commentaries of Remy d'Auxerre on Donatus and Priscian,[6] which last might more appropriately be classed among General Text Books, since, though professedly a grammatical work, it treats also of Dialectics, Rhetoric, Geography, Arithmetic, Music, and Astronomy,[7] composed in the tenth century ; the *Metricus de verbis deponentibus libellus cum commento*, written by Johannes de Garlandia in the eleventh century ; and the Grammar of Pierre Helie,[8] and the *Græcismus* of Everhard de Bethune, so called from the explanations of Greek words which it contains, and remarkable as being the first Grammar written in verse in order to make its study more attractive to youth,[9] composed in the twelfth

---

[4] Baehr Röm. Lit. ii. § 401.   [5] Cramer. Gesch. der Erz. in den Niederl. 66.   Mai. Classic. Auct. e. Vatican. vii. No. 8.
 [6] Pauly. Real Encyc.   Putsch Summul. der Lat. Gramm.
 [7] Baehr. Röm. Lit. 3er Suppl. 339.   [8] Hist. Litt. de France, v. 155.   Baehr. Röm. Lit. 3er Suppl. 419.   [9] Baehr. Röm. Lit. 3er Suppl. 365.   [1] Hist. Lit. de France, v. 128, 129.   [2] Ibid. 128. Baehr. Röm. Lit. 3er Suppl. 364.   [3] Baehr. Röm. Lit. 3er Suppl. 218, 618.   [4] Hist. Lit. de France, vi. 47.   [5] Ibid. 48.
 [6] Ibid. 119.   [7] Ibid. 47.   [8] Ibid. ix. 144, 147.
 [9] Cramer. Gesch. der Erz. in den Niederl. 258.

century : to these should be added the Dictionary entitled *Glosses Keroniennes*, produced in the eighth century, and attributed to the Monk Kero of St. Gall,[1] the Dictionary prepared under the direction of Salamon, Bishop of Constance, in the ninth century,[2] and the Lexicons of Balbi, Guilielmus Bretonus, and Ugutio, Bishop of Ferrara, compiled in the thirteenth century ; as also the books which were employed for the exercise of the pupils in reading and construing, as the Distichs of Cato, *Dionysii Catonis disticha de moribus ad filium*, which maintained its position as a first Latin book throughout the Middle Ages, and was translated into Anglo-Saxon, French, English, German, and Flemish, to serve the same purpose for beginners in those languages,[3] and the various other works which were composed for the use of those who had progressed beyond the first stage of learning, such as the *Doctrinale puerorum* of the Franciscan Alexandre de Ville Dieu,[4] the *Doctrinale altum seu liber parabolarum* of Alain de Lille, and the *Doctrinale* of Bernardin le Sauvage,[5] which were, like the Distichs of Cato, collections of moral precepts, designed to promote at the same time the progress of the pupils in knowledge and in virtue, by causing the text whose critical study exercised their intellectual faculties to become the means of imprinting noble sentiments in their hearts, while more advanced students imbibed the same pure morality from the pages of the Christian poets, Prudentius,[6] Avitus,[7] Arator,[8] Juvencus,[9] Prosperus,[1] Sedulius,[2] St. Paulinus,[3]

---

[1] Rud. von Raumer. Die Einw. des Christ. 123.   [2] Ibid. 128.
[3] Pauly. Real Eucyc.   [4] Hist. Litt. de France, xvi. 144.
[5] Cramer. Gesch. der Erz. in den Niederl. 260.   [6] Baehr. Röm. Lit. 1er. Suppl. Rud von Raumer. die Einw. des Christ. 104.
[7] Rud. von Raumer. die Einw. des Christ. 102.   [8] Ibid.
[9] Ibid. 103.   [1] Ibid   [2] Ibid. 106.   [3] Ibid.

and Theopistus,[4] whose strains, if they wanted the exquisite polish which gratifies the taste in the Heathen bards whose writings fill their place in modern Schools, were at least free from the licentiousness which depraves the soul.   For Logic they employed the dialectic writings of Aristotle, translated by Boethius in the sixth century,[5] subsequently rendered anew from an Arabic version by Michael Scot,[6] and also translated by William of Brabant, under the supervision of St. Thomas of Aquin, in the thirteenth century ; the versions of portions of the works of Porphyry by Boethius ;[7] the writings of Averroes ;[8] the Treatises of Boethius entitled, *Introductio ad categoricos syllogismos : De syllogismo categorico : De syllogismo hypothetico : De divisione : De definitione :* and *De differentiis topicis ;*[9] the Treatise *De dialecticâ,* composed by Alcuin in the eighth century ;[1] the Treatise of Raban Maur, *In Porphyrium et Aristotelem de Interpretatione,*[2] produced in the ninth century ; the Commentary on Porphyry by Gerbert, who flourished in the tenth century ;[3] and the *Summula Logica* of Pierre d'Espagne,[4] which, together with a dialectic work by Johannes de Sacro Bosco,[5] appeared in the thirteenth century: for Rhetoric, the writings of Cicero[6] and Quintilian ;[7] the Treatise of Priscian, *De præexercitamentis rhetoricæ ;*[8] the *Communis speculatio de rhetoricæ cog-*

---

[4] Hist. Litt. de France, ix. 144. 147.   [5] Pauly Real Encyc.
[6] Ibid.   [7] Ibid.   [8] Petr. Bles. Contin. ad Hist. Ingulf. Rer Angl. Scr. i.   [9] Pauly Real Encyc.   [1] Baehr. Rom. Litt. 3er. Suppl. 339.   [2] Ibid. 423.   [3] Hist Litt. de France, vi. 65.   ·   [4] Ibid. xvi. 103.   [5] Ibid. 104.   [6] Alain. de Lille Anti-Claudianus.   Petr. Bles. Contin. ad Hist. Ingulf. Rer. Angl. Scr. i.   [7] Petr. Bles. Contin. ad Hist. Ingulf. Rer. Angl. Scr. i.
[8] Baehr. Röm. Litt. ii. § 379.   Pauly Real Encyc.   Cramer Gesch. der Erz. in den Nederl. 258.

natione and the *Locorum rhetoricorum distinctio* of Boethius ;[8] and the *Dialogus de rhetoricâ et virtutibus* of Alcuin.[1]   For Arithmetic, the books most in favour were the Treatise of Priscian, *De figuris et nominibus numerorum et de nummis ac ponderibus ;*[2] the two books of Boethius, *De Arithmeticâ;*[3] and the Treatises of Beda, *De Arithmeticis numeris : De diversis speciebus numerorum et mensâ Pythagoricâ : De Arithmeticis propositionibus : De asse et partibus ejus et de ratione calculi : De numerorum divisione :* and *De ratione unciarum :*[4] for Geometry, Euclid ;[5] the two books of Boethius, *De Geometriâ ;*[6] and the Treatise on the Quadrature of the Circle by Francon, Bishop of Liege :[7] for Astronomy, the Treatises of Cassiodorus,[8] Beda,[9] Alcuin,[1] Raban Maur,[2] Adalbard,[3] Hincmar,[4] Francon,[5] Heriger,[6] and Sigbert ;[7] for Music, the work of St. Augustine, *De musicâ ;*[8] the Treatise of Beda, entitled *Musica theoretica et practica seu mensurata ;*[9] the five books, *De Musicâ,* of Boethius ;[1] and the Treatises of Hincmar of St. Amand, *De harmonicâ institutione* and *De Musicâ enchiriadis,* together with his *Commentatio brevis de tonis et psalmis modulandis.*[2] Such were the books generally used, in conjunction with

[9] Pauly Real. Encyc.   [1] Baehr. Röm. Lit. 3er. Suppl. 339.
[2] Pauly Real. Encyc.   [3] Ibid.   [4] Baehr. Röm. Lit. 2er. Suppl. 478. 479.   [5] Alain de Lille. Anti-Claudianus.   [6] Pauly Real. Encyc.   [7] Hist. Litt. de France, vii. 18.   Launoi De Schol. Celebr. c. xxv. p. 106.   [8] Pauly Real, Encyc.   [9] Baehr. Rom. Lit. 2er. Suppl. 478.   [1] Ibid. 3er. Suppl. 340.   [2] Hist. Litt. de France, v. 182.   Baehr. Röm. Lit. 3er. Suppl. 423.   [3] Hist. Litt. de France, v. 585.   [4] Ibid.   [5] Launoi De Schol. Celebr. c. xxv. p. 106.   Hist. Litt. de France, vii. 18.   [6] Hist. Litt. de France, vii. 207.   [7] Foppens. Bibl. Belg.   [8] Pauly Real. Encyc.   [9] Baehr. Röm. Lit. 3er. Suppl. 479.   [1] Pauly Real. Eucyc.   [2] Baehr. Röm. Lit. 3er. Suppl. 534.

the General Treatises of Capella, Cassiodorus, Isidore, and Alcuin, in the study of the Seven Liberal Arts, though of course all were not employed in every School, nor did each remain in vogue throughout the whole of the Middle Ages ; there were many others, also, whose use appears to have been confined to particular localities, such as the volumes frequently composed by Scholastics to facilitate the studies of their pupils, which were mostly compilations from the already existing Treatises of highest repute, and rarely passed beyond the Schools for whose peculiar use they were designed.   In many Monastic and Cathedral Schools the secular studies pursued extended beyond the limits of the *Trivium* and *Quadrivium* ; we have already seen that the *Origines* of Archbishop Isidore comprehended Treatises on Jurisprudence, Medicine, Chronology, History, and the various nations and languages of the earth, and to this work, which enjoyed a very high repute, and was in general use as a Text Book from the period of its production in the seventh century, must be added the Treatise *De universo*, composed by Raban Maur, Archbishop of Mayence, in the ninth century, which, in the section devoted to secular learning, treats of the Creation of the World, of Astronomy, of Physics, of Chronology, of the Earth, of Man, of Animals, of Plants, of Oceans and Rivers, of Metals, of the Phenomena of Nature, of the Philosophers, Poets, and Divinities of Paganism, of Numbers, Weights, and Measures, of Maladies and the Science of Medicine, of Navigation, of Agriculture, of Military Art, and of the ordinary apparatus of domestic life, such as houses, vestments, food and utensils ;[2] the *Mirouer du Monde* of Gauthier de Metz, an encyclopædic work produced in the

[2] Baehr. Röm. Lit. 3er. Suppl. 419. 421.

thirteenth century,[4] the *Speculum Magis* of Vincent of Beauvais, which consists of four parts, the *Speculum Naturale*,
the *Speculum Doctrinale*, the *Speculum Morale*, and the
Speculum Historiale, the first of these being divided into
six books, in the order of the six days of Creation, and
treating at great length of Quadrupeds, Birds, Fishes, Insects,
Plants, and Minerals, as well as of Geography, Agriculture,
and Mining; the writings of Albertus Magnus, which embrace many works on different branches of Natural History;
the *Margarita Philosophica*, the author of which is unknown;
and the numerous *Bestiaria*, *Volucraria*, and *Lapidaria*,
which were produced at various periods, and especially in
the thirteenth century. One of the stipulations made by
Charlemagne in founding the school at Osnabruck, in the
eighth century, was that the study of Greek should be
always there pursued,[5] an injunction which was so well
observed, that the biographer of the Abbot Herman deems
it a sufficient explanation of his habit of constantly carrying with him a Greek Testament, and using it in preference
to the Latin version, to note that he was educated in that
school;[6] at the Abbey of Tegernsee, in Bavaria, Greek
was cultivated with success, and a botanical garden formed
to facilitate that branch of study;[7] the linguistic attainments of the Monks of the Monastery of St. Martin are
manifested by the *Tetraples du Psautier*, containing in four
columns the Hebrew, Greek, Latin, and French versions
of the Psalms, which was there prepared under the direction

---

[4] Cramer. Gesch. der Erz. in den Niederl. 260.   [5] Baluz.
Capit. Reg. Fr. i. 245. 246. 419. 420.   Hist. Litt. de France, iv. 12.
Cramer. Gesch. der Erz. in den Niederl. 56. 57.   [6] Chron.
Cænob. Virg. Ottburg. ap. Paulin. Rer. et Antiq. Germ. Syntag.
[7] Jaeck. Galerie der Klöster Deutschlands. i.

of the Abbot Odo,[8] who also composed an Introduction
to the study of Theology, in which are cited many passages
of the Hebrew text of the Scriptures ;[9] Mechanics and
Medicine are enumerated by Aldhelm, in addition to the
Seven Liberal Arts, in his record of the subjects generally
studied in the Anglo-Saxon Monastic Schools ;[1] Natural
History and Jurisprudence were taught in the Cathedral
School at York,[2] in which Alcuin also learnt Greek and
the elements of Hebrew ; and Trithemius mentions the
Hebrew, Greek, and Arabic languages among the subjects
studied in the Claustral Schools, which were especially
dedicated to the cultivation of learning among the Religious.[3]

But, great as was the activity displayed in the cultivation
of the Liberal Arts, a yet higher zeal was manifested in
the pursuit of those Divine Sciences to which all secular
learning was regarded as merely auxiliary, valuable chiefly
because it facilitated the successful prosecution of those
higher studies which were deemed to be the noblest field

---

[8] Hist. Litt. de France, ix. 101.   [9] Ibid. vii. 116.   [1] Aldhelm. MSS. Reg. 6. B. viii. fol. 30.   [2] Alcuin. de Pont.
Eborac. 728.   [3] Trithemius. Chron. Hirsaug.—cf. also on the
studies at Fulda and St. Gall, Rud. von Raumer. Die Einw. des Christ.
199 ; in the Schools at Paderborn under Bishop Meinwerc, Vit. Meinw.
ap. Leib. Coll. Scr. Brunsw. i. ; in the Irish Monasteries, Aldhelm ap.
Usher Syll. 39 ; in the Schools of Archbishop Theodore, Beda Eccles.
Hist. l. iv. c. 2. ; in the Franciscan School at Paris, Wadding. Annal.
Minor. 1234 : and generally on the studies pursued in the English and
Continental Monasteries, Johan. Sarisb. Metalogicon, l. i. c. iv. p. 273. c.
vii. p.749. c. xiii p. 759. l. ii. c. x. p. 802. Dacher. Spicileg. ix. 22. In-
gulf. 509. 514.   Johan. Sarisb. Polycraticon, l. viii. c. xxii. p. 672.
Bulæi. Hist. Univ. Paris. i. 42. ii. 575.   Petr. Bles. Epist. vi. 8. ci.
157.   Guil. Malms. Prol. in l. ii. p. 143.   Ant. Wood Hist. Univ.
Oxon. 46. 52.   Selden Diss. in Flet. c. vii. § 3.   Beda Eccles. Hist. l.
iv. c 2.   Launoi De Schol. Celebr. *passim*.

for intellectual exertion;[4] holding the salvation of his
soul to be man's chief business upon earth, it was but
natural that the men of mediæval times should have sought
to make all their labours conducive to this end, whose
attainment was the highest aspiration of their lives. The
study of the Bible, designated by Raban Maur "the foundation of all true learning,"[5] was pursued with a vigorous
energy of which it is difficult to convey an adequate conception;[6] to enumerate the works which were composed
as aids to the comprehension of the Sacred Text would be
to present a catalogue of the larger portion of the works
written during the Middle Ages; in addition to the precious
volumes of the Fathers of the Christian Church, which
constituted alone an ample and incomparable Theological
Library, and which were multiplied with untiring industry,
and studied assiduously in the Schools, the earnest desire
of the Monks to facilitate the progress of the student gave
birth to innumerable works, whose character attests the
vast extent of their Biblical studies, and the fervour of the
holy zeal which animated them to unceasing toil in the
interpretation of the Inspired Volume. While some occupied themselves in the composition of General Treatises
specially designed to elucidate the text of Holy Writ, such
as the *De Universo* of Raban Maur, of which the first part
contains dissertations on God, on the Angels, on the Patriarchs, on the Prophets, on the remarkable personages
named in the Old Testament, on the Evangelists, on the

[4] " Quanquam scientia Trivii et Quadrivii in se habet veritatem, non
tamen est scientia proprie dicta, sed bene valet ad Sacram Scripturam
intelligendam." Diploma of Philip of Brabant to the University of
Louvain, 1428.   [5] Raban Maur. S. Instit. Cleric. iii. ii. col. 628.
          [6] On this subject cf. especially Rud. von Raumer Die Einw. des
Christ. 218. *et seq.*

Apostles, on the Martyrs, on the Articles of Christian Faith, on the several books of the Bible, on the Septuagint and other versions of Scripture, and on the Sacraments,[7] and others engaged in the compilation of Biblical Lexicons, such as the *Catholicon, seu dictiones quæ sæpe inveniuntur in Bibliâ et in dictis Sanctorum et etiam poetarum secundum ordinem alphabeti ordinate subjunctæ* of Balbi,[8] the *Opusculum difficilium vocabulorum Bibliæ* of the Franciscan Guilielmus Bretonus, and the *Mammotrectus* or *Gemma Gemmarum* of Johannes de Garlandia,[9] or of Concordances such as that of Hugues de St. Cher, which groups together in alphabetical order all the texts of Scripture in which the same word occurs,[1] a vast multitude devoted themselves to the labour of commenting on the Bible, in which they toiled with an energetic zeal whose fruits yet survive to attest their ardour in the cultivation of sacred learning. No one who is conversant with the character of mediæval literature can be ignorant of the fact that, of the fragment of its productions which remains to us, by far the larger portion consists of Commentaries on the Scriptures ; the labours of Beda, of the one hundred and thirty-nine works from whose pen sixty-four are of Biblical Criticism, are but a fair example of the spirit which animated the Religious, and impelled them to consecrate their untiring energies to the illustration of the Sacred Volume. Throughout the Middle Ages, that School was most renowned and most frequented within whose walls the study of the Scriptures had arrived at highest perfection, and the climax of the laudations bestowed upon the most distinguished

[7] Baehr. Röm. Lit. 3er. Suppl. 419. xvi. 142.   Cantu Hist. Univ. xii. 667. Gramm. Lips. ii. 92.   [8] Hist. Litt. de France. xvi. 142.   [9] Erasmi Colloq. Synod Gramm. Lips. ii. 92.   [1] Hist. Litt. de France, xvi. 70.

Scholastics by their Monastic biographers is invariably that they were eminent for their Biblical learning. In truth, even the secular literature of the Middle Ages breathes of the Bible in every page ; the tone of thought, the language, the imagery of these antique writers demonstrates the profundity of their Scriptural attainments, by showing that they had become so habituated to the forms of expression employed in Holy Writ that these naturally enveloped their own ideas ; it is impossible to cast even a cursory glance at the productions of the Scholars of those centuries without recognizing this pervading characteristic, which affords the strongest evidence that the Bible was to them a most familiar volume. But the assiduity with which the study of the Scriptures was pursued in the Middle Ages is sufficiently attested by the material fruits of its prosecution which have survived the wreck of centuries ; even were we without the countless testimonies of contemporaneous annalists, which alone constitute an irrefragable demonstration, the number of Biblical Commentaries yet remaining to us among mediæval MSS. would establish the zeal of our forefathers in the cultivation of this branch of sacred learning beyond the possibility of contradiction.

The character of education in the Middle Ages was essentially Christian ; knowledge was sought for, not as an end but as a means, and the end to which it was to be the means was the purification of. the heart and the elevation of the soul to God. The prayer with which Ambroise Autbert, Abbot of St. Vincent of Vulturne, in Italy, concludes his Commentary on the Apocalypse, " that it may please God to enable him to combine with human learning the practice of virtue, since, if he cannot enjoy the happi-

ness of joining them together, he would rather be looked
upon by men as a fool than as a learned man without
virtue, the object which he has proposed to himself in life
being, not the acquisition of renown for learning, but the attainment of salvation by the practice of Christian virtues,"[2]
embodies the spirit which dominated the mediæval mind;
for the men of those ages deemed, with Peter of Blois,
that "the highest wisdom is, not to study Plato or to dis-
engage the subtleties of Aristotle, but to love Christ, to
serve Christ, and in this most grateful and fruitful service
willingly, efficaciously, faithfully, and finally to remain;"[3]
and the encomium which Beda passes upon Fursey, who,
he says, "was a man of noble Scottish blood, but yet
more noble from the dignity of his mind than from the
elevation of his birth, since from his boyish days he had
particularly applied himself to reading sacred books, and,
as is most becoming in holy men, he was careful to prac-
tise that which he had learned he ought to do,"[4] expresses
the idea with regard to the ends to be attained by intellectual cultivation which presided over the Schools of
mediæval centuries. In a Monastic education the noble
example of the holy brotherhood was deemed of yet higher
value than the learning which was imparted by their tuition;
thus Eginhard, the secretary of Charlemagne, writing to
his son whom he had placed in the Abbey of Fulda, under
Raban Maur, says, "My son, study to imitate good manners, and take care that you never offend him whom I wish
you always to follow, but be diligent always to obey his
commands; learned in these things, and familiar with the
labours of those who surround you, you will want the ad-

---

[2] Mabillon. Tr. des Etudes Monast. 11.   [3] Petr. Bles. Serm. liii.
[4] Beda Eccles. Hist. l. iii. c. 19.

vantages of no vital science. As I advised you while present to exercise yourself in the study of oratory, so I again exhort you to leave nothing untouched of that noble science which you may acquire from the genius of that great orator; but, above all, remember to imitate those good manners in which he excels, for Grammar, Rhetoric, and all other studies of liberal arts are vain, and greatly injurious to the service of God, unless by Divine grace they are made subject to virtue;"[5] and Archbishop Anselm, addressing his nephew in the same spirit, says, "Apply yourself assiduously to Grammar, and exercise yourself more in prose than in verse; but, above all things, guard your manners and actions before men, and your heart before God, that when, by the favour of God, I shall see you, I may rejoice in your progress, and you may rejoice in my joy."[6] The relation between the teacher and the scholars was one of tender and intimate affection; "the master," says St. Bonaventura, " must be full of gentleness and humanity for his disciples, whom he should regard as his children, evincing towards them the tenderness of a mother with the wise firmness of a loving father;"[7] and the affectionate and admirable epistles which yet remain to us as tokens of the nature of the intercourse which prevailed in those ages between men and their former teachers, afford proof that this noble ideal often attained realization. Simplicity was the prevailing characteristic of mediæval learning; that fantastic rhetorical spirit which Lord Bacon admits to have sprung into life with the Reformation,[8] had then no being; men looked

---

[5] Mabillon. Act. SS. Ord. S. Bened. Præf. in Sæc. iii. § 8.
[6] S. Anselm. I. iv. Epist. 31.   [7] S. Bonavent. Spec. Novit. c. xiii.   [8] Bacon, Advancement of Learning.

not to the words but to the matter, and were better pleased
with high thoughts in homely garb, than with platitudes
disguised in sounding phrase.   Mabillon shows that learning was cultivated with the sole object of rendering men
more humble and charitable, more fervent in the love of
God, and more diligent in His service ;[9] and Dionysius the
Carthusian gives utterance to the motives which universally inspired the toils of Monastic Scholars, when he says,
" I confess that, as far as I am able to discern, after self-
examination, I am not conscious of having undertaken
these works through vanity or for any vile end, for the
sake of fame or of temporal advantage, but I engaged in
them in order that, by daily occupying myself in the
study of the Scriptures, I might become able to live
according to them, acquiring true humility, meekness,
and patience, which I greatly need."[1]   It was the influence
of this dominant Christian spirit which excluded the
classics from the schools of the Middle Ages ; men could
not conceive that any graces of style which these writers
might possess could compensate for the peril to which they
would expose the youthful mind by associating its earliest
impressions with the false theories of the Philosophers
and the licentious strains of the Poets of Paganism ; they
therefore substituted in their stead the Doctrinals, which
were collections of moral precepts and matters of useful
learning, and the writings of the Christian Poets, and
deemed that, however inferior these might be in respect
of rhetorical beauty, they had clearly profited by the exchange.   Still it must not be imagined that the Classics
were entirely neglected ; although they did not enter into

[9] Mabillon Tr. des Etudes Monast. Pref.   [1] De Arctâ Viâ
Salutis.   Protest. ad Superiorem.

the course of public instruction in the Schools, there were many who applied themselves to their study, as may be seen by glancing at their writings, in which numerous passages of ancient writers are employed to illustrate the verities of religion. Thus, for example, Rathere, who was successively Bishop of Verona and of Liege in the tenth century, in his *Agonisticon*, which he composed while in prison at Pavia, quotes from Cicero, Varro, Terence, Horace, Persius, and Seneca, though he had by him when he wrote no other book than the Bible ;[2] John of Salisbury, in his work entitled *De Nugis Curialium*, produced in the eleventh century, makes citations from more than one hundred and twenty ancient authors, including the greater number of the Classical writers ; among the books which Dionysius the Carthusian enumerates as having been studied by him, we find mentioned Plato, Proclus, Aristotle, Anaxagoras, and many others of the natural Philosophers ;[3] Withold of Corby, in the twelfth century, names among the writers who should be studied Pythagoras, Plato, Sophocles, and Simonides ;[4] Beda compiled two collections of extracts from Classical writers, the one entitled *Sententiæ seu axiomata philosophicæ*, the other *Ex selectis Ciceronis sententiis liber* ;[5] John Erigena lectured in the Palatine School on Plato, whom he denominated the greatest of the natural philosophers ;[6] Nanno of Friesland, who taught in the Palatine School under Charles le Chauve, composed commentaries on some of the writings of Plato ;[7] Paschasius Radbert makes many quotations from Plato and other

---

[2] Hist. Litt. de France, vi. 380. [3] De Arctâ Viâ Salutis.
[4] Martene Vet. Scr. xi. 334. [5] Pauly. Real. Encyc. [6] Johan. Erigen. De Divisione Naturæ, i. c. xxxiii. [7] Hist. Litt. de France, v. 658.

classical authors ;[8] the writer of the Life of Bishop Liet-
bertus of Cambray describes the last hours of that Prelate
in language taken from the *Apologia Socratis* of Plato and
the Treatise of Cicero *De Senectute ;*[9] and the writings of
Peter of Blois, Archdeacon of Bath in the twelfth century,
contain citations from Tacitus, Aristotle, Hippocrates,
Galen, Horace, Aulus Gellius, Justin, Juvenal, Lucan,
Ovid, Persius, Frontinus, Terence, Quintus Curtius, Theo-
phrastus, Plautus, Quintilian, Valerius Maximus, Virgil,
Vegetius, Livy, Martial, Macrobius, Statius, Cicero, Sue-
tonius, Plato, Sallust, and Seneca. Such men thought,
with John of Salisbury, that " though the Gentile without
Christ had not laid hold of the fruit of beatitude, yet we
see in them the shadows of virtues, as in the diligence of
Themistocles, the gravity of Fronto, the continence of
Socrates, the fidelity of Fabricius, the innocence of Numa,
the modesty of Scipio, the patience of Ulysses, the ab-
stemiousness of Cato, the piety of Titus ;"[1] but such
judicious application, by men of piety and experience, of
the really valuable portions of the writings of the ancients
to the illustration of the dogmas of revealed religion, was
very different in its influence from the promiscuous use
which is made of these Pagan authors in modern days,
when they are placed unreservedly in the hands of the
young, who have thus presented to them a mingled mass
of good and evil, in which they cannot be expected to
separate the truth from the error, so that their moral perversion progresses coincidently with their advancement in
learning. Such a practice prevailed at no period during
the Middle Ages, nor could it ever exist in a society in

[8] Mabillon Acta SS. Ord. S. Bened. Sæc. iv.   [9] Dacher. Spicileg.
ix.   [1] De Nugis Curialium, l. iii. c. 9.

which Christian ideas exerted so practical an influence upon the conduct of its members ; the Author of the *Gemma Animæ*, in the twelfth century, gives utterance to the views which were all but universal among the Religious of mediæval times, when he says : " It grieves me when I consider in my mind the number of persons who, having lost their senses, are not ashamed to devote their utmost exertions to the investigation of the abominable faults of the Poets, and the captious reasoning of the Philosophers, (which often bind irrevocably in the bondage of sin the mind which has withdrawn itself from God,) and are yet content to remain ignorant of those principles of Christianity by which the soul may attain to everlasting felicity in Heaven. Nothing can be more insane than to devote oneself to the study of the edicts of an usurper, neglecting the laws of the rightful sovereign ; and moreover, what can the soul gain by dwelling upon the strife of Hector, following the arguments of Plato, giving heed to the poems of Virgil, or listening to the elegies of Ovid, all of whom are now gnashing their teeth in the prison of the infernal Babylon, under the cruel government of Pluto ? But the highest profit is his who, examining the deeds and writings of the Apostles, is continually engaged in contemplating those who, we know, are now reigning in the Palace of the heavenly Jerusalem, with the King of Glory."[2] Life being regarded by the men of those days as a conflict between rival agencies, upon the issue of which depended the eternal destinies of the soul, they deemed that the legitimate end of education was to train the warrior for the strife, and to arm him with the weapons which would ensure his victory over the foe

[2] Prol. Bib. Pat. x. 1179.

who laboured for his perdition; knowledge they conceived to be valuable only when it served as a stimulant to virtue, and erudition then only precious when piety and humility made it instrumental to salvation. In striving to become Sages our ancestors forgot not that they were Christians; spiritual elevation was ever with them the chief end aimed at in intellectual cultivation. Such was, in truth, but the natural result of the circumstances which environed their education, for in those centuries the shrines of learning were within the walls of the sanctuary; Monasteries and Cathedrals threw open wide the gates of their Schools for the free entrance of all who sought instruction, and Bishops and Priests delighted to labour in the culture of the youthful mind; for the agencies of popular enlightenment, which were so abundantly dispersed in every land, the world was indebted solely to the watchful care of Holy Church, and the noble enthusiasm which animated the hearts of humble men who had consecrated their lives to God, and assumed the habit of religion.

It is evident, then, that the Church, denounced by Her adversaries as the foe of intellectual progress, manifested Herself, in the Ages of Her highest might, the zealous and active patron of the diffusion of knowledge, and that the energies of those who had specially dedicated themselves to Her service were employed with admirable success in the pious labour of augmenting and directing the agencies for the enlightenment of the people. To the zeal of Priests and Monks the men of the Middle Ages were indebted for the noble Libraries which arose in every land, and whose most precious volumes might be freely carried to the student's home, for the abundant Schools which were multiplied throughout Europe, in which the children of the poor received a substantial and Christian education, and for the renowned Academies in which were cultivated the highest branches of divine and human learning ; the vast machinery of instruction, whose component elements we have passed rapidly in review, was essentially a part of the ecclesiastical organization, and to the Church belongs the glory of having created the instrumentalities whose action conferred such priceless benefits upon the world. Not for Her exists the need to draw a veil over the History of the Past ; when crafty foes, eager to overwhelm Her with obloquy and reproach, assail Her with the imputation that Her longing is for the enslavement of the human mind, She points proudly for Her vindication to the centuries in which She reigned supreme, She recals the memory of the hooded Scribes whose patient toils guarded the monuments of ancient wisdom from the rude touch of destroying Time, of the pious Monks and holy Priests who laboured with unwearying zeal in the instruction of the multitudes who thronged their countless Schools, of the saintly Bishops in whom the humblest scholar found a patron and a friend ; demanding only to be judged by the deeds which signalized Her sway, Her sole answer to Her revilers is an appeal to those faithful records of the olden time which display Her noble diligence in the encouragement of learning, Her ceaseless exertions for the intellectual advancement of mankind.

THE CHURCH AND THE PEOPLE

IN

THE MIDDLE AGES.

THE CHURCH AND THE PEOPLE

IN

THE MIDDLE AGES.

FROM our abiding-place amid the stern realities of the
actual Present, whose annals are the sad chronicles of the
battles of sordid avarice waged by class against class, by
man against his fellow-men,—whose atmosphere is discordant with the jarring echoes of the groans of starving
poverty, and the hideous clamour of rampant and triumphant vice,—we look back into the dim and distant Past,
upon Ages which had but few features in common with
our own, and strive to penetrate the veil which hides from
us the generating causes of a state of things so little in
harmony with all that now presents itself to our contemplation.   In what light shall we regard the spirit of those
bygone centuries, the springs of action which moulded
their character, the soul which breathed into them a life
so peculiar in its visible manifestations ?   Are we to place
ourselves above or below our forefathers ? to believe that
we have outstripped them in the race, and soared aloft to
a perfection far beyond the reach of their attainment, or
to recognise in them attributes of excellence which dwell
not with their posterity, and to trace in their lives the

action of sublime impulses which in our own hearts have been suffered to slumber in inanition?

The career of Society during the last three centuries has been, we are told, a march of progress. But progress whither? Progress to Heaven or progress to destruction? Progress in the growth of noble Christian energies, in the development of generous holy sympathies, in the assimilation of the life of man on earth to the higher spiritual life which is his hope beyond the grave, or progress in the degradation and debasement of human souls, in the fostering of the evil tendencies of our fallen nature, in the subjugation of the heart of humanity to the slavery of vice? The question to which all importance belongs is not whether Society has advanced since the epoch which we are to consider; the life of man is ever a career of movement, and a stationary existence is impossible alike to an individual and to a nation. But there are two roads along which he may journey, leading to widely different goals; the material and the immaterial afford like fields for his cultivation; and the true point to be considered is which track he has chosen for his pilgrimage, what fruit he is to reap from the ripe harvest which has crowned his toils. He has tilled, and planted, and watered, and the earth has yielded forth a rich crop to reward his labours; thus far there can be no doubt that his husbandry has thriven, and that he possesses something more than his progenitors. But the fruits which he may gather, are they Apples of Sodom, or clusters of the Celestial Vine? Unquestionably in some respects the world has made vast advances; has its progress drawn it nearer to God? The development of material civilization has been startling; has it been accompanied by a commensurate spiritual elevation? The instrumentalities of improvement have multiplied abundantly; does the spirit of Society manifest that they are as faithfully and efficiently employed as the less elaborate machinery of antiquity? These are the considerations which must determine our estimation of the relative excellences of the Middle Ages and the nineteenth century, and resolve the question whether the vaunted progress of humanity has been a march of improvement or of deterioration.

It has been the habit of a large class of writers to speak of mediæval centuries, as eras of unmitigated despotism, to paint for our edification dismal pictures of vast multitudes of men groaning beneath the iron yoke of irresponsible power, holding life itself at the pleasure of Kings, mere playthings for the sport of Emperors; to lead us, in a word, to believe that in those ages the world contained but two classes, the Noble and the Slave, and that those who had not gentle blood within their veins not only possessed no political rights, but were condemned to something less than mere animal existence. Such has been the historic theory of many a modern annalist who has succeeded in deluding the too credulous public, and gaining for himself a chaplet of renown; and the huge mounds of rubbish which such writers have heaped up to hide the grave in which they have buried Truth, are yet venerated by the many as the veritable shrines of wisdom, the authentic Temples of the Historic Muse, whence issue her oracles to the world.

Pity it is that our Law of Libel is framed only for the protection of the good name of the living; were it extended to shelter the fair fame of the dead, many a renowned historian might be brought as a criminal to the bar of justice.   It seems no good reason that a man should be slandered with impunity, that he lived ten centuries ago ; our ancestors have assuredly a right to the protection of their reputation against the assaults of these rabid defamers of all that is most venerable in antiquity. But that which would be a crime against the living becomes too often a source of glory, when its victims have crossed the frontier of the tomb ; assail the credit of the humblest citizen, even by a whispered imputation, and the prison opens for you its gates, the law, voracious for damages, plunges its greedy hands into your pockets ; but slander by wholesale defamation the character of entire bygone generations, spreading your calumnies far and wide in thousands of printed volumes, and Society awards you a niche in the Temple of Fame, and crowns you as a Sage amid the plaudits of an admiring world. There are, of course, many honourable exceptions to this unhappily too general rule ; but assuredly few can rise from the perusal of the pages of Gibbon, or Hume, or Robertson, or Voltaire, or any of the vast horde of their disciples, without recognizing the wisdom of the great Frederick, who was wont to say to his Librarian, " Bring me my Liar," when he needed a volume of a modern historian.

Would we contend, then, that the Middle Ages were eras of absolute perfection, that in their political and social features the most microscopic eye can detect neither blot nor blemish to mar their faultless symmetry ?   Assuredly we would sustain no such visionary theorem ; we seek to depict the condition of a society of men, not to sing the fanciful praises of an ideal Utopia.   Precisely because they were societies of men, the nations of me-

diæval centuries were exposed to all the dangers which wait
on human imperfection, and which will attend it as long
as the world endures; for the Golden Age which shines
so brightly in the visions of philosophic dreamers has its
realization in other than earthly realms; so long as frail
mortals sway the sceptre of dominion, so long as fallen
man controls the operation of the institutions of society,
so long will the battle between the agencies of good and
evil be waged with unrelaxing energy. The men of the
Middle Ages suffered from physical woes; the enjoyment
of liberty, the possession of property, life itself, were exposed to all the aggravated perils incident to a transition
stage of society; they were not exempt from the moral
evils springing from human depravity, whose development was stimulated by the disordered condition of the
European world : but have we, who no longer suffer from
the peculiar disadvantages under which they laboured, so
far succeeded in vanquishing these antagonistic influences,
that we may be permitted to rail at the barbarism of our
ancestors because they sometimes succumbed to their
assaults ? Have we no poverty, have we no vice, have
we no corruption in this our nineteenth century? Have
we no paupers dying of starvation in our secluded
lanes, no criminals congregated within the walls of our
stately prisons, no poison of immorality tainting the life
blood of Society? We are blessed with more abundant
agencies of improvement; have we made good use of
our increased facilities? Compare the condition of Europe
in the past and in the present; weigh well the impediments which in the olden time opposed themselves to the
efforts of the wisest legislators : the incessant ravages of
war, equally baneful to the physical and moral welfare of

mankind, the difficulties interposed to mutual intercourse
between nations, and between different portions of the
same nation, by the perils and fatigues of long and ar-
duous journeyings, the obstacles existing to the general
diffusion of knowledge, in the labour and expense involved in the multiplication of literary productions which
have since disappeared before the march of invention :
contemplate the increase which has taken place in the facilities for augmenting the physical comforts of the Poor,
by the vast cheapening of all products of manufacturing
industry, and for elevating their intellectual condition by
the development of new means for the diffusion of books,
and the consequent augmentation of the instrumentalities
of mental cultivation ; and then, bearing in mind these
vast mutations, judge whether the general condition of
mankind is better in modern than in ancient days, considered relatively to the means existing at each period for
its improvement ;—what honest mind can hesitate to award
the palm to the centuries of antiquity ?   In some respects,
indeed, even the physical welfare of the masses has undergone a positive deterioration ; the amount of wages assigned in former ages to the labourer contrasts strikingly
with the remuneration accorded to the same classes in the
same countries at the present day.   Taking England as an
example, and reducing the sums enumerated in ancient
records to the standard of present value, we find that the
Statute of 23 Edward III. fixed the daily wages of a reaper
at 6*s.* 8*d.*, of an agricultural labourer out of harvest
time at 5*s.* 10*d.*, and of a woman haymaking or weed-
ing corn at 1*s.* 8*d.*, and enacted that the payment for
mowing an acre of grass should be 10*s.*, and for threshing

a Quarter of Wheat 6*s.* 8*d.* ; the accounts of the expenses of the army of Edward III. before Calais, record that 314 Masons, Carpenters, Smiths, Engineers, Tent Makers, Miners, Armourers, Gunners, and Artillery Men were paid, some £1 10*s.*, some £1 5*s.*, some 12*s.* 6*d.*, and the lowest 6*s.* 3*d.* per day ; in 1444 the wages of labourers employed in building were fixed by Parliament at 4*s.* 8*d.* per day, which was increased by an Act passed in 1496. Comparing the sums prescribed by these enactments with the prices of food at the same period, as detailed in the *Chronicon Preciosum*, compiled by Bishop Fleetwood from the accounts of the Bursars of various Monasteries, we find that the agricultural labourer could purchase a quarter of wheat in fifteen days, a fat sheep in four days, and a grass-fed bullock in fifty-five days, with his wages out of harvest time ; and the preamble to the 23 Edward III. specially designates " beef, mutton, pork, and veal," as " the food of the poorer sort " of the English people. Turning to the England of the nineteenth century, the contrast is melancholy and impressive. The labourer for mowing an acre of grass, for which his ancestor received 10*s.*, has now 3*s.* 6*d.* ; for threshing a quarter of wheat his recompense has diminished from 6*s.* 8*d.* to 4*s.* ; the wages of women employed in agriculture have fallen from 1*s.* 8*d.* to an average of 8*d.* per day, some being as low as 6*d.*, and the highest, instances of which are rare, not rising above 1*s.* ; the gains of men engaged in the same pursuit are reduced from 5*s.* 10*d.* to an average of 1*s.* 4*d.*, the highest payment being 1*s.* 8*d.* in harvest time for the same amount of toil for which 6*s.* 8*d.* was paid to the mediæval labourer ; so that, looking at the present prices of food, we perceive that whereas the peasant in the days

L

of Edward III. could purchase a quarter of wheat by the labour of fifteen days, his descendant in the present age must toil for thirty-six days to achieve the same result, and that he must work for forty-five days to procure the fat sheep which was obtained in four days, and for three hundred and forty-five days to buy the bullock which was gained in fifty-five days by his ancestor.   Glancing at the condition of the working classes in France in the same century, we find that an Ordonnance of the Seneschal of Poitou, in 1307, states the wages of Carpenters and Masons at one sous, equivalent to 5f. 70c., and of Agricultural labourers at nine deniers, equivalent to 4f. 28c. per day of modern value ;[1] but as these rates refer to the period of the stay of Pope Clement V. at Poitiers, they are probably somewhat above the ordinary standard, which may be fixed at 5f. for the former, and 3f. 50c. for the latter class of labourers, the wages of Journeymen Tailors being at that period one sous, six deniers, equivalent to 5f. 50c. per day ; at the same epoch the Setier of 240lb. of wheat averaged thirteen sous, equivalent to 48f.[2] or 22c. per lb., and the price of a Bullock was four livres, fifteen sous, equivalent to 391f. 88c., and of a Sheep six sous, eight deniers, equivalent to 27f. 50c.,[3] making the price of Beef 63c. and of Mutton 57c., or the mean price of flesh meat 60c. per lb. In the provincial towns of France at the present day the wages of Carpenters and Masons average 2f. 25c., of Journeymen Tailors 3f., and of Agricultural labourers 1f. 25c. per day, the cost of the Setier of Wheat being 38f.,

[1] Leber. Fort. Priv. au Moyen Age, 64.   In France, in the same century, the daily pay of a Crossbow man ranged from 3f. 44c. to 5f. 50c., and of a common foot-soldier from 2f. 75c. to 3f. 67c. Leber, 65, 66.   [2] Leber. Fort. Priv. au Moyen Age, 16.   [3] Ibid. 74, 75, 76.   See note (H) at the end of the volume.

or 16c. per lb., and the price of Beef 44c., and of Mutton 46c., making the mean price of flesh meat 45c. per lb. Calculating from these data, and allowing to each labourer one pound of meat and three pounds of wheat per day, it appears that the Carpenter or Mason in the fourteenth century had remaining after this expenditure £46 16s. 6d. per annum, while the same classes of workmen in the nineteenth century have but £16 10s. 6d.; that the Tailor of those days had a surplus of £53 2s., while his descendant in this age has but £25 13s. 6d.; and that the Agricultural Labourer of the olden time had left for other uses £28 per annum, while but £4 remains to him who follows the same pursuits at the present day.[4] But it is not alone in certain aspects of the material life that we discover the traces of positive deterioration; penetrating beyond the surface, we recognise the evidences of the sad mutation which the lapse of a few centuries has sufficed to consummate in the spiritual condition of the masses of humanity, replacing the living Faith of bygone generations by the sceptical egotism whose God dwells, not in Heaven, but in its own poor shallow brain; corrupting and poisoning the heart by withdrawing from it the life-giving current of fervent piety which pulsed through it in antique times, and substituting in its stead a cold, intellectual credence, from its nature necessarily destitute of vitality; supplanting principle by self-interest as the rule of human action, and sapping the foundations of morality by the influence of

---

[4] Comparing these wages with the price of wheat at each epoch, it results, that in France, in 1307, the Carpenter or Mason received yearly 7114 lb., the Tailor 7825 lb., and the Agricultural Labourer 4979 lb of wheat, while in 1853 the Carpenter or Mason receives only 4401 lb, the Tailor 5868 lb., and the Agricultural Labourer 2445 lb. of wheat per annum.

the specious utilitarianism whose regards are centred upon earth, whose Paradise ends at the threshold of the tomb ; destroying, in a word, the Catholic people, whose hearts were the sanctuary of religion, and raising up in their stead a degraded populace, debased alike in their bodies and their souls. True, the Middle Ages had their physical woes, their poverty, and their sufferings ; but these were combated by agencies very different from those which array themselves against the same evils at the present day, and the spirit which pervaded society deprived them of more than half their terrors. Poverty to a Catholic heart, suffering to a pure conscience, death to an upright soul : these are not the highest calamities that can afflict humanity. In the Ages of Faith all these afflictions were battled against with manly energy ; but when the physical woe was victor, the resignation of the vanquished was far other than the resignation of despair ; in his breast was lodged a talisman which the sacred hands of Holy Church had planted nearest to his heart, whose presence called to his dying lips a joyous smile, and nerved him for the endurance of the trials and sufferings of existence. The afflictions which chastised the body were recognized as the agencies which purified the soul by the expiation of suffering, and opened wider for it the portals through which it might enter Heaven ; religion solved the mystery which becomes to rationalism the parent of despair, and solaced the pains of the sufferer by the assurance of recompense in eternity. Some men there were in those ages, as there have been in all periods of the world's history, and will be as long as earth endures, who lived at enmity with God, and toiled for their own perdition ; but among the vast majority of mankind Faith was the ruling spirit of life, devotion the dominant principle of action, salvation the aim and object of existence. Truly, as regards the moral health of humanity, the contrast between the trembling leper and the robust and vigorous man is not greater than between the multitudes of the nineteenth century and the people of Catholic antiquity.

It was precisely because they were Catholic, that the Middle Ages enjoyed these abundant blessings. The history of human progress is the chronicle of the triumphs of the Church, crowning Her unceasing warfare against the varied agencies of evil ; Her power was the safeguard of liberty, Her influence the parent of intellectual development, Her teaching the unique source of that spiritual vitality which was the especial characteristic of mediæval centuries, and whose extent is the unerring index of the veritable advancement of society ; through Her instrumentality the relics of barbarism disappeared from the social organization, and the dominion of Pagan ideas over the hearts of men gave place to the empire of Religion. It remains for us to consider the means which She adopted for the attainment of these admirable results, and to investigate the nature of the instrumentalities which She employed for the amelioration of the political, and intellectual, and moral condition of mankind.

Three principal evils may be noted, as resulting from the operation of principles inherent in the constitution of Feudal Society : the deification of force, arising from its essentially military character; the exclusion of all who were born beyond the pale of nobility from access to political dignity or influence, consequent upon its strictly hereditary organization ; and the depression of the physical condition of the masses, springing from its concentration of wealth in the hands of a few proprietors. Such were the prominent defects of Feudalism, whose pernicious tendencies it became the aim of the Church to mitigate, and, as far as might be possible, to destroy, by calling into operation such antagonistic agencies as were best fitted to counteract their influence, and to avert the perils with which they threatened the well-being of humanity.

In the then existing condition of Europe it was plainly inevitable that military prowess should command high renown, and pave the way to eminent authority. In the infancy of nations, at the moment of the emergence of the new society from the chrysalis of antecedent barbarism, when the convulsive throes which have accompanied its emancipation from its antique bonds are succeeded by the impotence of immaturity, the Great Captain is necessarily the most honoured, because the most indispensable of citizens ; powerless for its own defence, the State finds in its chief warriors the sole protectors of its existence, the only efficient safeguards of its integrity ; at an epoch when the sword is the arbiter of the national destiny, the rule of the soldier is an unavoidable necessity, and martial supremacy becomes invariably the stepping-stone to empire. It may not be amiss, however, to remark, that the nature of the modes of warfare which prevailed in those remote centuries, and which continued to be employed during the most illustrious period of the Middle Ages, ensured the possession of qualities which, though not the highest that can adorn humanity, are at least worthy of hearty and reverent admiration, by the hero who gathered laurels in the field of strife ; the battles of those days were contests of personal valour, in which the combatants fought man to man, and the high-born shared the peril with the humble ;

they had no devices by which a single puny arm could mow down a score of brave warriors as they stood, but hand to hand they struggled, and victory resulted from the valour of the Man, and not from the force of the Artillery. Their Generals did not, as in modern engagements, retreat from the peril in which they had placed their soldiers, and watch the progress of the fight from an adjacent eminence, secure from personal danger ; when Richard Cœur de Lion besieged Cyprus, " being armed, he leaped from his galley and struck the first blow in the battle, and before he had time to strike a second he had three thousand of his warriors fighting at his side ;"[5] and such was ever the habit of the warlike leaders of the olden time ; not unfrequently the chief captain fought on foot, that his followers might see that he had placed flight beyond his reach, and was resolved to conquer or to die. In our own day, war has become a game of tactics, in whose perils the commanders are too wise to share ; and with the change in the engines of military strife has come an immense depreciation in the value of personal prowess in the combatants. Of small account is the valour of the warrior, when death may be borne to him upon a bullet fired from behind a hedge ; little avails the courage of the advancing column, when the volley poured forth from the blazing mouths of fifty cannon mows them down as they advance to meet the foe. Bravery renders no man bullet-proof ; the most indomitable heroism makes but a poor figure when pitted against a cannon-ball ; when a warrior may fall by the hand of a far-off and unseen foe, it matters little whether he be a Bayard or a Parolles. But in the battles of earlier days personal valour was the chief element

[5] Richard of Devizes, § 60.

which decided the issue of the strife for victory ; and valour, in itself no mean attribute of man, is in most cases the index of yet higher qualities in its possessor.   The truly brave man is rarely a bad man ; his courage seldom lacks the alliance of many kindred virtues, linked with it in close companionship in his heart.

Still, it is obvious that the supremacy assigned by Feudalism to the sword was a dangerous feature in its constitution ; and as it was clearly impossible in the then existing condition of society to annihilate the preeminence of the warrior, it remained for the Church to correct the evil tendencies of this element of the social organization by Her action upon the individuals who were specially subject to its operation, by the introduction of an agency which should elevate and ennoble the military character, and realize, by the union of valour with sanctity, the ideal of the Christian warrior.

The material aspects of Chivalry, glorified in the strains of poets, and depicted with glowing enthusiasm even in the annals of sober chroniclers, have enchained the world in fascinated admiration ; the pomp of its gorgeous pageantry, the brilliance of its heroic deeds, the romantic charm of its perilous achievements, have so entirely engrossed the attention of mankind, that the elements of its true grandeur have been forgotten or unperceived ; the splendour of its external character has been suffered to eclipse the majesty of the sublime idea of which its visible glories were but the poor accoutrements, to which its outward panoply was but secondary in dignity and importance. The Order of Knighthood was in great measure a religious institution; assuming its place midway between the Church and the Feudal Aristocracy, it derived from each a portion of its character; but the features which were stamped upon it by Feudalism were but few and insignificant, as compared with those which were imparted to it by Religion. Assimilated in its ideal to the type of that Spiritual Knighthood, of which it was the martial emblem—and which, bound like it by the obligation of solemn vows, proving itself like it by achievement and suffering, and rising like it by noble deeds to glory, sought like it its reward not on Earth, but in Heaven; and clothed, by the religious ceremonies of its investiture, the lengthened fasts, the nights passed in prayer in the Church, the nocturnal watching of the armour before the Altar, the white robe and the bath which symbolised a second baptism, and the high ecclesiastical solemnities which accompanied the reception of the knightly grade, with an essentially sacred character; its Christian origin was no less eminently displayed in the obligations which were imposed by its laws, and the principles which formed the basis of its organization. In an especial manner the champions of the Church, the Knights were at the same time the sworn guardians of the weak, the pledged vindicators of the oppressed; all that was feeble and defenceless claimed as a right their aid; neither the rank of the wrong-doer nor the superior force of a mightier adversary deterred them from braving the perils of the holy war which they waged for the extermination of injustice. But the discharge of these admirable duties constituted not the sum of their obligations; not only did the duty of the Knight compel him to the performance of deeds of martial valour and self-sacrificing heroism, it also exacted from him a scrupulous integrity of life, failing in which, he incurred degradation from the dignity of Knighthood. The Code of Chivalry was the

first to consecrate a principle unknown to the warriors of
Pagan ages, and which the influence of Christian ideas
could alone have called into existence; the sentiment of
Honour became through its instrumentality the soul of the
Knightly character; Purity, Fidelity, Courtesy, Humility,
and Devotion were proclaimed by its teaching indispensable elements of heroism, attributes which could alone
give dignity to valour, and merit for it a glorious renown.
We cannot fail to be struck by the immense power which
a purely moral agency exercised in the government of this
institution, in the very infancy of society, for the dreaded
penalty of the infraction of the laws of Knighthood was no
material chastisement, but simply attaint of reputation; and
it is only by calling to mind the dominion which religion
then swayed over the hearts of men, that we can arrive at
a full comprehension of a phenomenon so remarkable in
its singularity. The ideal of Knightly Honour was the
ideal of Christian Perfection; he who was disloyal to his
vows was necessarily unfaithful to his religion : little cause
have we then to wonder that in ages so especially signalised
by their spiritual exaltation, the hearts which no peril of
flood or field could daunt, shrunk appalled from the shadow
of dishonour, and preferred death to the tarnished fame
which spoke a blemished soul. A fundamental analogy
was recognized between the two grand orders of Chivalry
and the Priesthood; the Knights were Warrior Priests, as
the Priests were the Knights of Spiritual Chivalry; bound
alike to the observance of spotless purity, to the practice
of exalted virtues, each waged the same unceasing war
against iniquity—the Priest with the spiritual arms of
sacrifice and prayer; the Knight with the temporal weapons
which he had consecrated to the service of religion, and

dedicated in an especial manner to the protection of the weak and the vindication of the oppressed.

For proof of the influence which these ideas exercised over the minds of our forefathers, it needs but that we should contemplate the history of those glorious enterprises which were the peculiar offspring of Chivalry, and which its spirit alone could have inspired. In this age the Crusades would be impossible, not because we are of less martial mould than our ancestors, but because we are dead to the impulses which prompted them to engage in perilous undertakings, without calculating the chances of worldly loss or gain, from a simple sense of duty to God, and in the sole hope of benefitting their own eternal destiny. It was not the result of the struggle, but the performance of duty by struggling, that chiefly occupied the attention of those who enrolled themselves beneath the banner of the Cross ; their labours were undertaken, not so much to secure the attainment of the ends proposed, as to fulfil an obligation of conscience. The motto of the Crusaders, " Diex li volt," was at once the motive and the justification of their enterprise ; if they triumphed in the fight, they thanked God for the victory ; if they were vanquished, they deemed the eternal reward of perseverance cheaply purchased by death upon the battle-plain. Once inspired by the conviction that it was their duty to rescue the sepulchre of Christ from the hands of the Infidel, the Monarch, the Noble, and the Knight abandoned the joys of home, the luxuries of wealth, and the allurements of honourable ambition, and journeyed to a far-off land, not to conquer a rich inheritance, but to screen one sacred spot from the access of pollution ; their pilgrimage was undertaken, not to swell the revenues, to augment the power, or to extend the dominions of their own nation, but to discharge a duty, whose performance brought no temporal reward; they stopped not to consider whether it was probable that they would have strength to overcome the force of the enemy, but, having once assumed the sacred symbol of self-devotion, they went rejoicing on their way, reposing all trust in God, and well assured that it would be better for their souls that they should leave their bones to bleach upon the Syrian sands, than that they should live disobedient to the call that summoned them to join the consecrated band. The modern world, in whose cold heart the flame of antique Faith glimmers fitfully in half extinction, may denounce the Crusades as wild outbursts of fanatical zeal, mad schemes of perilous adventure, romantic offsprings of bigoted knight-errantry; it is the world's time-honoured privilege to deride what it cannot comprehend, and to launch its scornful sneers at all that lies beyond the grasp of its calculating utilitarianism; but the gibes of rationalism change not the intrinsic character of these sublime enterprises, which were in their very essence sacrifices of all worldly advantages at the shrine of conscience, right earnest offerings of life and energy to God. If it had been objected to an old Crusader that his undertaking, to use the favourite jargon of our own times, tended to no practically useful result, he would have answered, that it tended to save his own soul, and that this was the most practically useful result within the range of his apprehension.

In a warlike age, when the dominion of the sword was an unavoidable necessity, a condition inseparably appertaining to the existing structure of society, the grand desideratum was obviously the creation of an indissoluble alliance between the might of force and the power of conscience; and this was the end proposed and attained by the institution of Chivalry, which, in its origin, a re-action against the excesses of Feudalism, a recorded protest of brave and generous hearts against the lawless oppression of the weak by chieftains whose power owned no restraint of conscience, achieved the most illustrious of triumphs over its adversary, by permeating with its own spirit the institution against whose invasions of justice it had been in its birth arrayed, and causing its noble principles to become in the end so intimately interwoven with the dominant sentiments of Feudal Society, that the proudest Baron learned to prize more highly the renown of knightly fame, than his ancestral heritage of nobility. But one agency could have effected this mighty regeneration—the supreme authority of religion; no other power could have breathed this new spirit into the soldier's heart, inspired with this new vitality the warrior's soul; the Church, by surrounding the forms of knightly investiture with the consecrating pomp of ecclesiastical ceremony, by imparting to the ideal of the knightly character the attributes of exalted purity and immaculate integrity, and by introducing into the code of knightly duty the obligation to the rigid observance of the most essential virtues of the Christian life, sanctified the institution of Chivalry, and attained a triumph which no other agency could have secured over the unruly passions of humanity. At the same time, She called in the aid of other instrumentalities to repress the dominion of violence; the institution of the Truce of God, which forbade all hostilities between vespers on Wednesday evening and the hour of dawn on Monday morning, under the fearful penalty of excom-

munication, incurred by any man who should assault his
enemy within the period thus prescribed,[6] and the establishment of the Right of Sanctuary, which made the pre-
cincts of the House of God the inviolable shelter of the
fugitive, and raised a consecrated barrier between the op-
pressor and his victim, were Her protests against the omnipotence of the sword, bulwarks erected by Her for the
protection of society against the inroads of the spirit of
lawless force, too often incident to a military domination.

But the infusion of these noble principles into the
character of the warrior, grand and substantial as were
the benefits which it secured to society, was necessarily
limited in its operation to the moral elevation of the class
whose power was derived from hereditary transmission,
and left untouched that element of the Feudal organisation which made noble birth the sole title to political
authority; the improvement of the character of the
Nobles, admirable as was its influence upon the spirit of
their administration, still left the powers of government
centred in their hands, and removed not the barrier which
obstructed the rise to eminence in the State of those who
inherited no ancestral dignity.   This evil, then, remained
to be overcome by the development of an agency which
should ensure to high endowments an open avenue of ad-

---

[6] Such were the conditions of the Truce of God, as first formally
established in Aquitaine, in 1041.   This institution was speedily extended to other countries ; in England, the periods during which all acts
of hostility were interdicted by its provisions, were the Ember Days,
the whole of Advent and Lent, the Vigils and Festivals of Our Lord,
of the Blessed Virgin, of the Apostles, and of All Saints. and all Sundays, reckoning from nine o'clock on Saturday evening until dawn on
Monday morning.

vancement, however humble might be the origin of their possessor.

It must be borne in mind, however, that, even at the period when Feudalism had attained its most mature development, the inhabitants of Towns, though excluded from all share in the control of the acts of the supreme sovereignty, retained yet a considerable control over their local affairs, and swayed an important influence in the direction of their domestic administration. The Roman Empire, essentially a Federation of Municipalities, had converted the municipal sovereignty of the cities which became subject to its sway into a mere administrative organization; at its fall each Town resumed in some measure its ancient privileges, and, although in all cases subject to the authority of an external superior, conserved to itself a large share of power in the regulation of its internal government. True, it was not until the thirteenth century that the Towns achieved their complete enfranchisement; but still, in the earliest times succeeding the dissolution of the Western Empire, the burgesses retained some share of independence, and preserved the right to elect Magistrates, who, sometimes alone and sometimes in concert with an officer nominated by the Suzerain, directed the affairs of the community. Occasionally they enjoyed yet greater privileges; often the right of the Feudal superior was limited to the monopoly of certain specified revenues, or to the reception of a fixed annual tribute, and not unfrequently the Towns became themselves Suzerains, and had vassals subject to their authority; but even those which possessed less extensive immunities conserved an independent municipal existence, impaired and enfeebled, doubtless, by being subject to the frequent invasions of force, and exposed to the assaults of armed injustice, but nevertheless retaining considerable vitality. We are not to conclude, therefore, that the people were entirely destitute of political influence, because they had no share in the control of the general government; their municipal privileges, enjoying a practical existence long before they were efficiently and finally guaranteed against infraction, compensated to a great extent for the privation of other powers; if the rights of the Subject were few and unimportant, those of the Citizen were numerous and substantial in their character.

Yet it was obviously desirable that these privileges should receive a wider extension, and that an avenue should be opened for the advancement of men of distinguished abilities, who possessed not the qualification of exalted lineage, to a share in the direction of the government of the nation. Such was the problem whose solution could alone restore the equilibrium destroyed by the hereditary character of Feudalism, and remedy the most signal defect in its constitution, the exclusion from all political power of the lowly born, whose capacities fitted them for the exercise of authority; and the Church, in providing within the circle of Her own institutions an agency for the accomplishment of this result, presented a means for the introduction of this new element into the political organization, affording all requisite facilities, and at the same time maintaining the indispensable safeguards demanded by the true interests of Society.

By one path alone was it permitted to the humble aspirant to advance to dignity; the avenue of warlike achievement, through which the Feudal chieftains had marched to supremacy, was closed to those who sought to rise from lowly rank to eminence; the endowments of mind were the sole title by which they could claim elevation to authority. But mental capacities, divorced from the spiritual attributes whose alliance is the consecration of intellect, constituted no valid qualification; the men of the Ages of Faith well knew that the mantle of the Philosopher is the favourite livery of Satan, and that the enemy of mankind disguises in the specious and winning axioms of seeming wisdom the poison which kills the soul, and they demanded of the man who would achieve eminence by the power of his genius, that he should first give evidence that his genius was of God, by consecrating his life to the service of religion. Those who shrunk not from this test found no obstacle to their onward career, and the pilgrimage whose starting point was the peasant's hut terminated in the council chamber of the Sovereign. To the humblest born the gate of the Monastery stood ever open, the holy brotherhood welcomed with joy the lowliest postulant who sought admission to the Cloister; the Monk, whose moral and intellectual qualifications fitted him for the Priesthood, received, whenever he might seek it, the grace of Ordination; and the Priest, whose learning and sanctity had advanced him to ecclesiastical eminence, found himself in possession of an influence in the councils of the nation, even transcending that which was swayed by the nobles who had derived their jurisdiction from hereditary transmission. The highest offices in the State were most frequently occupied by illustrious Churchmen; the Barons, who represented the dignity of earthly power, ceded precedence to the Prelates, who typified the majesty of Divine authority; the lordly chieftains, beneath whose standards had gathered the armed hosts of many a glorious field, whose pennons had fluttered on the plains of Palestine, whose gallant deeds had gilded with new renown names ennobled by illustrious ancestry, yielded pre-eminence to the servants of the Sanctuary, whose nobility was in their own learning and their own sanctity, and who, having advanced from the humblest ranks by their own worth alone, were emphatically the Heroes of the People. The peasant, whose lot in life had been cast with the lowliest, became the Mitred Abbot, or the puissant Prelate, the equal of him who had been born his Feudal lord; or, rising yet higher, attained to the supremacy of the Universal Church, and, seated in the Chair of Peter, received the loving homage of entire Christendom. The history of the Bishops and Pontiffs of the mediæval times abounds with brilliant examples of such triumphs of genius over poverty, achieved through the instrumentality of the Church, whose agency, bridging thus the gulf between the high-born and the humble, and enabling exalted worth to rise from obscurest rank to eminence, provided, at the same time, an admirable safeguard against the perversion of the means thus created for the elevation of the truly meritorious to the promotion of the schemes of mere worldly ambition, in the vows of poverty and continence which marked the first stage of the pilgrimage, and which, involving the eternal renunciation of the objects ever dearest to the heart of the selfish intriguer for power, the accumulation of wealth and the foundation of illustrious and powerful family, opposed a barrier to the rise of the demagogue as insurmountable as that which was presented to the advancement of the unbeliever.

True, the many were compelled to rest content with the station assigned to them by birth; wherever eminence is he prerogative of exalted merit but few can hope to achieve distinction, and the examples, numerous and brilliant as they are, of the rise of the humble to dignity, which are presented in the annals of mediæval history, are but the exceptions to the general rule, which enforced the jealous conservation of the constituted organization of society. But the spirit of those ages discovered no intolerable evil in this preservation of the social classification ; our mediæval ancestors were strangers to the restless ambition which fills the minds of men at the present day, leading them to view the existence of a superior as an injustice, and to regard their own worldly elevation as the grand end of their existence. They had firm faith in the existence of a Divine government of the world, and implicit reliance on the justice of the dispensations of Providence ; they believed that they were placed in their allotted ranks of life, not by virtue of an " accident of birth," since they had not attained to the conception of a chance-medley direction of the Universe, or of the possibility of casualties in the administration of Omnipotence, but because God willed it ; and, deeming that every station had its special duties, whose performance was the assigned vocation of humanity, they considered that it was their plain duty to address themselves zealously to the fulfilment of the obligations attached to the position which had been accorded to them by Him who alone knew what was best for the welfare of their souls. Theirs was a veritable contentment ; not an unwilling submission to circumstances which they would have avoided if they could, but to which they accommodated themselves because there was no escape, but a contentment which had its source in a firm, practical faith in the wisdom of God and His ever-watchful care for the happiness of His faithful children, and which, instead of pretending to make the best of a bad position, believed with earnest trustfulness that the position was really the best, since it had resulted from the will of the Almighty. They deemed that every man had his vocation, some to rule and some to obey, some to shine in the possession of honourable dignities and some to shine only in the faithful discharge of Christian duties and the pious endurance of the toils and sufferings of virtuous poverty, and that the highest merit of every man lay in the due performance of the work proper to his own vocation ; they conceived that the true ends of the Christian's ambition were to be found not in Time but in Eternity, and that the labours which filled up the years of his probation were to be devoted, not to raising himself in worldly rank, but to fitting his soul for Paradise. The Serf and the King, placed at opposite extremities of the social scale, and filling widely different parts in the pageant of the hour, knew that they were alike mere wayfarers amid the scenes of earth, pilgrims towards that common home whose threshold was the grave ; for each the world was a mere school of trial, the salvation of their souls the business of existence ; and they whose lot had been cast by the Supreme Ruler of the Universe in the humblest sphere repined not at the dispensation of His Providence, since they knew that for them, as for the loftiest, were reserved prizes to be toiled for with patient perseverance, transcending in their unfading splendour the fleeting glories of earthly grandeur, and often easier of attainment by the peasant in his hut than by the wearer of the diadem of empire. Faith made a bed of roses of the couch of thorns, and the lowly blessed the sufferings which opened wider for them the gates of Heaven.

But while thus teaching the humble to seek consolation amid their afflictions in the contemplation of the bliss reserved for them in eternity, the Church failed not to exert Herself strenuously to procure the abatement of the physical ills which pressed so heavily upon the multitude, and to ameliorate the temporal condition of the masses of mankind. Charged by Her Divine Founder with the special guardianship of His Poor, and placed in the midst of a society in which the concentration of property in the hands of a few condemned the many to the sufferings of poverty, She laboured with unrelaxing energy to mitigate, as far as might be possible, the evils resulting from this unequal distribution of wealth, striving to assuage the corporal wants of her children as well as to guard them against the perils which assailed their souls. Teaching the rich to regard their vast possessions as a trust of which they were but stewards for the benefit of humanity, and exalting to highest rank among the duties of the Christian life the ministration to the wants of the necessitous, She at the same time provided a means for the realization of the charitable aspirations which were called into life by the influence of Her monitions, by becoming Herself the Grand Almoner of Society, and charging Herself with the administration of the wealth which was consecrated to the use of the poor by the devotion of the opulent. The Monasteries were the agency which served to correct to a great extent the unequal apportionment of wealth incident to the Feudal organization; their possessions were the property of the poor, their coffers were the treasury of the indigent, each new donation conferred upon them by their pious benefactors was an augmentation of the resources of the multitude. The wealth of the Church was the opulence

of the People ; the riches committed to Her keeping by
the saintly munificence of many successive generations,
were employed by Her to alleviate the varied woes of
suffering humanity ; Her ministering hand relieved the
physical distresses of the necessitous, and provided the
means for the intellectual and spiritual elevation of the
multitude.   The triumph of Her adversaries in England
in the sixteenth century gave birth to a very different
spirit towards the indigent ; the champions of the Reformation, perverting to vile uses and squandering in
profligate excesses the treasures which had been consecrated by Her to the relief of the lowly,[7] denounced
poverty as a crime, and levelled against its victims the
most severe enactments.   The Statute of 27 Henry VIII.
c. 25, decreed that all persons found begging should for
the first offence lose their ears, and for the second suffer
death as felons : by the Act of 1 Edward VI. c. 3, it was
provided that upon a beggar being brought by any person
before a Justice of the Peace, he should be marked with
the letter V, branded with a red hot iron on his breast, and
adjudged as a slave for two years to the individual thus

---

[7] Bale, the Protestant Bishop of Ossory in Ireland, and one of the
most virulent among the adversaries of the Church, says " A great
part of this treasure was turned to the upholding of dice-playing,
masking and banqueting, yea (I would I could not by just occasion
speak it) of bribery, whoring, and revelling." Bale apud Strype, i. 346.
The profligacy with which the Church property was squandered by
Henry VIII. may be judged from a few examples cited by Stow, who
states that the King on one occasion made a grant of a Religious House
to a gentlewoman for presenting him with a dish of puddings which
pleased his palate, that he played away many thousands a year belonging to the Monasteries, and that Jesus Bells, belonging to a steeple not
far from St. Paul's, London, were lost at a single throw of the dice to
Sir Miles Partridge.   Stow, Survey of London, Farringdon Ward.

presenting him, who was empowered to compel him to wear an iron ring on his neck, arm, or leg, and authorized to feed him on bread and water and scraps of refuse meat, and to employ him in any species of work, however vile it might be, enforcing his obedience by beating, chaining, or otherwise, as he might see fit ; if the slave absconded and remained absent fourteen days, he was to have the letter S burnt with a hot iron on his cheek or forehead, and to be made a slave for life ; if he attempted a second time to escape, he was to suffer death as a felon. Such were the tender mercies towards the Poor by which Protestantism signalized the advent of its supremacy in England ; but wherever the Church held sway, the spirit of charity reigned with undivided empire. In the hour of temporal need the humble turned to Her for the succour which was never sought in vain, and the gifts which the mighty laid upon Her Altars beame the heritage of the destitute.

Such were the grand agencies which the Church called into existence to counteract the prominent evils of Feudalism ; becoming the parent of the Institution of Chivalry, She wedded sanctity to valour, and effected an alliance between the might of the warrior and the purity of the Christian ; opening to all, without regard to their worldly station, the road to ecclesiastical eminence, and providing special facilities for the entrance of the lowly into Her ministry, She annihilated the obstacles which obscure birth presented to the rise of genius to authority, and enabled the worthiest to ascend from humble rank to influence ; leading the rich to devote a large share of their worldly means to the foundation and endowment of the Institutions which She created for the benefit of the Poor, She restored to a considerable extent the disturbed equilibrium in the distribution of wealth, and opposed an enduring barrier to the inroads of physical destitution. If the actual condition of Society fell short of Her sublime ideal, if the passions of men, obstructing the realization of Her grand designs, succeeded in preventing the full practical development of Her conceptions, not to Her is to be ascribed the blame. Doubtless the evils against which She contended were not wholly eradicated by Her exertions; among the military chieftains there were still many whose hearts were dead to the noble impulses which She strove to impart to the Knightly character, whose deeds were outrages on humanity, whose lives presented few traits of Christian heroism; the power of Her prelates, the Heroes of the People, the representatives of the intellectual element in the political organization, was unceasingly struggled against, and occasionally for a time overpowered, by the antagonistic principle against which it was arrayed; the wealthy often turned a deaf ear to Her monitions, and refused to second Her endeavours to ameliorate the condition of the multitude: yet, by the blessing of God upon Her labours, the energetic warfare which She waged unceasingly against evil was crowned with triumphs, whose brilliance was but augmented by these temporary reverses, and whose substantial results were of incalculable value to mankind.

But it was not by these means alone that the Church was eminently instrumental in promoting the welfare of humanity: Her indirect agency was yet more extended in its sphere of action; the influence of Her teaching, permeating the entire structure of society, wrought the most essential changes in the character of legislation, the tone of literature, the conditions of the social relations, and the spirit of the individual life ; the sublime truths which it was Her mission to proclaim as the guiding principles of human thought, the regulating laws of human action, became, through Her exertions, the basis of Philosophy and the soul of practical existence. In all that was most admirable in the Ages of Faith we behold the trophies of Her victories, and the evils which survived Her assaults owed their preservation, not to Her apathy in the discharge of Her sacred trust, but to the strength of the inborn corruption which impelled men to thwart Her efforts and to become accomplices in their own destruction.

In Her action upon the spirit of legislation the Church was the first to proclaim the right of man to liberty. Before the advent of Christianity, slavery was recognised as the inevitable condition of the majority of mankind ; the most enlightened Sages of the Heathen world, far from condemning the usage which consigned the multitudes to bondage, perceived in this institution a necessary element of political society. At Athens there were 40,000 slaves, and but 20,000 citizens ;[2] at Rome, of the 1,200,000 inhabitants which it contained towards the close of the Republic, there were scarcely 2000 who possessed property,[2] and one individual sometimes owned several thousand bondmen ;[1] and the doctrine that some men were born slaves, enunciated by Aristotle, was accepted as irrefragable by the wisdom of Pagan antiquity. Slavery certainly formed no integral element of the Feudal organization ; the Suzerain and the Vassal were the sole parties whose existence was contemplated in its constitution, and whose mutual relations were regulated by its provisions ; yet

[2] Larcher in Herod. i. note 258.   [2] Cicero de Offic. ii. 21.
[1] Juvenal. Sat. iii. 140.

M

Feudalism, born and cradled among the ruins of the Roman
Empire, had conserved that portion of the institutions
which had preceded it, and perpetuated a form of personal
servitude, milder, it is true, in its nature, and in some important respects considerably ameliorated in its character,
but still grievously oppressive to those who were condemned by it to serfdom.   Against the evil feature thus
grafted on the system, of which it formed no necessary
element, the Church arrayed Herself in vigorous antagonism ;
the taint which Feudalism had derived from antecedent
barbarism engaged Her earnest efforts for its eradication.
True, She counselled not the Serf to rise in insurrection
against his Lord, and to achieve by violence his redemption,
for rebellion is never Her chosen agency for the amelioration
of the condition of humanity ; but while She inculcated
upon the humble the duty of obedience to those whom the
law recognised as their superiors, and presented to them,
as the reward of entire resignation to the Divine dispensation which had fixed their lot on earth, the consolations
of religion and the assurance of beatitude in eternity,
She laboured no less assiduously to elevate their temporal
condition, by bringing Her influence to bear upon their
Feudal masters, and combating with the precepts of Christian charity the Pagan ideas whose surviving force alone
maintained Slavery in existence.   Alike by teaching and
by example, She manifested Herself the champion of the
bondsman ; in the sixth century St. Gregory the Great
gave liberty to his slaves, whom he described as free by
nature, but placed by an unjust law under the yoke of
servitude ; and when Pope Alexander III., in the twelfth
century, proclaimed in the name of the Universal Church
the right of every Christian to exemption from bondage,

he but gave formal utterance to the principle which had
animated Her teaching in all ages of Her existence.   To
the Nobles who desired to propitiate the mercy of the Almighty She proposed the manumission of their Serfs as
among the most acceptable of the deeds of mercy, and the
acts of enfranchisement attest the nature of the influence
which dictated them, by the almost invariable avowal of
religious motives as the ground of their concession.   Undoubtedly Her progress was slow towards the entire realization of Her design ; a revolution which disowns the
aid of force, and seeks to achieve its triumph by the agency
of persuasion, marches ever with tardy steps to victory ;
but Her success, though gradual, was enduring, and Serfdom, succumbing at length beneath Her prolonged assaults,
was annihilated beyond the possibility of resuscitation.

Equally beneficial was Her influence on the character of
criminal jurisprudence ; the nature of the principles by
which She sought to regulate this important branch of
government is best exemplified by a comparison of the
provisions embodied in the laws of the Visigoths, which
were the product of the labours of the Spanish Clergy
in the Councils of Toledo, with the enactments of barba-
rian legislation.   In all antecedent Codes the material
damage was recognized as the essence of the crime, the
feature which was to regulate the assignment of the penalty,
which consisted chiefly in a material reparation ; the ecclesiastical legislators regarded only the moral element, the
intention of the offender, and proportioned the punishment
to the intrinsic demerit of the criminal, so far as this could
be determined by the circumstances which accompanied the
commission of the offence : at the same time they substituted for the simple oath which was resorted to by other

nations for the decision of judicial enquiries, a careful and deliberate examination of the evidence by the Judge, and a full investigation of all the facts which could tend to throw light upon the cause, and conduce to the discovery of the truth.[2]   Striving ever to temper with mercy the severity of human justice, and often, through Her ministers, rescuing criminals from the death to which they had been doomed by the law, that they might end their days in penitence and prayer in the seclusion of Monastic Cells, She presented to the world, in Her penitential inflictions, the model of a system of penality in perfect accordance with the dictates of the most exalted wisdom; Her canonical punishments were designed not only to provide for the imposition of the temporal chastisements due to sin, but to excite the awe of the spectators by the exhibition of salutary examples, and to move the souls of the sinners to repentance, and promote their reconciliation with God; the principles which the world is in our own day beginning slowly to recognize as the essential basis of sound and efficient penal legislation were enunciated centuries ago by the Church, and constantly developed by Her in practical application.

In Her action upon the intellectual life of humanity, Her agency was productive of no less eminent benefits to mankind.   The spread of popular enlightenment was the object of Her zealous and unremitting labours; within the circle of Her own organization abundant means were provided, as well for the instruction of the humble as for the extended pursuit of the highest branches of divine and human learning.   In the Minor Schools of the Monasteries, as well as in the Parochial Schools, the children of the poor received a substantial and Christian education, and in all

[2] For. Jud. l. ii. tit. i. 21.

of these, tuition was imparted without fee or charge to all who sought the benefits of mental cultivation ; the spirit which breathed in the epistle of Pope Alexander III. to the French Bishops, in which he declared that knowledge should not be exposed for sale, but should be offered gra‑tuitously to all,[3] inspired the hearts of the teachers of the olden time, who desired no reward for their toils other than the sweet consciousness of the blessings which were con‑ferred upon humanity by their exertions ; even in the days of Sigbert, Beda declares that in England " all who sought to be instructed, especially in sacred reading, had masters at hand to teach them;"[4] and this was equally true of every European land throughout the whole of the Middle Ages· Learning reposed in the shadow of the Cross, and Know‑ledge, purified by its union with Faith from the contaminations which convert it into a snare to weak souls and a tempter to destruction, was made accessible to the lowliest among the people by the ministrations of the Monastic Teachers, who, with a wise perception of the true ends of intellectual culture, made the progress of their pupils in spiritual per‑fection the grand object aimed at in the enlightenment of their minds. In the Major Schools of the Monasteries, and in the Cathedral Schools, were provided ample facilities for the pursuit of the higher branches of erudition ; Gram‑mar, Logic, Rhetoric, Music, Arithmetic, Mechanics, Mathe‑matics, Geometry, and Astronomy were cultivated in these academies with admirable success, and in many the course of secular studies received a yet wider extension ; in all, the study of the Scriptures was pursued with an unweary‑ing assiduity which evinced the fervent piety of the antique heart, and which has left its monuments in the Scriptural

[3] Martene. Vet. Scr. ii. 853.   [4] Beda. Eccles. Hist. l. iv. c. 2.

Commentaries which constitute so large a proportion of the literature of mediæval centuries. The most eminent Prelates distinguished themselves by the zeal with which they watched over the Cathedral Schools, welcoming with benevolent affection the strangers who flocked to them from foreign lands, sustaining the indigent with temporal aid, and labouring personally in the work of instruction ; and in the latter portion of the mediæval period, the Universities, which multiplied so rapidly that not less than fifty-six were founded before the close of the fifteenth century, attracted vast crowds of students, those of Paris, Oxford, Bologna, Salamanca, and Prague acquiring speedily an European fame, and many others attaining an almost equal eminence. Bishops and Ecclesiastics of high rank received under their care youths of noble family, whose advancement in knowledge and virtue engaged their assiduous labours, and who received from them the same advantages which were conferred by the Parish Priests on the children of the Poor ; and the Monastic Libraries, abundantly scattered throughout Europe, and freely offering their books to the perusal of all who sought for them, afforded to all classes the largest facilities for the prosecution of intellectual pursuits. Whatever may have been the extent of popular ignorance— a question which has been made the theme of much vague declamation, but with regard to which it is by no means easy to arrive at a satisfactory judgment from the meagre evidence within our reach—it certainly owed not its existence to the absence of means for its removal; the Church provided an instrumentality of instruction amply commensurate with the requirements of mankind, the benefits of which were accessible to the humblest classes of society.

Nor was Her influence less admirable upon the character

of Literature; the position in which She placed the Scholar, and the spirit with which She animated intellectual exertion, conferred the most exalted blessings on humanity. In the present age, the literary life is fettered by conditions which divert it from its rightful aims, and convert the arms of virtue into weapons for her own destruction. The pen has become an instrument of gain ; literature has degenerated into a craft, pursued as a means of subsistence ; the Author, whose high vocation it is to combat the corruption of humanity, and to become the pioneer of Society in all moral and intellectual advancement, reduced to absolute dependence upon popular favour for his daily bread, is the slave of the antagonistic influences against which it is his mission to wage perpetual warfare. Upon the sale of his works depends the prolongation of his existence ; if he would live, he must consult the tendencies of the public mind, deal tenderly with popular vices, and avoid contention with the prejudices of the multitude ; it is not for him to direct, but to obey, and his reward is great in proportion as he is false to his vocation. His task should be to raise the minds of the many to the elevation of his own ; it is only by assimilating his own intellect to the low level of the general intelligence, that he can secure the patronage which is his only safeguard against starvation ; and the more unscrupulously he panders to the corruption of humanity, the more abjectedly he cringes to the frivolous taste of the multitude, flattering its prejudices, nourishing its ignorance, compounding with its errors, and stimulating its evil passions, the more rapidly will he attain to opulence and renown. The smaller the intrinsic worth of his productions, the more abundant is his pecuniary reward ; the price of books being regulated by their size and bulk, and the Romance which occupies a few months in its composition bearing as high a price as the Treatise which embodies the results of the study and meditation of years, the labours of fancy and of thought would receive a vastly disproportioned recompense, even if their fruits found an equal sale ; but the public buys by hundreds the works of the Novelist, and by scores the writings of the Philosopher, the Historian, and the Divine.   The popular mind, dominating the agency which should direct it, and pouring its abundant largesses into the lap of its corrupters, advances constantly in a gradually progressive depravation ; already the love of solid learning has given place to a morbid craving for the excitement supplied by imaginative creations ; frivolity corrupts the tone of literature, and enervates the intellectual energies of humanity. Unquestionably Fiction has its high utilities ; guided by the inspiration of noble principles it becomes a valuable ally of Philosophy, and exercises an important instrumentality in the moral elevation of humanity ; but the agency which is valuable under due restraint becomes pernicious when exalted to supreme dominion : doubtless it has in our own day its great masters, writers whose rank is high among the true poets of the age—whose potent touch awakens into tuneful vibrations the hidden chords of gentle sympathies, who with the torch of fancy rekindle in the heart the flame of virtue ; but the miserable scribblers of vapid and worthless romances, whose trashy wares crowd the shelves of our booksellers, are no more worthy of a place in the same class with them, than the playwright who shapes the last new novel into a melodrama is worthy to be ranked as a dramatist by the side of Shakspere. The evils which characterise the tone of modern literature

are but the legitimate offspring of the conditions attached to
literary labour ; frivolity will reign supreme, and literature
will continue to be an echo of the passions and prejudices
of the multitude, so long as the Author remains the slave
of the public, owing his bread to popular favour, and remunerated in the inverse ratio of the value of his productions. Such was not the position of the mediæval Scholar,
who sought to devote his life to intellectual exertion.
Retiring within the hallowed shelter of the Monastic Cell,
and relieved from all dependence upon popular appreciation,
he was enabled to tread in peace the paths of learning,
and to achieve those triumphs of patient zeal whose fruits
yet remain to us as monuments of the diligence and erudition of antiquity ; placed above the necessity of humour-
ing the prepossessions of mankind, he launched his censures fearlessly against the corruptions of society, and condemned the vices alike of the humblest and of the most
exalted ; abjuring the pursuit of wealth by the vow of
poverty, and sheltered against the perils of destitution, he
could be tempted neither by the dread of want nor by the
allurements of avarice to disobey the voice of conscience.
Literature was in those ages not a craft, but a vocation,
and the intellectual labourer was enabled, by the agency of
Monasticism, to secure for himself a position the most advantageous for the efficient discharge of the duties of his
exalted mission ; a position in which he was neither ener-
vated by wealth nor harassed by poverty, in which an
assured competence supplied his daily wants, and an insurmountable barrier protected him from the temptation
to barter his genius in exchange for opulence. The fall of
the Monasteries annihilated the independence of literature;
in the age which immediately succeeded their subversion,

the Author was the slave of the few, the protegé of the great, the servitor of the wealthy patron whose favour supplied him with the means of existence ; in our own day he has become the slave of the many, feeding upon the bounty of the public, dependent upon the patronage of the multitude. Literature has changed masters during the past three centuries, but it has never doffed the livery of servitude, and under each form of bondage the highest recompenses have been earned by the prostitution of intellect. The Monastic Institute guarded the Scholar from the debasement to which he has been consigned by its overthrow, and the sanctification of Learning achieved by its agency breathed an admirable spirit into the intellectual life. Wisdom became the handmaiden of Sanctity, Religion trimmed the lamp of Science, and Poetry, pouring its richest treasures into the lap of Faith, embalmed in its strains the pious thoughts which found their echo in the sympathies of every Christian soul.

Thus moulding and directing the agencies which sway a general influence over Society, the Church achieved a not less signal success in the changes which she wrought in the character of those domestic relations whose tone is the unerring index of the moral status of humanity. By Her instrumentality the blot which defaced the civilization of the most polished nations of antiquity was obliterated from the social organization ; the degradation of Woman, universal beneath the sway of Paganism, disappeared before the march of Her influence, and the revolution thus effected in the spirit of social existence secured the most essential benefits to mankind. It has been the fashion to ascribe to the Germanic nations a large share in the achievement of this mighty regeneration; the purity of their morals and the high

development among them of the family relations have been
extolled by historians, and pointed to as the germ of the
sentiment which ripened to maturity in the spirit of Chivalry,
and restored to Woman the influence which had been
denied her in the heathen world ; but the authorities from
whom alone we derive our knowledge of the manners of
these barbarians amply attest the futility of the theory
which would assign to them the glory of having been in
this respect the pioneers of the advancement of humanity.
The Germans, it is true, rendered especial homage to
virginity, regarding it as an attribute which elevated its
possessors almost to the rank of divinity, and placed them
in special relations with celestial beings:[5] but this sentiment was by no means peculiar to them alone ; the
idea that continence is eminently pleasing to God, and indispensable to the perfection of sanctity, is one of those
innate truths which develope themselves in the human
mind in all ages and in all countries, under the most ad-
verse conditions of climate, of temperament, and of religion.   At Athens we find the Hierophant bound to the
most rigorous continence,[6] and the Priestesses of Ceres, to
whom the law assigned most exalted importance, consecrated to perpetual virginity,[7] the sacred fire in the Temple
of Minerva tended only by Virgins, and women of all
classes bound to offer a sacrifice to Diana on their marriage,
in expiation of the species of profanation which it involved ;[8] at Rome we find Numa prescribing virginity to
the Vestals, in order, we use the language of Livy, that he
might give them a sacred and venerable character,[9] the

---

[5] Tacitus. Germ. c. viii.   [6] Potter. Greek Antiq. i. 182. Origen
contra Cels. c. vii. 48. Pliny Nat. Hist. xxxv. 13.   [7] Lettres sur
l'Histoire, ii. 577.   [8] Schol. in Theocr. Idyl. xi. 66.   [9] Livy i. 29.

fire in the temple of Minerva tended by Virgins as at Athens, and the Priest who had guarded continence through life placed by Virgil in the Elysian Fields ;[1] in Egypt and in Ethiopia we discover that celibacy was obligatory on the Priesthood ;[2] in Peru we encounter, not only Priests bound to perpetual continence,[3] but consecrated Vestals, upon whom the violation of their vow entailed the same punishment as at Rome ;[4] among the Chinese we meet with Virgins dedicated to religion, and receiving special honours from the Emperor after having observed their vows during the space of forty years ;[5] among the Mexicans we find a precisely similar institution ;[6] in every quarter of the globe the veneration of virginity as a sacred attribute has been intimately interwoven with the religious ideas of mankind.[7] The Germans undoubtedly shared this widely diffused sentiment, but in the relations of domestic life the position of Woman among them was scarcely superior to that which she held among other nations of antiquity. The wife was purchased from her parents for a pecuniary equivalent ;[8] the husband exercised over her an authority as extensive as that which had been swayed by her father, to whose guardianship she reverted in case of widowhood, and her life was occupied in the toils necessary for the sustenance of the family ;[9] polygamy and concubinage were permitted in the husband, while the adulterous wife was visited with the most signal punishment.[1]

[1] Virgil. Æneid. 66.   [2] Bryant. Mythology Explained, i. 281. iii. 240. Porphyr. de Abstin. iv. 364.   [3] Carli. Lett. Americ. i. 19.
[4] Ibid. 8. 9.   [5] M. de Guignes. Voyage à Pekin, ii. 279. 357.
[6] Humboldt. Vue des Cordillieres, i. 237.
[7] De Maistre. Du Pape, i. 293.   [8] Cf. the Ancient Laws of the Germans, Langobards and Saxons.   [9] Tacit. Germ. c. xxvi. Faureil. Hist. de la Gaule Merid. c. xi.   [1] Tacitus Germ. c. xviii. xix.

In such a state of society we seek in vain for the germs of that immense development of female influence which marked the most striking contrast between mediæval centuries and the ages which had preceded them ; the manners of the Germans were in perfect harmony with the principle of force, which constituted the basis of their social organization, and whose supremacy necessarily involves the subjection of all that is intrinsically feeble ; their mythology, depicting the degradation of the Valkyrs from the dignity of Goddesses to the station of simple mortals as soon as they yielded to the power of love, reflected the tone of popular sentiment, and typified the immense distance which, in their estimation, separated the Virgin from the Wife, the former being reverenced as holding a rank not far below divinity, the latter actually maintaining a position but little above a slave.

From a higher than human agency proceeded the impulse which gave birth to this stupendous advancement of humanity ; the veneration of the Mother of God, which the teaching of the Church inculcated on Her children, the affectionate reliance on the intercession of Mary which Her lessons generated in their hearts, alone sufficed to raise woman from her debasement, and to snap asunder the chains which had bound her in the Heathen world. Fulfilling the prediction which the Spirit of God had breathed through her sacred lips, at the moment which witnessed the consummation of the august miracle which brought redemption to mankind, the Ages of Faith exhausted the resources of art in their efforts to give expression to their reverence and affection for her whom they loved to designate their Mother, and in the depth of whose maternal solicitude they found the source of solace in their woes, of strength in their temptations, of hope in their despair. The earth was gemmed with gorgeous sanctuaries, raised to perpetuate her glory; the Poet, the Painter, the Sculptor, and the Sage dedicated to her service the energies of their genius; the most illustrious Saints devoted their lives to labouring for the extension of her empire over the hearts of men, and taught the feeble to implore from her the aid which no suppliant ever craved in vain. The world resounded with the praises of the humble maiden, whose sublime perfection had elevated her to the sovereignty of the angelic hosts, and who, in the exaltation of her celestial dignity, retained the tenderest sympathy for the mortals whose nature she had shared on earth, whose trials and sufferings she had partaken during her sorrowful career; all Christendom poured out its soul in homage to that glorious being, in whom it recognized the type of immaculate purity, the personification of all ideal loveliness; Monarchs and Nobles made barefoot pilgrimages to her Shrines, and erected Churches in her honour, and the humblest placed their labours under her patronage, and, secure in her protection, defied the perils which assailed their souls. Sanctioned by the testimony of innumerable miracles, and marked by not less signal evidences of Divine approval in the eminent graces which it was the daily means of imparting to her suppliants, the veneration of the Blessed Virgin grew constantly in fervour, as the world beheld the augmenting proofs of the power of her intercession; the preaching of St. Bernard was followed by the foundation of new Orders of Religious specially dedicated to her service; the Franciscans, by the promulgation of the dogma of the Immaculate Conception, gave new radiance to her glory, and the introduction of the devotion of the Rosary by St. Dominic consecrated to her praise, in obedience to her revealed command, the most exquisite of all exercises of piety. In the thirteenth century the universal reverence of mankind found utterance in the establishment of that Order, whose founders chose the title of Servites, or Serfs of Mary, as the expression of their joyful allegiance to her sovereignty; and the Order of the Carmelites, offering to the world the sacred garb of the Scapular, which the Blessed Virgin had herself delivered to St. Simon Stock, and appointed as the peculiar livery of her servants, presented a new bond of alliance between her clients, and enrolled in its widespreading confraternity the multitudes who sought to shelter themselves beneath her guardian care. The tenderest relation of humanity was deified in the veneration which Mary received from united Christendom; in her the penitent beheld the Mother and the Mediatrix, the loving parent and the potent intercessor, eager to bless as she was all-powerful to save; the sinner who implored her aid appealed not alone to the clemency of the Queen of Heaven, the chosen minister of God's mercies, but to the tender sympathy of the woman who had been a weeping mourner upon earth, and to whose maternal love her Divine Son, expiring upon the Cross, had commended the entire family of mankind. It was impossible that a religion which thus enshrined as the object of ardent devotion the favoured handmaiden of God, whose obedience had cancelled the curse entailed upon the world by the rebellion of Eve, and re-opened to man the gates of Heaven, should fail to operate a mighty revolution in the position of that sex of which she was the inmaculate type, whose noblest attributes were in her exalted to perfection; " in our relations with women," says a poet of the thirteenth century, " we should ever bear in mind that the Mother of Christ was a woman ;"[2] and the fervent veneration which the Christians of those remote centuries cherished for the Blessed Virgin, shedding its sanctifying influence on the relations of domestic life, imparted a new tone to social existence. The absurd reproach unceasingly urged against the Church, that the tendency of Her teaching is to chill the holiest human sympathies, and to blight the tender ties which link humanity in the bonds of mutual affection, is best refuted by the contemplation of the spirit of the ages in which She reigned supreme ; no other epoch in the history of the world presents such admirable models of conjugal perfection, such eminent examples of the union of the energy of passion with the purity and simplicity of religion. Among the Saints whose memory She has enshrined in glorious recollection, we find the types of the Christian spouse ; in the wedded life of the heroic St. Louis of France with his beloved Marguerite, and of the gentle St. Elizabeth of Hungary with the noble Duke Louis, we recognize the realizations of the ideal of Christian marriage, in which the passionate love of human hearts was rendered immortal by the sanctifying influence of Faith, and gained new vigour from the sacramental grace which consecrated the impulses of affection. Love was in those ages a tree whose bright blossoms budded upon earth, but whose fruits ripened in eternity ; the passion which had been sanctioned by the benediction of the Church, less refined and subtilized, perhaps, than the sentiment of later days, but infinitely

. [2] Frauenlob, poem of the thirteenth century, cited by M. de Montalambert. Hist. de St. Eliz. de Hongrie, i. 121.

more profound, became stronger and more enduring with each advance in spiritual perfection, and, looking for the consummation of its bliss in Heaven, grew in tenderness as the pilgrims drew nearer to their home. The language of mediæval centuries manifested the spirit which animated society ; the epithet " amorous," was employed as a title of high praise, denoting the possession of the attributes of moral excellence in exalted perfection ; Froissart declares of King Wenceslaus of Bohemia, that he was " noble, wise, and amorous," and the literature of chivalric days affords innumerable examples of the similar application of an expression which in modern times would bear a widely different signification. The purity of the antique heart was reflected in its poetical creations ; during the greater portion of the Middle Ages, imaginative literature was devoted to the portrayal of the delights of lawful love, and fancy wreathed its most alluring beauties around the pictures which it enshrined of conjugal affection ; it was not until towards the close of the mediæval epoch that fiction selected for its theme the fortunes of unconsecrated passion, and commenced the career of depravation on which it has since hurried with fearful strides. Until then the tale commenced where modern novels end ; the marriage, or at the least the betrothal of the lovers, was the indispensable foundation of the interest which encircled their destinies ; the sanctification of human affections by the benediction of the Church was recognized as the sole source of their perfect development, the agency which imparted new fervour to the tender sympathies of Christian hearts, and stamped passion with the seal of immortality. The scenes which the Poets of those ages have embalmed in most exquisite

narration, are scenes of wedded life ; many a sacred legend, such as those of St. Alexis, of St. Nothburghe of
Suabia, and of St. Matilda, presented to the popular mind
the most admirable models of conjugal purity and fidelity,
and the same spirit breathed through the strains of the
secular muse, and animated the most romantic productions
of mediæval literature.   For the conservation of the
sanctity of marriage, the Church waged vigorous conflicts
with the most potent Sovereigns ; the outraged Queen,
repudiated by the sensual Monarch who sought freedom
for the gratification of unholy passions, driven with igno-
miny from her realm, and abandoned by the courtiers of
her prosperous days, found in Her supreme head the
champion whose spiritual power was vigorously wielded
to redress her wrongs ;[3] nor is that among the least glorious of the pages of her history, which records that, in
the age in which Luther and Melancthon rewarded the favour of the Landgrave of Hesse Cassel by the concession of
the privilege of polygamy, She preferred the relinquish-
ment of wealth and power to the betrayal of the just cause
of an injured wife who had appealed to Her for protection, and chose rather to sacrifice Her sway in England
than to lend Her ear to the solicitations of a libertine.

Throughout all classes of society, Faith shed sanctifying influence on the individual life ; the tender relation-
ship which the doctrines of antique Christianity established
between the members of the Church Militant on Earth

[3] The history of Tietberge of Lorraine, of Berthe and Ingelburge
of France, of Mary of Arragon, and of Adelaide of Bohemia, may serve
as examples of the zeal with which the Church maintained the sanctity of marriage, and the success with which the arms of Her spiritual
power were employed for the correction of the disorders of licentious
sovereigns.

and the Saints of the Church Triumphant in Heaven linked mankind in closest intimacy with the spiritual world; from the Monarch to the lowliest labourer, each found among the illustrious servants of God, whom the Church had canonized in glory, a special model for his imitation, the contemplation of whose perfections aroused him to holy emulation, whose patronage brought blessings upon his undertakings, whose prayers obtained rich graces for his soul. No rank or condition of life was without its representative in the army of celestial intercessors; and the memory of these consecrated heroes, who had triumphed by obedience over the corruptions of the flesh, and grasped the crown of immortality, was cherished in the hearts of men with devoted and affectionate veneration. In this characteristic alone may we discover an unerring index of the elevated tone of mediæval morality; the character of a people may be read in the qualities of the heroes who command its highest reverence, and they who offered the homage of their souls to the victorious warriors of the Cross, whose lives were the realization of ideal sanctity, manifested the purity of their own hearts in their sympathetic appreciation of the attributes most admirable in humanity. Throughout the Christian world, a spirit of fervent devotion to the Saints of God reigned supreme among mankind; around these centres of popular affection art clustered its most transcendent beauties, and poetry entwined its most alluring charms; the pencil of the painter drew inspiration from his theme, in portraying the heroic sufferings of the Martyrs of the Faith, and giving visible presentment to the miraculous displays of Divine power which had borne testimony to the sanctity of the servants of Heaven, and literature enshrined in a

thousand sublime and touching legends the memory of
the special manifestations of His favour with which God
had crowned the intercession of His elect.   It is the
fashion of modern scepticism to sneer at these records of
the wondrous interpositions of Providence, so precious to
Catholic antiquity : yet they who are content to regard
them as simple allegories, mere mythic expressions of the
sentiments of the multitudes who cherished them in their
affections, must behold in them unanswerable evidences of
the exalted spiritualism of mediæval centuries ; for each
one of these traditions was a formal recognition of the
omnipotence of Faith, a signal example of the triumph of
the invisible over the material, a noble vindication of the
eminence of sanctity.   All the prodigies recorded in the
biographies of the Saints were regarded as tokens of the
Divine approval which rewarded the purity of their lives
and the entire devotion of their souls to God ; the veneration which these spiritual heroes received from mankind
was the spontaneous utterance of its reverence for the
sublime virtues which had adorned their illustrious careers.
To the mind of the Catholic these antique legends : for him
no mythic fables, but the faithful narratives of the dealings
of God with his forefathers : speak with a far higher sig-
nificance ; beholding the miracles yet wrought by the
relics of the Saints, the abundant graces yet vouchsafed to
their celestial intercession, he sees no reason to marvel at
the signal manifestations of Divine favour which illustrated
their living labours ; witnessing the supernatural displays
of His power by which the Almighty yet responds to the
prayers of His Church, he recognizes in their more frequent recurrence in bygone centuries the promised reward
accorded to the ardent Faith which reigned supreme in

the mediæval soul : in these momentary suspensions of
the ordinary laws of the Universe he perceives nothing
incredible, since they were effected by Him who gave
those laws their being, nothing trivial, since the slightest
incident which displayed the operation of Almighty power
was as forcible an evidence of Divine interposition as the
most stupendous manifestation of the might of Omnipotence, nothing uncalled for, since each was wrought to
promote the salvation of human souls, by exhibiting
to mankind a signal indication of the special graces
accorded to those whose lives were dedicated to the service of Heaven.   But, view them as we may, it is impossible to deny the vast sway which these traditions exercised over the world, and the admirable influence which
they exerted upon the spiritual advancement of humanity.
Truly has an illustrious Catholic writer of our own day
averred, that the simplest Catholic legend has gained more
hearts to God than all the dissertations of the Philosophers ;[4] for these sacred histories, enshrined in the inmost
hearts of the people, and constituting, in truth, the popular
literature of the age, were embodiments of the highest
lessons of Christian morality, illustrated by the practical
examples of the Saints, and enforced by the commemoration of the miraculous gifts which had rewarded their
triumphs over the corruptions of frail mortality ; their tendency was to lead man to a clearer perception of his relations with the spiritual world, and, exhibiting to his view the
heavenly goal of his earthly pilgrimage, to point out to him
the means by which he might achieve victory over the agencies which conspired for his perdition.   Amid the temptations and sufferings of life, the humblest drew consolation

[4] M. de Montalambert, Hist. de St. Eliz. i. 136.

from the assurance that the glorified Saints of God cherished
for him a loving sympathy, and aided him in his struggles
with their prayers, and, selecting for his special patron
some one among the triumphant soldiers of the Cross
whose earthly lot had borne resemblance to his own, found
in his virtues the model for his imitation, in his victories
over the flesh the promise of his triumph, in the miracles
which had borne testimony to his sanctity the assurance
of the eternal rewards which awaited his perseverance, in
his intercession the agency which gained needful graces
for his soul. Mankind dwelt in tender intimacy with the
hosts of Heaven ; the Communion of Saints was no dry
dogma of the schools, but a reality of daily life; each
Christian recognized in the Queen of Heaven the gentle
Mother whose help was never asked in vain, in the Saints
the brethren who longed and laboured for his salvation, in
the Angels the guardians who watched over his soul and
guided it in the road to Paradise. All Nature discoursed
to humanity of God ; the phenomena of the material
world were to the pious hearts of the olden time the
symbols of eternal truths ; the Earth was to them a vast
volume, in whose every page the eye of Faith might read
the mystic lessons traced by the finger of Omnipotence.
Many a holy legend records the sympathy which linked
the pure in heart with the entire family of creation ; the
savage denizens of the forest dwelt in kindly intercourse
with saintly hermits, fed from their hands, and laboured
in their service ; the feathered choristers of the woods
lent their notes to swell the anthems of pious cœnobites,
and warbled requiems over their graves ; the flowers of
the field inclined their heads in homage when the body of
a Saint was borne by to its earthly sepulchre ; roses and

anemones sprang from the soil which had drunk the blood
of martyrs, and lilies gemmed the spots which had been
watered by their tears. From the cradle to the tomb, the
Christians of mediæval days lived in familiar converse with
the unseen world; in the habits of animals, the properties
of plants, the qualities of minerals, they recognized the
types of spiritual truths, in the phenomena of the Universe
the emblems of the mysteries of Religion. The flowers,
at once the most beautiful and the most abundant of the
marvels of creation, were especially chosen by our forefathers as the exponents of this pious symbolism; the
Ages of Faith had their floral language, widely different
in its character from that which modern Europe has bor-
rowed from the Eastern world, a language which discoursed,
not of human passions but of spiritual aspirations, whose
emblematic utterances were moral precepts and monitions
of the excellence of sanctity. The opening spring beheld
the meadows resplendent with souvenirs of Heaven, in the
flowers whose names recalled to memory the virtues of
illustrious Saints, and among which an innumerable multitude of the loveliest bore the blessed name of Mary, so
dear to the antique heart; the floral wreaths which Monastic scribes loved to entwine around their delineations of
the scenes of the life of Christ, and of the sufferings of
the Martyrs, in the margins of sacred volumes, were no
mere artistic adornments, but pictorial homilies, whose
meaning was familiar to all, garlands of holy thoughts
whose every blossom was a lesson to the soul.

Such were a few of the principal agencies which the
Church, in the Ages which may in some sense be designated especially Her own, employed for the elevation of
humanity, consolidating political liberty, vivifying in-

tellectual energy, dignifying the domestic relations, and
exalting the tone of individual life, among the multitudes
who owned allegiance to Her spiritual sway, and recognized in Her the divinely appointed guardian of society.
It would be at once a pleasant and a profitable task to
trace out more minutely the varied ramifications of Her
influence, and to exhibit in more extended detail the mul-
tiform instrumentalities which She employed to subserve
the great end of Her earthly mission, the promotion of
the temporal and eternal welfare of mankind ; but enough
has been displayed to manifest the spirit which animated
Her exertions, and to demonstrate that all veritable human
progress had its source in Her zealous and unremitting
labours.   True, She succeeded not in achieving a complete victory over the evils with which She waged ceaseless warfare ; the Ages whose general characteristics we
have passed rapidly in review had their sins, their vices,
their corruptions ; all men bowed not their hearts to the
influence of Her teaching, even when yielding external
homage to Her authority, and some were found in those
centuries, as in all epochs of the history of the world, in
whom the strength of human corruption triumphed over
the impulses of grace, who gloried in the bondage of iniquity and conspired with Satan for their own perdition.
Yet these were but exceptions to the healthy tone of
general morality ; while a few among the rich and powerful abandoned themselves to the control of guilty passions,
and sullied their lives by the perpetration of heinous crimes,
religion held its sanctuary in the hearts of the people,
and was sheltered, as in an impregnable fortress, in the
affections of the multitude.   The evils which assailed
the vast masses of society were purely material in their

character ; life, liberty, and the peaceable possession of property were perilled, it is true, by many dangers ; physical woes abounded, as they must at all times inevitably abound in the infancy of nations ; bodily privations harassed the poor, and the calamities incident to frequently recurring war troubled the repose of all classes of men : but these temporal afflictions left intact the purity of the soul.   Simplicity and Faith, twin sisters so linked in mutual sympathy that the death of either causes the survivor to pine into decay, held supreme dominion over the antique heart, and the agencies of evil encountered an antagonistic force which vanquished their most vigorous assaults, in the fervent and practical piety which breathed throughout the lives of the Christians of the mediæval world.

What indications do we discover, in the existing aspect of Society, of progress beyond the condition of these antique centuries ?   Assuredly that progress alone deserves the name, which bears direct relation to the ultimate ends of man's existence, that advancement alone confers substantial benefits on mankind, which gives new vigour to the spiritual life, and nurtures the growth of holy aspirations in the soul ; however striking may be the increase of the appliances of material civilization, however remarkable the extension of the means of merely intellectual cultivation, these agencies secure no real advantages to mankind, if their growth be not accompanied by a commensurate augmentation of the power of religion over the hearts of men, a corresponding development of its influence upon their daily lives.   Such is the essence of Christian civilization, which aims chiefly at the cultivation of the interior life, and regards all other improvements as

N

subordinate instrumentalities, valuable only in so far as
they are conducive to its promotion : is such the character
of the civilization whose fruits surround us in the nineteenth century?   Look where we will, we perceive the
evidences of a spiritual degeneration co-extensive with our
material progression ; a frightful corruption pervades the
entire frame of society, and poisons the life-blood of humanity.   Even our physical amelioration is but partial in
its operation ; among the poor, the woes which harassed
the mediæval world rage with yet greater vigour than in
the olden time ; famine and disease are familiar guests in
the homes of the humble, and starvation strikes down its
victims in the midst of plenty ; not only relatively, but
absolutely, the bodily condition of the lowly has become
less advantageous in the lapse of centuries, and threatens
to undergo yet farther deterioration.   Unchecked com-
petition, the modern alchemy which casts the blood and
sinews of the artizan into its crucible, and converts the
base metal of the labourer's flesh into golden ingots
in the coffers of the capitalist, has reduced the wages
of the toiler to augment the wealth of the millionaire ;
the command which the working man possesses over the
necessaries of life is far inferior to that which was enjoyed
by his ancestor, and when want assails his dwelling, if he
seeks for the treasures which the pious care of his Christian forefathers consecrated to God for the relief of the
necessitous, he finds that they have passed into the hands
of laic proprietors, who dissipate in luxury the fruits of
their sacrilegious plunder, while those for whose solace it
was destined are sinking by slow starvation into the grave.
While the physical sufferings of the poor have increased
in actual intensity, not only by the diminution of the wages

of labour, but also by the destruction of the agencies which formerly existed for the succour of the destitute, the altered spirit of society renders these woes yet more onerous to the afflicted; if, in the olden time, the career of man on earth was a journey along a path bestrewn with thorns, the sufferings of the pilgrimage were forgotten in the contemplation of the goal; the true source of the bodily evils which afflict humanity was understood, the justice of their infliction recognized, and their utility to the soul, when accepted in a spirit of pious resignation to the will of God, comprehended by the sufferer; these corporal visitations became the aliment of spiritual growth, the instrumentalities which served to promote the purification of the heart. In the men of modern days the woes which awakened holy aspirations in the minds of their ancestors generate only repining and despair; existence has become entirely secularized; the spirit of materialism has obtained universal dominance in practice, even among those who repudiate it in theory, and the pursuit of the riches and pleasures of earth is the chief occupation of their lives. To gain wealth, or power, or renown among men, to leave a fortune to his family, or a great name to his posterity, is the aim whose attainment engrosses each man's most abundant energies; and he who succeeds not in acquiring opulence or distinction generally resigns himself to despondency, and deems that he has failed to achieve the grand end of his existence. ".Put money in thy purse," is the precept which echoes in the ears of childhood, and is enforced upon the mind of youth by the practical conduct of the seniors whose example is to be the model for its imitation; his own elevation above the rank in which he was born is the task which each man proposes himself at the opening of his career ; the world and its glittering prizes are to him the business of to-day, and he defers ever till the morrow the contemplation of the mysteries of eternity.   Undoubtedly the agencies which might be made conducive to real advancement are within our reach in far greater profusion than they were at the command of our forefathers ; but the machinery which is efficacious for the encouragement of virtue, is equally available for the propagation of depravity, and the tokens of veritable progress are to be recognized, not in the multiplication of instrumentalities, but in the abundance of the good fruits which have resulted from their application. The Printing Press is a blessing or a curse, according to the manner of its employment : if it has aided to enlighten many minds, it has also served to poison many souls; if it has afforded wholesome nutriment to the intellect, it has also furnished noisome food to the evil passions of corrupt humanity ; if it has diffused the works of genius, it has disseminated as widely the licentious creations of disordered fancy : equally at the command of the teachers of truth and the emissaries of error, it is not easy to determine whether it has rendered more abundant assistance to the propagandism of vice or to the preaching of religion.   So far as regards the masses, however, there can be no question that its evil influence has greatly preponderated ; the literature which circulates among the poor is, with few exceptions, fearfully corrupting in its tendency ; the holy legends which formed the popular literature of the mediæval world, the common delight of the Peasant, the Scholar, and the King, have been replaced by licentious tales and chronicles of guilt ; the sacred histories, each one of which was a solemn monition of the destinies of

humanity, a formal recognition of the affinities which link
the visible with the unseen world, an admirable example
of holy life, a sweet assurance of the ceaseless vigilance
of God over His people, have been supplanted by sensual
romances which cloke beneath alluring imagery the native
hideousness of vice and palliate profligacy by specious
sophistries, and narratives of iniquity which serve as hand-
books to neophytes in crime, and guide them in the broad
road to perdition.   Our schools are less abundant in proportion to our population, the blessings of education are
less accessible to the humble, than in the days when
every Monastery opened the gates of its school for the
free entrance of all searchers after instruction ; the access of the lowly to eminence is less easy than in
the ages which beheld Urban IV., the son of the shoe-
maker, Adrian IV., the son of the English labourer, and
Sylvester II., the son of the peasant of Auvergne, wielding
the spiritual sceptre of the Christian world, and in which
the most powerful section of the Aristocracy was composed of men who had risen from obscure birth to dignity,
by the union of sanctity with learning in the service of the
Church of Christ: wealth is now the first qualification
demanded in those who are to sway authority, and knowledge is guarded in a casket which may be opened only
with a golden key.   All the thoughts, all the actions
of men have reference to earth and its enjoyments ;
the simple piety of antique days, the loving trust in
God which animated the mediæval heart, the spontaneous and affectionate reverence for all that is pure and
holy which characterised the people of the olden time,
have passed into extinction among the multitudes, who
live but for the pleasure of the passing hour, and give

scarce a thought to Heaven.   Worldliness is the ruling spirit of the age ; education is controlled by a narrow utilitarianism, which regards as of chief importance the cultivation of the faculties which have a marketable value, and disdains to busy itself in the nurture of the qualities whose reward lies beyond the grave.   Religion is a Sunday garment, laid aside at other times as sadly incommodious for working wear ;   men live as if this world were their eternal home instead of their school of brief probation, as if death were the end of being, and not the beginning of our true existence.

Since the advent of Christianity, the Church and the World have been engaged in perpetual conflict ; in modern days the World has achieved a temporary triumph, and usurped the prerogatives of the foe whose power so long protected mankind from its machinations.   Has humanity profited by the revolution which has paralysed for a while the might of its divinely appointed guardian, and reduced the spiritual arm to subjection to the temporal authority ? The most strenuous upholders of the system which has replaced the Christian polity of antique days themselves bear testimony to the discomfiture which has hitherto attended their efforts to rule society without the aid of the Church, protracted as they have been over a period of three hundred years, during which the instrumentalities of advancement have been undergoing constant augmentation ; with one consent they denounce the wide-spread corruption which is the legitimate offspring of their own teaching, the depravity of the people whose morals are the practical development of the spirit of their own philosophy; differing widely as to the means of cure, all are agreed as to the existence of the disease which has seized upon the vitals of humanity, and manifests its presence in multiplied and constantly increasing symptoms. Varied are the schemes propounded by the social reformers of our day for the restoration of the health of society, but all are alike defective in their theoretical basis, in their avowed aim, and in the machinery of their practical operation : in their theoretical basis, because they start from the assumption that man is naturally good, and needs only the careful nurture and development of his proper faculties to arrive at absolute perfection ; in their avowed aim, because they fix the paradise of their dreams on earth, and direct their efforts solely to the elevation of the physical and intellectual condition of humanity during its pilgrimage from the cradle to the tomb ; in the machinery of their practical operation, because they are designed to act upon society in the aggregate, and propose by the agency of general laws to affect the amelioration of the condition of mankind.   All these projects carry within themselves the seeds of their failure ; they are utterances of the longings of earnest minds which feel the thick darkness of the present and crave for light, but, not knowing that light comes alone from Heaven, delve down into the caverns of Earth and bury themselves in yet deeper gloom.   Individual sanctification is the first step in social regeneration, and this is to be achieved by action, not upon the masses but upon the units which compose them, not by general laws but by particular ministrations ; the nurture of personal holiness is the sole agency which can secure the redemption of men from evils both temporal and eternal, and this is to be effected, not by concentrating their regards upon earth and directing their chief attention to the search after material advantages, but by elevating their minds to the comprehension of their spiritual destiny, and teaching them to regard all temporal gifts in their true light, as merely secondary objects, valuable only in so far as they become conducive to the salvation of the soul, positive evils when they tend to withdraw the mind from meditation on the mysteries of the unseen world; the purification of the hearts of the people is the only true safeguard of the welfare of society, and this is to be attained, not by development alone, but by repression, not only by cultivating man's better sympathies, but by battling against the innate corruption of his fallen nature, which the grace of God is alone potent to destroy. The world has lost the perception of these eternal truths, whose recognition lies at the root of all true progression; and the social reformers of the day, ignoring their verity, and modelling their systems in direct contravention of their monitions, can but succeed in sinking humanity yet lower in spiritual degradation.

For the woes which afflict mankind there is but one medicament; one hand alone can pour balm into the wounds whence is ebbing the life-blood of Society, and restore to its diseased and palsied frame the vigorous vitality which animated it in antique days; all merely human remedies will serve but to aggravate the evils which we seek to cure, if their application be not preceded by the revival of the empire of religion. The glorious spirit which breathed in the hearts of the men of mediæval times had not its source in the influence of secular institutions, but owed its being to the guardian agency which checked and counterbalanced their pernicious tendencies, and shielded the world from the evils which would have resulted from their uncontrolled operation; all that was admirable in Christian antiquity, all that made the Middle Ages illustrious, and sheds a halo of deathless renown around their memory, all that secured to our ancestors the possession of blessings whose revival after the lapse of centuries is now the problem for the solution of the true philanthropist, all, in short, that is memorable and beautiful in bygone centuries, owed its existence, under God's blessing, to the Church ; and our chief ground of hope for the future destinies of the world lies in the recollection that this holy Parent, whose pious care instilled these sublime ideas into the minds of our buried forefathers, yet survives in unaltered majesty, yet lives to herald the auspicious birth of a new Age of Faith, when the deluded votaries of self-will, having sought in vain in the barren fields of Heresy for peace, shall fly for repose to the bosom of the tender Mother of the Christian world. In Her the spiritual life has its unique source ; She alone possesses the treasures of sacramental grace, the assurance of eternal life, the promise of Divine protection ; beyond Her pale there may be seeming energy, but there can be no true vitality ; the activity of the sectaries is to the vigour of Her children as the contortions of the galvanized corpse to the healthy movements of the living frame. Deprived of the sanctifying influences which She is alone empowered to impart, man strives in vain to emerge from the abyss into which he has been precipitated by his innate depravity ; no other than Her instrumentality can suffice to achieve his deliverance from the thraldom of corruption, and to restore to humanity the living Faith and purity of heart which belonged to it in antique centuries ; and when Error shall have run its course, and Her separated children are again gathered into the one Fold of Christ, it is by Her anointed hand that Society shall be baptized into a new existence.

In the present age the Church languishes in apparent prostration : but God forgets not His Vicegerent ; they who have remained faithful to Her in Her adversity, undaunted by the perils which the unbelieving regard as presages of Her destruction, undismayed by the clamorous exultation of the foes who rejoice in the hope of Her annihilation, await in patient confidence the moment of Her inevitable triumph, well knowing that neither the machinations of the world nor the devices of the powers of darkness can impede the advent of Her final victory, though the hour, the means, and the manner of its achievement are yet hidden in the inscrutable counsels of the Eternal.   Even in the lands which still participate in the spiritual blessings of communion with the Head of Christendom, Her power is paralysed by the usurpations of the temporal authority, which has bereft Her of the influence which She swayed in olden times, and left Her impotent to give realization to Her sublime aspirations for the welfare of mankind ; among the multitudes who own external obedience to Her sway, the poison of modern rationalism has tainted many hearts, and the flame of Faith, dwindled to a glimmering spark, gives but little visible token of its existence : but Her abasement is but for a season ; the spirit of antique Christendom slumbers, but its sleep is not the sleep of death.   In other sections of Her ancient empire the plague of Heresy has wrought yet deadlier ravages ; humanity has repudiated the gentle Mother whose loving cares were lavished on its infant years, in whose arms it found shelter from every peril, whose lessons guided it in the road to Heaven ; in the fulness of its daring pride it has repulsed the faithful monitor whose warnings grated unwelcomely upon its carnal ear, and abandoned itself to the domination of its own corruption ; scorning the precepts which the voice of God pronounced through Her sacred ministry, it has preferred the dictates of its erring reason to the utterances of inspiration, and worshipped as oracles of eternal truth the ideas which the malignity of its fallen nature has generated in its own feeble brain : but its impious rebellion has brought no peace into its soul ; in the bitter warfare of a hundred rival sects, all appealing, and with equal right, to the same authority for the sanction of their discordant doctrines, in the secularization of human existence by the influence of a pervading worldliness, the legitimate offspring of rationalistic principles, which extinguishes all moral energy in the hearts of men and annihilates all spiritual vitality in their souls, it is reaping the fruits of its disobedience ; and assuredly a day will come when the memory of the abundant blessings which were showered upon it by the ministrations of the holy guardian of its infancy will waken it to remorse, and it will seek to be clasped once more in Her fond embrace, to listen once again to the teaching of that sacred voice which breathed the maxims of eternal truth beside the cradle of its early days. Truth dies not, though Error may lull it for a while into a trance ; and the light of Faith, now hidden beneath a cloudy veil of false Philosophy, shall in time to come again beam through the darkness, to bless and beautify the world.

APPENDIX.

APPENDIX.

NOTE A. (Page 154.)

MONASTERIES DESTROYED IN ENGLAND BY THE DANES.

BERKSHIRE . . . . Abingdon, Cholsey.
CAMBRIDGESHIRE . . . . Ely, Horningsey, Soham.
CUMBERLAND . . . . St. Bees, Carliol.
DERBYSHIRE . . . . Repingdon.
DEVONSHIRE . . . . Exeter.
DORSETSHIRE . . . . . . Cern, Warham, Winburn.
DURHAM . . . . Ebbchester, Wermouth.
ESSEX . . . . Chich.
GLOUCESTERSHIRE . . Boxwell, Derehurste, Gloucester.
HAMPSHIRE . . . . Winchester.
HEREFORDSHIRE . . . . Leominster.
HUNTINGDONSHIRE . . St. Neots.
KENT . . . . Folkestone, Shepey, Thanet.
LINCOLNSHIRE . . . . . Bardney, Icanhoc, Croyland.
MIDDLESEX . . . . Westminster.
NORFOLK . . . . East Dereham.
NORTHAMPTONSHIRE . . Bucclesworth, Bredon, Wermundsey, Repingas,
 Wockingas, Dormundecastre, Poykirk.
NORTHUMBERLAND . . Hexham, Tinmouth.
OXFORDSHIRE . . . . . . Oxford.
SHROPSHIRE . . . . Wenlock.
SOMERSETSHIRE . . . . Bath, Froome.
STAFFORDSHIRE . . . . Hehanburghe, Stone.
SURREY . . . . Chertsey.
WARWICKSHIRE . . . . Coventry, Warwick (*two*).
WILTSHIRE . . . . Ambrosebury.
YORKSHIRE . . . . Beverley, Gilling, Lastingham, Whitby.

NOTE B.   (Page 154.)

MONASTERIES DESTROYED IN ENGLAND AT THE NORMAN CON-
QUEST.

BEDFORDSHIRE ...... Bedford.
BERKSHIRE   ., ... Brandanfield, Reading.
CHESHIRE .... Runcorn.
CORNWALL .... Petrocstow.
CUMBERLAND   ...... Dacor.
DURHAM. .... Gateshead.
GLOUCESTERSHIRE   .. Beccanfield, Berkley, Cheltenham, Cirencester,
                     Tettan.
HAMPSHIRE   .... Redbridge, Sapalanda.
KENT .... Canterbury, Thanet.
LINCOLNSHIRE ...... Peartan.
NORTHAMPTONSHIRE. . Oundle, Wedon-on-Street.
STAFFORDSHIRE. ..... Strenshall, Tamworth.
SUFFOLK. .... Burgh Castle, Hadleigh, Stoke.
SUSSEX .... Chichester, Ferring, Readingham.
WORCESTERSHIRE .... Bitumæum, Blockley, Hehanbiri, Kiddermin-
                     ster, Kemesey.
YORKSHIRE   .... Calcaria, Crayke, Elmete, Ripon, Walton.

NOTE C.   (Page 154.)

MONASTERIES DESTROYED IN FRANCE BY WAR.

N.B.—*The figures within brackets refer to the volume and page of the
Gallia Christiana in which the history of the Monastery is contained.*

PROVINCIA ALBIENSIS.—Conchæ. *Goths*, A.D. 371.   *Saracens*, A.D.
730 (i. 235.)

PROVINCIA AQUENSIS.—S. Eusebii. *Saracens*, (i. 337)—S. Crucis.
A.D. 1361, (i. 384.)—Bevons. (i. 508.)

PROVINCIA ARELATENSIS.—Mons Major.   *Saracens*, (i. 603.)—S.
Victor. *Vandals. Wisigoths*, A.D. 464.   *Normans*, A.D. 867, (i.
679.)—S. Salvator. *Danes*, A.D. 867.   *Saracens*, A.D. 923, (i. 695.)
—S. Maria de Nazareth, A.D. 1359, (i. 704.)—La Manarre. A.D.
1243, (i. 761.)

PROVINCIA AUXITANA.—Passanum. *Saracens.   Normans*, (i. 1012.)
—S. Petri de Regula. *Normans*, A.D. 848, (i. 1215.)—S. Severi de

Russitano. *Saracens*, (i. 1244.)—S. Savini. *Saracens. Normans*, (i. 1247.)—S. Petri de Tasqua. *Often destroyed*, (i. 1259.)

PROVINCIA BITURICENSIS.—S. Outrille. (ii. 120.)—S. Petri Puellarum. A.D. 1012. (ii. 121.)—Beata Maria de Salis. Sæc. IX. (ii. 122.) S. Laurent de Bourges. (ii. 172.)—Barzelle. *English*, A.D. 1313, (ii. 204.)—Cournon. *Danes*, (ii. 320.)—S. Allyre. *Normans*, A.D. 916, (ii. 323.) —Solignac. *Saracens*, (ii. 566.)—S. Augustin de Limoges. *Danes*, (ii. 575.)—Tulle. *Normans*, (ii. 661.)—Le Monastier S. Chaffre. *Saracens*, A.D. 732, (ii. 762.)—Clavas. *Often destroyed*, (ii. 730.)

PROVINCIA AQUITANICA II.—S. Croix de Bourdeaux. *Saracens*, (ii. 858.)—S. Œmiliani. *Saracens and others*, (ii. 881.)—S. Romain de Blaze. A.D. 1341, (ii. 883.)—S. Maurin. *English*, (ii. 994.)—S. Cybard. *Normans*, A.D. 868, (ii. 1030.)—S. Auzony. *Normans. English*, (ii. 1050.)—S. Jean d'Angely. *Normans*, A.D. 867, (ii. 1096.)—S. Hilaire le Grand. A.D. 863, (ii. 1223.)—S. Cyprien. *Normans*, (ii. 1230.)—Brantosme. *Normans*, (ii. 1490.)—Terasson. *Civil War. Danes*, (ii. 1532.)

PROVINCIA CAMERACENSIS.—S. Gery. *Normans*, A.D. 881. *Huns*, A.D. 895. *Hungarians*, A.D. 953, (iii. 73.)—Soigny. *Normans*, A.D. 880, (iii. 75.)—Morselle. *Frieslanders*, A.D. 680, (iii. 77.)—Walers, (iii. 77.)—Crespin. *Normans*, A.D. 870, (iii. 100.)—Liesse. *Hungarians*, (iii. 123.)—Premy. Sæc. XVI. (iii. 166.)—Maroilles. *Normans*, (iii. 227.)—Marchiennes. *Normans*, A.D. 851, and A.D. 879, (iii. 393.)—Hasnon. *Normans*, A.D. 880, (iii. 399.)—Mont St. Eloy. *Normans*, A.D. 880, (iii. 426.)—Hennin Lietart. *Normans*, (iii. 438.)—Maroeul-lez-Arras. (iii. 442.)—Monstier sur Sambre. *Normans*, (iii. 579.)

PROVINCIA COLONIENSIS.—S. Ursulæ et Sodalium. *Attila*, A.D. 451, (iii. 771.)—S. Petri Leodensis. *Normans*, A.D. 881, (iii. 933.)—S. Mariæ Aquisgrannensis. *Normans*, (iii. 933.)—S. Mariæ et S. Severi Messensis. *Normans*, (iii. 937.)—Susteren. *Normans*, (iii. 997.)

PROVINCIA LUGUDENSIS I.—Aisnay, (iv. 234.)—Savigny. *Often destroyed*, (iv. 259.)—S. Seine. *Saracens*, A.D. 731, (iv. 695.)—La Fontaine de Beze. *Civil War. Vandals. Saracens. English. Normans*, A.D. 888. A.D. 937, (iv. 704.)

PROVINCIA MECHLINIENSIS.—Renay. *Normans*, A.D. 880, (v. 29.)—Einham. Sæc. X. A.D. 1379. A.D. 1382. A.D. 1452. A.D. 1568, (v. 33.)—Helichem. *Often destroyed*, (v. 104.)—S. Pierre de

Gand. *Normans*, A.D. 851, and A.D. 880, (v. 185.)—Oost eecklo.
Sæc. XVI. (v. 227.)—Capella de Thosan. Sæc. XVI. (v. 260.)—
Sostendael. A.D. 1758, (v. 263.)—S. Trudo in Odeghem. *Danes.*
Normans, (v. 281.)—Wormhoult. *Normans*, (v. 325.)—S. Jeanne
de Therouanne. A.D. 1538, (v. 327.)—Zonebecka. A.D. 1578, (v.
352.)—Grevendael. A.D. 1474, (v. 390.)—Binderen. *English*,
A.D. 1571. A.D. 1588. (v. 409.)—Limpurg. A.D. 1504, (v. 749.)
Odenheim. A.D. 1525, (v. 752.)—Eschaw. *Hungarians*, (v. 847.)
Altorfuim. A.D. 1260, (v. 878.)—Rheinthat. (v. 944.)—Ma-
rienaw. A.D. 1525, (v. 944.)—Heckbach. (v. 1095.)—Friden-
weyler. (v. 1101.)—S. Blasii in Northeim. A.D. 1128, (v. 1114.)

PROVINCIA NARBONIENSIS.—Jaucels. *Saracens*, Sæc. X. (vi. 398.)—
S. Claire de Beziers. *English.* Sæc. X. (vi. 422.)—S. Baudilius.
Saracens, (vi. 469.)—Psalmodium. *Saracens*, A.D. 793, (vi. 471.)
S. Guillem du Desert. *Saracens*, A.D. 804, (vi. 580.)—Gigeau.
(vi. 856.)—S. Salvator Carcassonensis. A.D. 1209. A.D. 1250,
(vi. 934.)—Rien Nette. *Goths*, (vi. 1023.)—Arles, (vi. 1083.)—
S. Genesius de Fontanis. A.D. 891, (vi. 1105.)

PROVINCIA PARISIENSIS.—Lagny. *Normans*, (vii. 490.)—Notre
Dame d'Argenteuil. *Normans*, (vii. 507.)—S. Martin des Champs.
Normans, (vii. 515.)—Traniel. A.D. 1629, (vii. 640.)—Laval.
(vii. 642.)—S. Geneveive. *Normans*, A.D. 856, (vii. 700.)—Iverneaux. (vii. 849.)—L'Abbaye au Bois. A.D. 1650, (vii. 906.)—
Leves. Sæc. IX. (viii. 1211.)—S. Pierre en Vallée. *Normans*, A.D.
857. *Often destroyed*, (viii. 1214.)—Bonneval. *Normans.* *English*, (viii. 1235.)—Coulombs. *Normans. English.* Sæc. XIV.
(viii. 1248.)—St. Avit. *Normans*, (viii. 1289.)—St. Cyr. *English*,
(viii. 1296.)—St. Jean en Vallée. A.D. 1591, (viii. 1311.)—St.
Avit. *Normans. English*, A.D. 1428, (viii. 1512.)—St. Lifard.
Vandals, (viii. 1513.)—Bonne Nouvelle. *English*, (viii. 1515.)—
St. Pierre en Pont. *Danes*, Sæc. IX. (viii. 1516.)—Micy. *Normans.*
Sæc. IX. *English*, Sæc. XIV. (viii. 1527.)—Fleury. *Normans and
others*, (viii. 1540.)—S. Loup. *English*, (viii. 1571.)—S. Euverte
Normans, Sæc. IX. *English*, Sæc. XIV. Sæc. XV. (viii. 1575.)
—Beaugency. *English*, Sæc. XIV. (viii. 1579.)—Voisin. Sæc. XIII.
English, Sæc. XV. (viii. 1588.)—Lieu Notre Dame. *English and
others*, (viii. 1592.)—Rabais. *Normans. English*, (viii. 1680.)—
Chage. *Normans*, Sæc. IX. Sæc. XVI. (viii. 1716.)—Notre Dame
d'Ormont. *English*, Sæc. XV. (viii. 1722.)

PROVINCIA REMENSIS.—S. Thierri. *Normans*, Sæc. IX. *Hungarians.*

A.D. 954 (ix. 182).—S. Medard. *Normans*, A.D. 884 and A.D.
886. *Hungarians*, A.D. 901; A.D. 1418. *English*, A.D. 1419;
A.D. 1436. *Charles V.*, A.D. 1544 (ix. 409.)—Orbais. *Hun-
garians and others*, (ix. 423.) — Chesy. *Normans*, A.D. 887.
English, A.D. 1414 (ix. 428.) — S. Remi. *English*, Sæc. XV.
Civil Wars, A.D. 1589 (ix. 451.)—Longport. *English*, (ix. 474.)
—Argensoles. *Often destroyed*,(ix. 479.)—L'Amour Dieu. *English*.
Charles V., (ix. 481.)—Braine. (ix. 489.)—S. Vincent de Laon.
Normans. *English*, A.D. 1539 (ix. 567.)—S. Jean de Laon. A.D.
1112 (ix. 588.)—S. Nicolas au Bois. *English*, A.D. 1418 (ix. 611.)
—Ribemont. A.D. 1590 (ix. 615.)—Calvaire. A.D. 1596 (ix. 627.)—
Montreuil. *Often destroyed* (ix. 639.)—Insula. *Normans*. (ix. 776.)
—Fontanidum. *Normans*, (ix. 776.)—S. Lucianus. *Normans*, A.D.
845. *English*, A.D. 1346 (ix. 779.) — S. Geremarus. *Normans*, A.D.
906. *English*, Sæc. XIV. *and others*, (ix. 787.)—Britulium.
English, A.D 1427 (ix. 799.)—S. Paulus. *Normans*, A.D. 851
(ix. 812.)—Mouchi le Peroux. *English*, (ix. 847.)—S. Sauveur
de Vertus. *English*, (ix. 939.)—S. Fursæus. *Normans*, A.D. 882,
(ix. 1036.)—S. Eloi de Noyon. *Normans*, A.D. 860. *English*.
A.D. 1472. A.D. 1507 (ix. 1056.)—S. Quentin en l' Isle. A D.
1148. A.D. 1557. *English*. *Flemish*. *Burgundians*. *Spaniards*,
(ix. 1081.) — Le Mont St. Quentin. *English*. *Burgundians*.
Spaniards. *Civil War* (ix. 1102.)—S. Barthelemi de Noyon. A.D.
1557 (ix. 1115.)—Ham. *Spaniards*, (ix. 1120.)—Fervagues. A.D.
1580. A.D. 1595, (ix. 1136.)—Vermand. *Huns*, (ix. 1139.)—S.
Valery. *Normans*, A.D. 859. and A.D. 881. *English*, A.D. 1088, and A.D.
1360. and A.D. 1422. *Burgundians*, A.D. 1433, (x. 1231.)—S.
Riquier. A.D. 1095. A.D. 1131. *Normans*, Sæc. IX. *Burgundians*. A. D. 1421, *Civil War*, A.D. 1475. *Spaniards*, A.D. 1554,
(x. 1242.)—Corbie. *Normans*, A.D. 859. *Danes*, A.D. 880. Sæc.
X., (x. 1264.)—S. Josse-sur-Mer. *Normans*, Sæc. IX. *English*,
(x. 1289.)—S. Austreberte. *Normans*, A.D. 1032, (x. 1319,)—
Willencourt. (x. 1344.)—S. Jean-lez-Amiens. A.D. 1358. *Spaniards*, A.D. 1597, (x. 1355.)—Le Parc aux Dames. *English and
others*, (x. 1515.)—Blanzy. *Normans*, (x. 1589.)— Samer. *Normans*, (x. 1593.)—Auschy les Moines. *Normans*, A.D. 881, (x.
1598.)—Dodeanville. (x. 1611.)—S. Vulmer. (x. 1612.)—Beaulieu. *English*, A.D. 1390, (x. 1614.) — Licques. *Spaniards*, (x.
1618.)

PROVINCIA ROTOMAGENSIS.—Pentale. *Normans*, (xi. 120.)—S. Sidonius. *Normans*, Sæc. IX., (xi. 122.)—S. Sauve. *Normans*, (xi. 122.)—Evrardi Ecclesia. *Normans*, (xi. 124.)—Andilega. *Normans*, A.D. 900, (xi. 131.)—Loguin. *Normans*, (xi. 132.)—Septem Molæ. *Normans*, (xi. 133.)—St. Ouen. *Normans*, A.D. 841, (xi. 136.)—St. Vaudrille. *Normans*, A.D. 756, and A.D. 862, (xi. 156.) —Jumiége. *Normans*, A.D. 841, (xi. 186.)—Fecan. *Normans*, A.D. 841, (xi. 201.)—Le Bec. *English*, A.D. 1356, and A.D. 1418, (xi. 221.)—B. Maria de Prato. A.D. 1417. A.D. 1450. *English*, (xi. 241.)—Le Treport. *English*, A.D. 1339, and A.D. 1413, and A.D. 1535, (xi. 246.)—St. Martin d'Aumale. A.D. 1393, (xi. 275.)— Montwillier. (xi. 281.)—S. Saens. *English*, A.D. 1450, (xi. 324.) —Belosanne. (xi. 334.)—Revier. *Normans*. (xi. 404.)—S. Vigor. *Normans*. (xi. 404.)—Les Deux Jumeaux. *Normans*, (xi. 406.) —Liviay. (xi. 408.)—S. Etienne de Caen. *English*. (xi. 421.)— S. Laurent de Cordeillon. (xi. 439.) — Le Mont St. Michel. *English*, (xi. 512.)—Les Blanches. *English*, (xi. 555.)—S. Taurin. *Normans and others*, (xi. 626.)—Jory. Sæc. XI. *Normans*, (xi. 652.)—S. Serenicus. *Danes*. (xi. 712.)—Fontenay. *Normans*, (xi. 713.)—S. Martin. (xi. 713.)—Almenesches. *Normans*, A.D. 870, (xi. 736.) — St. Evreul. Sæc. IX., (xi. 814.)— Bernaicus. A.D. 1590. *English*, A.D. 1563, (xi. 830.)—Preaux. *English*, (xi. 836.) —Nanteuil. *Normans*, (xi. 912.)

PROVINCIA SENONENSIS.—S. Gervais. A.D. 1015. *Normans and others*, (xii. 117.)—S. Remy. *Normans*. A.D. 886. A.D. 1033, (xii. 118.)—S. Symphorien. (xii. 125.)—S. Hilaire. *Normans*, A.D. 876, *and others*, (xii. 126.)—Notre Dame du Charnier. *Normans. English*, A.D. 1358. A.D. 1417, (xii. 127.)—Ferrieres. *Normans. English*, (xii. 157.)—S. Pierre de Melun. A.D. 577. *Normans*, A.D. 845, and A.D. 848. *English*, (xii. 171.)—Chaume. *Normans*, (xii. 184.)—Ville Chasson. *English*, (xii. 188.)—S. Jean. *Normans*, A.D. 887, (xii. 195.)—S. Germanus. *Huns*, (xii. 358.)—B. Maria de Caritate. *Vandals* A.D. 743, *and again*, (xii. 403.)—Sessiacum. *Normans*, Sæc. X., (xii. 358.)—S. Germanus. *Normans*, A.D. 887, and Sæc. X., (xii. 365.)—Rigny. (xii. 460.)—St. Marianus. *English*, A.D. 1358, (xii. 471.)—St. Gon. *Normans*, (xii. 532.)— Monstier la Selle. *English*, A.D. 1358, (xii. 540.)—St. Loup. *Normans*, A.D. 889, (xii. 584.)—St Maurice en Valais. *Vandals. Lombards*, A.D. 574. *Saracens*, A.D. 765, and A.D. 900, (xii. 773, 789.)

PROVINCIA TOLOSANA.—St. Sernin. *Saracens*. A.D. 721, (xiii. 91.) —Mas Garnier. A.D. 1216. *English*, (xiii. 115.)—S. Clara de

Alta Ripa. Sæc. XIV., (xiii. 147.) — Valnegre. (xiii. 200.)—
Soreze. *Saracens. Normans.* Sæc. IX. *Hungarians,* Sæc. X.,
(xiii. 257.)

PROVINCIA TREVIRENSIS.—S. Symphorianus. *Normans,* A.D. 882.
(xiii. 516.)—S. Martinus. *Normans.* A.D. 882, (xiii. 522.)—Notre
Dame des Martyrs. *Normans,* (xiii. 566.)—Metloc. Sæc. X., (xiii.
570.)—Prum. *Normans.* A.D. 898, (xiii. 591.)—S. Anna Trevirensis. (xiii. 649.)—S. Martinus. A.D. 1552, (xiii. 826.)—S.
Magdalena. A.D. 1396, (xiii. 1262.)—Dom Evre. A.D. 1587, (xiii.
1357.)— Renivremont. *Hungarians,* A.D. 910, (xiii. 1408.)

NOTE D. (Page 155.)

MONASTERIES DESTROYED IN FRANCE BY FIRE.

PROVINCIA ALBIENSIS.—S. Privati. A.D. 1667, (i. 111.)

PROVINCIA BITURICENSIS.—S. Laurent de Bourges. *Often destroyed.*
(ii. 172.)—Fenieres. *Often destroyed,* (ii. 401.)—Les Chases. (ii.
452.)—La Regle. (ii. 610.)

PROVINCIA AQUITANICA II.—L'Isle Chauvet. A.D. 1588, (ii. 1432.)

PROVINCIA COLONIENSIS.—Tuy. A.D. 1376, and A.D. 1416, (iii. 753.)

PROVINCIA LUGUDENSIS I.—S Claire de Mont Brison. A.D. 1520, and
A.D. 1524, and A.D. 1699, (iv. 313.)—La Bussiere. (iv. 495.)

PROVINCIA MECHLINIENSIS.—Helichem. *Often destroyed,* (v. 104.)
—Hoydonck. A.D. 1564, (v. 410.)—Frawen Alb. A.D. 1508, (v.
761.)—St. Thomas Argentoratensis, A.D. 1144, (v. 832.)—Seltz.
A.D. 1258, (v. 834.)—Schutteren. A.D. 937, (v. 852.)—Schwar-
zach. Sæc. VIII., (v. 874.)—Guttnow. A.D. 1323, (v. 938.)—
Weingarten. A.D. 1053, (v. 1150.)—Ruti. A.D. 1706, (v. 1023.)

PROVINCIA NARBONENSIS.—S. Genesius de Fontanis. A.D. 1642, (vi.
1105.)

PROVINCIA PARISIENSIS.—L'Abbaye au Bois. A.D. 1661, (vii. 906.)—
Tiron. A.D. 1450, (vii. 1259.)—S. Jean au Vallée. A.D. 1215, (viii.
1311.)—L'Etoile. Sæc XIII. (viii. 1401.)—Fleury. (viii. 1540.)
S. Euverte. Sæc. XII. (viii. 1575.)

PROVINCIA REMENSIS.—S. Corneille de Compeigne. (ix. 435.)—Mo-
rienval. (ix. 448.)—St. Remi. (ix. 451.)—Le Mont St. Quentin.
(ix. 1102.)—Fervagues. A.D. 1557, (ix. 1136.)—Vermand. A.D.
1142, (ix. 1139.)—St. Claire de Chauny. A.D. 1558. A.D. 1567,
(ix. 1143.)—S. Riquier. A.D. 1487, (x. 1242.)—Corbie. A.D.

1137. (x. 1264.)—S. Sauve. A.D. 1536, (x. 1297.)—Samer. A.D. 1155, (x. 1593.)—Licques. A.D. 1674, (x. 1618.)

PROVINCIA ROTOMAGENSIS.—St. Ouen. A.D. 1136 ; A.D. 1201 ; A.D. 1248, (xi. 836.)—B. Maria de Prato. A.D. 1243 ; A.D. 1351, (xi. 241.)—Valmont. (xi. 279.)—St. Amand de Rouen. A.D. 1126 ; A.D. 1248 ; A.D. 1709, (xi. 286.)—Beaubec. A.D. 1383, (xi. 301.) Conches. A.D. 1357. (xi. 638.)—Lira. A.D. 1138, (xi. 645.)—St. Severus. (xi. 914.)

PROVINCIA SENONENSIS.—Notre Dame du Charnier. A.D. 1180, (xii. 127.)—Notre Dame pres Provins. (xii. 130.) S. Germanus. A D. 1064, (xii. 365.)—Notre Dame des Prez. A.D. 1591, (xii. 613.)— S. Maria. *Often destroyed*, (xii. 672.)—S. Maurice en Valais. A.D. 940 ; A.D. 1320 ; A.D. 1347 ; A.D. 1384 ; A.D. 1551 ; A.D. 1693, (xii. 773, 789.)

PROVINCIA TOLOSANA.—Prouille. A.D. 1715, (xiii. 316.)

PROVINCIA TREVIRENSIS.—Munster. (xiii. 600.)—St. Thomas. (xiii. 644.)—St. Catherina. (xiii. 645.)—Omnes Sancti. A.D. 1447, (xiii. 653.)—St. Vincentus. A.D. 1705, (xiii. 918.)—Renivremont. A.D. 1057, (xiii. 1408.)

NOTE E. (Page 155.)

MONASTERIES DESTROYED IN FRANCE BY SECTARIES.

PROVINCIA ALBIENSIS.—Mercoria. *Often destroyed.* (i. 111.)—Ardorellum. (i. 79.)

PROVINCIA AUXITANA.—Sorde. (i. 1061.)—B. Maria de Comba Longa. (i. 1143.)—S. Johannis de Castella. A.D. 1568, (i. 1182.) S. Gerons. A.D. 1569, (i. 1184.)—Montis Martiani. A.D. 1561 ; A.D. 1569, (i. 1187.)—Sarrances. (i. 1302.)

PROVINCIA BITURICENSIS.—S. Gildas. A.D. 1623, (ii. 155.)—Font Gombaud. (ii. 168.)

PROVINCIA AQUITANICA II.—Clairac. *Albigenses*, Sæc. XIII ; Sæc. XVI. (ii. 941.)—S. Maurin. *Albigenses*, Sæc. XIII. and Sæc. XIV. ; Sæc. XVI. (ii. 944.)—Perignac. Sæc. XV. (ii. 952.)—S. Auzony. A.D. 1658, (ii. 1029.)—Madiori. (ii. 1126.)—La Frenade (ii. 1133.)—Quincy. Sæc. XVI. (ii. 1290.)—S. Severin. (ii. 1348.)— Mauleon. A.D. 1587, (ii. 1391.)—Moureilles. (ii. 1396.)—La Chaume. (ii. 1400.)—Orbestier. (ii. 1428.)— Lieu Dieu en Jard. (ii 1445)—La Bugue. A.D. 1575, (ii. 1501.)—La Pierouse. (ii. 1505.) Boschaut. (ii. 1506.)

PROVINCIA CAMBRACENSIS.—Spinlieu. A.D. 1578, (iii. 191.)

PROVINCIA COLONIENSIS.—Tuy. A.D. 1583, (iii. 753.)

PROVINCIA LUGUDENSIS I.—Savigny. *Often destroyed*, (iv. 259.)— St. Claire de Mont Brison. A.D. 1562. (iv. 313.)

PROVINCIA MECHLINENSIS.—Cortenberg. A.D. 1572, (v. 53.)—Oost- eeckloo. (v. 227.)—S. Godolena. A.D. 1577, (v. 284.)—Les Dunes. A.D. 1577, (v. 284.)—Merckem. Sæc. XVI. (v. 326.)—S. Jean de Therouannes. (v. 327.)—Binderen. A.D 1566, (v. 409.)—Cau- waeter. A.D. 1566, (v. 411.)—Voortense. Sæc. XVI. (v. 424.)— Breidnawe. A.D. 1549, (v. 586.)—Otterburgum. A.D. 1648, (v. 596.)—Limpurg. A.D. 1556, (v. 749.)—Usserthal. (v. 760.)— Eschaw. (v. 847.)—Constantiense Scotorum. A.D. 1534, (v. 930.) —Gultnow. (v. 938.)

PROVINCIA NARBONIENSIS.—Font Chaude. (vi. 266.)—St. Martin de Lez. (vi. 290.)—St. Afrodise. A.D. 1562, (vi. 386.)—Jaucels. Sæc. XVI. (vi. 398.)—Ville Magne l'Argentiere. Sæc. XVI. (vi. 404.)—Notre Dame de la Font de Nismes. Sæc. XVI. (vi. 508.) S. Guillem du Desert, Sæc. XVI. (vi. 580.)—S. Sauveur. Sæc. XVI. (vi. 601.)—Gorjan. Sæc. XVI. (vi. 606.)—Valsauve de Bagnols. A.D. 1522, (vi. 657.)—Amarice. Sæc. XVI. (vi. 831.)— Montoliou. A.D. 1170 ; A.D. 1209 ; A.D. 1226, (vi. 972.)—Villa Longa. Sæc. XVI. (vi. 1018.)—Rien Nette. Sæc. XVI. (vi. 1023.)

PROVINCIA PARISIENSIS.—Iverneaux. (vii. 849.)—Bonneval. A.D. 1568, (viii. 1235.)—Coulombs. A.D. 1567, (viii. 1248.)—Tiron. A.D. 1562, (viii. 1259.)—Josaphat. A.D. 1564, (viii. 1279.)—S. Nicasio. A.D. 1561, (viii. 1288.)—S. Cyr. *Twice destroyed*, (viii. 1296.)— S. Jean en Vallée. A.D. 1568, (viii. 1311.)—L'Eau. A.D. 1568, (viii. 1326.)—Grand Champ. A.D. 1568, (viii. 1332.)—S. Launier. A.D. 1567, (viii. 1352.)—Bonne Nouvelle. (viii. 1515.)—Micy. Sæc. XVI. (viii. 1327.)—Fleury. (viii. 1540.)—S. Loup. (viii. 1571.)—S. Euverte. Sæc. XVI. (viii. 1575.)—Beaugency. A.D. 1562. (viii. 1579.)—La Cour Dieu. Sæc. XVI. (viii. 1583.)— Voisins. (viii. 1588.)—Lieu Notre Dame. (viii. 1592.)—Rebais. (viii. 1680.)—St. Faron. A.D. 1562, (viii. 1689.)

PROVINCIA REMENSIS.—St.Thierri. Sæc. XVI. (ix. 183.)—St. Etienne. A.D. 1567, (ix. 182.)—St. Medard. A D. 1567, (ix. 409.)—Orbais. (ix. 423.)—Long Pont. (ix. 474.)—L'Amour Dieu. (ix. 480.)— Lieu Restaure. Sæc. XVI. (ix. 502.)—St. Vincent de Laon. Sæc. XVI. (ix. 567.)—Nogent sous Couci. A.D. 1567, (ix. 603.)—S. Nicolas aux Bois. A.D. 1567, (ix. 611.)—S. Sauveur de Vertus.

(ix. 939.)—La Charmoie. Sæc. XVI. (ix. 971.)—St. Eloi de Noyon.
A.D. 1591 ; A.D. 1649. (ix. 1056.)—Le Mont St. Quentin. (ix.
1102.)—St. Claire de Chauny. A.D. 1571, (ix. 1143.)—St. Valery.
A.D. 1568 : A.D. 1591, (x. 1231.)

PROVINCIA ROTOMAGENSIS.—St. Ouen. A.D. 1562, (xi. 136.)—St.
Vaudrille. A.D. 1566, (xi. 156.)—Le Bec. A.D. 1563, (xi. 221.)—
B. Maria de Prato. A.D. 1562, (xi. 241.)—Le Treport. A.D. 1560,
(xi. 246.)—St. George de Rocherville. (xi. 269.)—St. Etienne de
Caen. A.D. 1562, (xi. 421.)—Le Mont St. Michel. (xi. 512.)—
Les Beauches. (xi. 555.)—S. Taurin. A.D. 1565, (xi. 626.)—Lira.
(xi. 645.)—Ivry. A.D. 1563, (xi. 652.)—St. Martin. A.D. 1563 :
A.D. 1568, (xi. 713.)—Preaux. (xi. 836.)

PROVINCIA SENONENSIS.—St. Pierre de Melun. (xii. 171.)—Ville
Chasson. (xii. 188.)—S. Germanus. A.D. 1567, (xii. 365.)—Rigny.
(xii. 460.)—S. Marianus. A.D. 1567, (xii. 471.)—Bella Aqua.
A.D. 1567, (xii. 534.)—Nesle la Reposte. (xii. 536.)—Notre Dame
de Sezanne. Sæc. XVI. (xii. 578.)

PROVINCIA TOLOSANA.—Mas Garnier. *Albigenses*, A.D. 1574, (xiii.
115.)—St. Sernin. A.D. 1562, (xiii. 122.)—Eaunes. Sæc. XVI.
(xiii. 124.)—L'Oraison Dieu. (xiii. 140.)—La Capelle. A.D. 1570,
(xiii. 143.)—Mas d'Asile. A D. 1570, (xiii. 201.)—Bellus Locus.
Sæc. XVI. (xiii. 286.)—Bolbone. Sæc. XVI. (xiii. 289.)—Soreze.
A.D. 1567 ; A.D. 1575, (xiii. 357.)

PROVINCIA TREVIRENSIS.—Beselich. (xiii. 522.)—Wadegassen. (xiii.
658.)—Merkingnen. (xiii. 826.)—Hornebacum. (xiii. 831.)—
Vaux en Ornois. A.D. 1575, (xiii. 1113.)—Dom Evre. A.D. 1524 ;
A.D. 1565, (xiii. 1357.)—Belchamp. A.D. 1587, (xiii. 1361.)

NOTE F. (Page 155.)

MONASTERIES SUPPRESSED IN ENGLAND BY HENRY VIII.

BEDFORDSHIRE. *Benedictines*, Elstow, Mergate. *Cistercians*, War-
don, Woburn. *Augustinians*, Bissemede, Caldwell, Dunstaple,
Newenham, Harwolde. *Gilbertines*, Chicksand. *Knights Hospitallers*, Melchburn.

BERKSHIRE. *Benedictines*, Abingdon, Hurley, Reading. *Augustinians*, Bustleham, Pougheley. *Trinitarian Friars*, Donington.

BUCKINGHAMSHIRE. *Benedictines*, Snelleshall, Ankerwyle, Merlow,
Meuresley. *Cistercians*, Bittlesden. Medmenham. *Augustinians*,
Missenden, Noctell, Burnham. *Premonstratensians*, Lavinden.
Bonhommes, Esserug. *Grey Friars*, Aylesbury.

CAMBRIDGESHIRE. *Benedictines*, Ely, Thorney, Chateris, Ikelington, Swaffham. *Augustinians*, Anglesey, Barnwell. *Gilbertines*, Cambridge, Fordham, Mirenand. *Minoresses*, Denny. *Knights Hospitallers*, Chippenham, Shengay.

CHESHIRE. *Benedictines*, Birkenhead, Chester (2). *Cistercians*, Combermere, Vale Royal. *Augustinians*, Norton. *Knights Hospitallers*, Yvele, Barrow.

CORNWALL. *Benedictines*, Truwardraith. *Augustinians*, Bodmin, St. Germans, Launceston.

CUMBERLAND. *Benedictines*, St. Bees, Wetherall, Armethwait, Seton, *Cistercians*, Calder, Holme Cultram. *Augustinians*, Carlisle, Lanercost.

DERBYSHIRE. *Benedictines*, King's Mead. *Augustinians*, Darley, Greisley, Repingdon, Brisol. *Premonstratensians*, Beauchief, Le Dale.

DEVONSHIRE. *Benedictines*, Exeter, Pilton, Tavistock, Totness, Polleshoo. *Cluniacs*, Barnstaple. *Cistercians*, Bockland, Buckfastre, Dunkeswell, Ford, Newenham. *Augustinians*, Frethelstoke, Hertland, Plympton, Cornworthy, Legh. *Premonstratensians*, Torr.

DORSETSHIRE. *Benedictines*, Abbotesbury, Cern, Milton, Sherburn, Shaftesbury. *Cistercians*, Bindon, Tarent.

DURHAM. *Benedictines*, Durham, Finchall, Jarrow, Weremouth.

ESSEX. *Benedictines*, Colchester, Colum, Hatfield Peverell. Hatfield Regis, Walden, Berking, Hedenham. *Cluniacs*, Prittlewell. *Cistercians*, Coggeshall, Stratford, Tiltey. *Augustinians*, Berden, Chich, Colchester, Dunmowe, Lighes, Thremhall, Waltham. *Premonstratensians*, Bileigh. *Black Friars*, Chelmsford. *Crutched Friars*, Colchester, *White Friars*, Maldon.

GLOUCESTERSHIRE. *Benedictines*, Gloucester, Stanley, Tewkesbury, Winchelcombe. *Cistercians*, Flexely, Hayles. *Augustinians*, Cirencester, Gloucester, Lantony. *Knights Hospitallers*, Quenington.

HAMPSHIRE. *Benedictines*, Winchester (2), Hyde, Rumesey, Wherwell. *Cistercians*, Beaulieu, Netteley, Guarrer, Winteneye. *Augustinians*, Bromere, Motisfont, Portchester, Southampton, Twinham. *Premonstratensians*, Tychfield. *Knights Hospitallers*, Badeisley.

o

HEREFORDSHIRE. *Benedictines,* Hereford, Leinster. *Cluniacs,* Clifford. *Cistercians,* Dore. *Augustinians,* Flanesford, Wigmore, Wormeleye, Acornbury, Lymbroke.

HERTFORDSHIRE. *Benedictines,* St. Albans, Hertford, Redburn. Cestrehunt, Flamstead, Sopewell. *Augustinians,* Royston, Wymondealey. *Gilbertines,* Hitchin. *White Friars,* Hitchin. *Black Friars,* King's Langley.

HUNTINGDONSHIRE. *Benedictines,* St. Neots, Ramsey, Hinchinbrooke. *Cistercians,* Salterey. *Augustinians,* Stonely, Huntingdon.

KENT. *Benedistines,* Canterbury (3), Dover, Feversham, Folkestone, Rochester, Malling, Shepey. *Cluniacs,* Horton. *Cistercians,* Boxley. *Augustinians,* Bilsington, Canterbury, Cumbwell, Leedes, Dertford. *Premonstratensians,* Bradsole, Langdon. *Trinitarian Friars,* Muttinden. *Knights Hospitallers,* Peccham, Swingfield.

LANCASHIRE. *Benedictines,* Holand, Lythorn, Penwortham. *Cistercians,* Furnes, Whalley. *Augustinians,* Buscough, Konisheved, Kertmel. *Premonstratensians,* Cokersand.

LEICESTERSHIRE. *Benedictines,* Langley. *Cistercians.* Gerondon. *Augustinians,* Bradley, Bredon, Ulverscroft, Kirley, Landa, Leicester, Osulveston, Grace Dieu. *Premonstratensians,* Croxton. *Knights Hospitallers,* Dalby, Hether, Rotheley.

LINCOLNSHIRE. *Benedictines,* Bardney, Belvoir, Crowland, Lincoln, Spalding, Stamford (2), Fosse, Grimesby, Humbersteyn, Stanfield. *Carthusians,* Eppworth. *Cistercians,* Kirksted, Louth Park, Revesby, Swineshed, Vandey, Cotham, Goukwelle, Greenfield, Heyminges, Lekeburn, Stykeswold. *Augustinians,* Bourn, Ellesham, Hyrst, Kyme, Maikeby, Newsted, Nocton, Thorneton, Thornholme, Torkesey, Wellow. *Premonstratensians,* Barlings, Hagueby, Neubo, Neus, Tupholm, Irford. *Gilbertines,* Alvingham, Bullington, Catteley, Haverholm, Holland Brigge, Lincoln, Newstede on Ancolm, Ormesbey, Sempringham, Sixhill. *Knights Hospitallers,* Bruer, Egle, Wilketon.

MIDDLESEX. *Benedictines,* Westminster, Kilborne, Clerkenwell, Halwell, St. Helens, Stratford. *Carthusians,* London. *Cistercians,* St. Mary of Graces. *Augustinians,* St. Bartholomew, Elsing Spittle, London. *Brigettines,* Syon. *Minoresses,* London. *Trinitarian Friars,* Hounslow. *Black Friars,* London. *Grey*

Friars, London. *Crutched Friars*, London. *White Friars*, London. *Knights Hospitallers*, London.

MONMOUTHSHIRE. *Benedictines*, Bergavenny, Monmouth, Stroguil, Eisk. *Cluniacs*, Malpas. *Cistercians*, Grace Dieu, Llantarnam, Tintern. *Augustinians*, Lantiony.

NORFOLK. *Benedictines*, Hulme, Binham, Horsham, Norwich, Wymondham, Blackborough, Cairo, Thetford. *Cluniacs*, Bromholm, Castleacre, Thetford. *Cistercians*, Marham. *Augustinians*, Beeston, Buckenham, Cokesford, Flitcham, Hempton, Hickling, Pentney, Thetford, Weyburn, Walsingham, Westacre, Weybridge, Crabhouse. *Premonstratensians*, West Dereham, Langley, Wendling. *Gilbertines*, Shouldham. *Trinitarian Friars*, Ingham. *Black Friars*, Lynn. *White Friars*, Burnham, Lynn. *Grey Friars*, Walsingham. *Knights Hospitallers*, Carbroke.

NORTHAMPTONSHIRE. *Benedictines*, Peterborough, Katebi. *Cluniacs*, Northampton, De la Pré. *Cistercians*, Pepewell, Sewardesley. *Augustinians*, Canons Ashley, Chacomb, Castle Hymel, Northampton, Rothwell. *Premonstratensians*, Sulby. *Grey Friars*, Northampton. *White Friars*, Northampton. *Black Friars*, Northampton. *Knights Hospitallers*, Dingley.

NORTHUMBERLAND. *Benedictines*, Farn Island, Lindisfarne, Tinmouth, Halystane, Lambley, Nessham, Newcastle. *Cistercians*, Newminster. *Augustinians*, Bamburgh, Brekenburne, Hexham, Ovingham. *Premonstratensians*, Alnewick, Blanca Landa.

NOTTINGHAMSHIRE. *Benedictines*, Blythe, Marshe, Walingwels. *Cluniacs*, Lenton. *Carthusians*, Beauvale. *Cistercians*, Rufford. *Augustinians*, Felley, Newstead, Shelford, Thurgarton, Workesop. *Premonstratensians*, Wellbeck, Brodholm. *Gilbertines*, Mattersey.

OXFORDSHIRE. *Benedictines*, Egnesham, Durham College, Godestow, Stodely. *Cistercians*, Bruercay, Rewte, Tame. *Augustinians*, Burcester, Dorchester, Oseney, Wroxton, Goring. *Gilbertines*, Clattercole.

RUTLANDSHIRE. *Augustinians*, Brooke.

SHROPSHIRE. *Benedictines*, Bromfield, Morfield, Shrewsbury. *Cluniacs*, Wenlock. *Cistercians*, Bildewas, Brewood. *Augustinians*, Chirbury, Hagmon, Lilleshull, Wombridge. *Premonstratensians*, Hales. *Knights Hospitallers*, Halston.

SOMERSETSHIRE. *Benedictines*, Athelney, Bath, Dunster, Glastonbury, Michelney, Bearwe, Canyngton. *Cluniacs*, Montacute. *Carthu-*

sians, Henton, Witham. *Cistercians*, Clyne. *Augustinians*, Bar-
lynch, Bruton, Byrkeley, Keynsham, Taunton, Wospring, Bristol.
Buckland. *Knights Hospitallers*, Combe.

STAFFORDSHIRE. *Benedictines*, Burton, Tutbury, Brewood. *Cluniacs*,
Dudley. *Cistercians*, Crokesden, Dieulacres, Hulton. *Augustinians*, Roucester, De Sartis, Stafford, Stone, Trentham.

SUFFOLK. *Benedictines*, Bury, Eye, Hoxne, Bungay, Redlingfield.
Cluniacs, Wangford. *Cistercians*, Sibton. *Augustinians*, Ble-
burgh, Butley, Herlyngflete, Ipswich, Ixworth, Letheryngham,
Woodbridge, Campsey, Flixton. *Premonstratensians*, Leystone.
Minoresses, Brusyard. *Knights Hospitallers*, Batisford.

SURREY. *Benedictines*, Chertsey. *Cluniacs*, Bermondsey. *Carthusians*, Shene. *Cistercians*, Waverley. *Augustinians*, Aldebury,
Merton, Reygate, Southwark, Tauregge.

SUSSEX. *Benedictines*, Battell, Boxgrave, Easeborne, Ruspar. *Cluniacs*, Lewes. *Cistercians*, Robert's Bridge. *Augustinians*,
Hastings, Michelham, Tortington, Wolinchmere. *Premonstratensians*, Dureford.

WARWICKSHIRE. *Benedictines*, Alenceaster, Anecote, Coventre,
Heanwood, Oldbury, Pollesworth, Wroxhall. *Carthusians*, Co-
ventre. *Cistercians*, Combe, Mereval, Stonely, Puiley. *Augus-
tinians*, Erdbury, Kenilworth, Maxstoke, Studley, Warwick,
Atherstone. *Fontevrauld Nuns*, Nun Eaton. *Trinitarian Friars*,
Thelesford. *White Friars*, Coventre. *Black Friars*, Warwick.

WESTMORELAND. *Premonstratensians*, Hepp.

WILTSHIRE. *Benedictines*, Malmesbury, Kemton, Wilton. *Cluniacs*,
Farleigh. *Cistercians*, Kingswood, Stanleigh. *Augustinians*,
Bradenstoke, Bradley, Ivychurch, Lacock. *Gilbertines*, Marle-
burgh, Pulton. *Fontevrauld Nuns*, Ambrosebury. *Bonhommes*,
Edindon. *Trinitarian Friars*, Efton.

WORCESTERSHIRE. *Benedictines*, Evesham, Malvern Major, Malvern
Minor, Pershore, Worcester. *Cistercians*, Bordesley, Cokeshill,
Weston. *Fontevrauld Nuns*, Westwood.

YORKSHIRE. *Benedictines*, Grosmont, Middlesburgh, Richmond,
Selby, Whitby, York (2), Arden, Arthington, Brunnum, Handale,
Kelynge, Mareis, Maryke, Molesby, Monketon, Rosedale, Thikhed,
Clemensthorp. *Cluniacs*, Monk Bretton, Pontefract. *Carthu-
sians*, Kingston, Mount Grace. *Cistercians*, Ryland, Fountains,
Joreval, Kirkstall, Melsa, River, Roche, Sallay, Nun Appleton,

Basedale, Elreton, Esseholt, Hanepole, Kekdon, Kirkleghes, Sinningthwait, Swinhey, Wyckham. *Augustinians*, Bolton, Burlington, Drax, Feireby, Giseburn, Haltemprice, Helagh Park, Kirkham, Marton, Newburgh, Nostell, Tockwith, Warter, Widkirk. *Premonstratensians*, Corham, Egleston, Richmond. *Gilbertines*, Ellerton, Malton, Oveton, Watton, York. *Trinitarian Friars*, Knaresborough. *Knights Hospitallers*, Beverley, Mount St. John, Newland, Ribstane.

ANGLESEY. *Benedictines*, Glaunach.

BRECKNOCKSHIRE. *Benedictines*, Brecknock.

CARMARTHENSHIRE. *Benedictines*, Cadweli. *Cistercians*, Alba Landa. *Augustinians*, Carmarthen. *Premonstratensians*, Tallagh.

CARNARVONSHIRE. *Benedictines*, Bardsey. *Augustinians*. Bethkelert.

CARDIGANSHIRE. *Benedictines*, Cardigan. *Cistercians*, Strata Flonda, Llanleir.

DENBIGHSHIRE. *Cistercians*, Maynan, De Valle Crucis.

FLINTSHIRE. *Cistercians*, Basingwerk.

GLAMORGANSHIRE. *Benedictines*, Gwenny. *Cistercians*, Margan, Neth.

MERIONETHSHIRE. *Cistercians*, Kinner.

MONTGOMERYSHIRE. *Cistercians*, Ystrat Marchel, Llanlugan.

PEMBROKESHIRE. *Benedictines*, St. Dogmael, Pembroke, Pilla. *Augustinians*, Haverford. *Knights Hospitallers*, Slebach.

RADNORSHIRE. *Cistercians*, Cumhyre.

NOTE G.   (Page 163.)

COST OF RICHLY ILLUMINATED MSS. IN THE FOURTEENTH AND FIFTEENTH CENTURIES.

THE data given in the text refer solely to MSS. without paintings or illuminations, and bound in the most ordinary style; but some details with regard to the sums paid for richly ornamented and elegantly bound volumes may not be without interest for the reader. The subjoined particulars are taken from various authentic sources, but chiefly from the catalogue, made in 1427, of the Library of Charles d'Orleans, a wealthy noblemen and accomplished poet, who flourished in the fifteenth century, the various prices enumerated being reduced to their equivalents in money of the present day.

Date.	Enumeration of Objects.	Cost in Modern Value.		
		£	s.	d.
1388	*Heures de Notre Dame à IX Psaumes et XIX leçons*, bought of Henri Maristoch, bookseller at Paris.	8	13	11
1390	*Livre de chant*, bought of Raoul le Gay, Premier Sumellier of the King's Chapel.	38	15	0
1393	Book entitled *Le dit royal*, bought of Jean Froissard, Priest and Canon at Chimays	38	15	0
1394	Various books, among which were *une Bible en Latin, le roman de Boesce de Consolation*, and *le Jeu des Echez*, together	521	9	3
	Un racionnel des divins offices, bought of Henri de Trenon, bookseller	193	5	7
	Histoires scolastiques en Français, bought of Etienne Angevin, bookseller at Paris	178	4	10
	Paid at various times to the Scribes and Illuminators engaged in copying and illuminating the book entitled *le Mirouer hystorial*, and other books	1024	7	9
1395	*Unes croniques de France ystoriées*, complete, and adorned with miniatures, bought of Guillaume Deschamps, bookseller	415	1	3
1396	*Le livre des propriétez*, and *le livre des Fables d'Ysopet*, bought of Guillaume de Tignonville, Chamberlain to Louis, Duke of Orleans	173	19	0
	Two volumes, one entitled *Josephus en maniere de croniques*, and the other *Romain Lanceloz*, purchased together for	391	7	10
	Two volumes, containing, the first, *le livre du Trésor, le livre de Julius César, le livre des Roys, le Secret des Secrez*, and *le livre de Estrille Fauveau ;* the second, *le Romaunt de la Rose, le Testament maistre Jehan de Mehun*, and *le livre des Echez moralisé ;* the whole illuminated in gold and silver, and adorned with paintings, bought of Jacques Johan, grocer, and citizen of Paris	130	9	3
	Cost of parchment and other necessary provisions furnished for the Scribes engaged in copying *le livre de la Cité de Dieu, les livres des Ethiques et Politiques, le livre du Ciel et du Monde*, and *la grant Bible*	193	5	7
1397	The *livre de Valerius Maximus* in French, bought of Gilles Malet, Knight, and Maitre d'Hotel to the King	217	8	9
	A *Breviaire* in two volumes, bought of Andry Dessoubzlourme, Knight	387	10	5
	Livre ou est le fait des Romains, written in French, compiled from Isidore, Suetonius, and Lucan	347	18	7

Date.	Enumeration of Objects.	Cost in Modern Value.		
		£	s.	d.
1397	A *Tite Live*, and a *Boesce de Consolation*, translated and written in French, bought of Pierre de Véronne	579	8	11
	Paid to Guillaume de Villiers for the binding of sixty-two volumes £ *s.* *d.*			
	For the covering, being about 5*s.* 2*d.* per volume... .... 15 19 6			
	For seven skins, being about 4*s.* 6*d.* each 1 11 8			
	For 23 clasps, being about 3*s.* 10*d.* each 4 8 10			
		22	0	0
	Paid to Jean d'Esture, for twenty pairs of silver clasps, gilt, and enamelled with the arms of the Duke of Orleans, furnished for twenty volumes of his library (being about £4 11*s.* per clasp). £ *s.* *d.*			
	For the silver employed 80 14 0			
	For the workmanship, gilding, and enamelling 74 7 10			
	For silk for these clasps 6 15 7			
		161	17	5
1398	A volume entitled *l'Apostille maistre Nychole de Lyre*, bought of Guillaume Daniel, Priest ...	579	8	11
	A *Concordance sur la Bible*, bought of Jean de Marson, Master of Arts and Scelleur of the University	193	5	7
	Le livre des problemes de Aristote, translated into French by Evrard de Contis, *maistre en medicine*, bought of Jean Doche, Master of Arts, and Student at Paris.........................	152	4	2
	Paid for parchment and other necessary provisions for the Scribes and Illuminators who are engaged in copying and illuminating the *grant Bible glosée*, the *Croniques de Burgues*, the *Lamentations St. Bernart*, the *livre de l'Empereur Celestiel*, and other books	483	4	0
	Paid to Jean d'Arras, bookseller of Paris, for having re-stitched and bound in good leather with four clasps, two on the front and one at the top and bottom, a book called *Gyron le Courtois*	2	18	0
1399	Paid to Sevestre Trente, Merchant of Lucca, residing in Paris, for five quarters of green damask and two ells and a quarter of thin green satin, sold by him to the Duke of Orleans, for the making and lining of two coverings, one for the *Breviaire*, and the other for the *Heures* of the Duke..	20	15	6

Date.	Enumeration of Objects.	Cost in Modern Value.		
		£	s.	d.
1401	Paid to Jacques Richier, for binding a large volume in leather, elaborately tooled, garnished with ten bosses and four clasps, and with several silk markers	5	15	11
	Paid to Huguet Foubert, bookseller and illuminator of books, residing at Paris, for illuminating with gold azure and vermilion two small books, and binding them in leather (apparently in a single volume.)	7	4	11

NOTE H.   (Page 280.)

PRICES OF VARIOUS ARTICLES OF NECESSITY AND LUXURY IN FRANCE IN THE FOURTEENTH AND FIFTEENTH CENTURIES.

THE subjoined data, selected from the elaborate and carefully compiled tables of M. Leber, published in his *Essais sur l'Appreciation de la Fortune Privée au Moyen Age,* will probably be new to most English students, and will form a valuable aid to the appreciation of the cost of existence during the period to which they refer.   It has been deemed more convenient to group together the various prices relating to the same species of commodity than to follow the strictly chronological order adopted by M. Leber, as the reader is thus enabled to perceive at a glance the various fluctuations in value which the same article underwent during the period which our facts embrace.   It should also be noted that, in order to avoid minute fractional sums, the franc of French money at the present day has been taken at tenpence in the reduction of the various prices to English standard ; should it be desired, therefore, to attain a precisely accurate result it will be necessary to deduct 1s. 1d. in the pound or about one nineteenth from the amount quoted in the table.

Date.	Enumeration of Objects.	£	s.	d.		Cost in Modern Value.		
						£	s.	d.
1372	Wheat, the setier of 240lb.	0	19	9½	the pound[1]	0	0	1
1418	" "	4	11	8	"	0	0	4½
1440	" "	0	14	7½	"	0	0	0¾
1444	" "	1	14	4½	"	0	0	1½
1449	" "	0	11	4¾	"	0	0	0½

[1] From the price of a pound of wheat, it is easy to calculate the price of bread.   Thus, in 1372 wheat being at 1d. per pound, the price of the loaf of 2lb. 4oz. of common bread is stated at 2½d. ; 10 per cent. being added for the cost of fabrication.

Date.	Enumeration of Objects.	£	s.	d.		Cost in Modern Value.		
						£	s.	d.
1458	Wheat, the setier of 240lb.	1	7	9	the pound	0	0	1½
1492	" "	0	17	2¼	"	0	0	0¾
1498	" "	1	2	11	"	0	0	1½
1500	" "	0	17	2½	"	0	0	0¾
	Average of the 14th Cent. the Setier £2; the pound					0	0	2
	" " 15th Cent. " £1 3s. 6d. "					0	0	1¼
	" " both Centuries " £1 11s. 2d. "					0	0	1½
1372	Common Loaf of 2lb. 4oz.....					0	0	2½
	Best Bread, Loaf of, 2lb. 1oz.					0	0	4¾
1448	Loaf sufficient for a day's food for a man					0	0	2
1302	A small Ox					13	1	3
1313	A Bullock					16	6	6¾
1314	An Ox					20	12	6
1341	A Bullock					9	11	8
1372	A Calf					1	10	9¾
1411	Two Cows and a Calf					11	0	0
1426	A Cow					11	5	2¼
1427	A Calf					2	6	8
	An Ox					4	13	4
1440	A Calf					2	5	6½
1449	A Cow					3	7	2¾
1458	A Fat Bullock					13	9	8¼
1470	A Calf					0	19	7
	A Bullock and a Cow					15	0	0
1476	A Calf					1	2	11
	Average price of a Bullock or Cow					9	14	6¼
	The Bullock being supposed of average weight, the price of Beef would be per pound...........					0	0	3¾
	Average price of a Calf					1	13	1¼
1312	A Sheep...........................					1	2	11
1341	"					1	3	0⅛
1376	"					1	6	5½
1397	"					0	19	9½
1411	"					0	17	10½
1418	"					0	8	10½
1421	" (the finest)					2	4	2½
1427	"					1	10	0
1458	"					0	11	8½
1470	"					0	5	0
	Average price of a Sheep....................					1	1	0
	The Sheep being supposed of average weight, the price of Mutton would be per pound.........					0	0	5¼

Date.	Enumeration of Objects.	Cost in Modern Value. £	s.	d.
1312	A Pig	2	10	0
1328	A Fat Pig	2	5	10
1376	A Pig	5	7	10¾
1406	"	4	1	6
1418	"	2	18	3
1426	"	0	12	0
1440	"	0	9	4
1458	"	1	14	10½
1493	"	0	8	7
	Average price of a Pig	2	5	4¼
1375	Old Wine, the pint	0	1	3½
	New Wine "	0	0	8
	Wine "	0	0	6½
1385	" "	0	0	5¾
1390	" "	0	0	7
1398	" "	0	0	4¾
1406	" "	0	0	11
1411	" "	0	0	7
1415	Good Wine "	0	0	3½
1417	Wine "	0	0	1½
1421	Best Beaune Wine, the pint	0	2	5½
	Best French Wine "	0	1	7½
	Common Wine "	0	0	9¾
1424	New Wine "	0	0	1¾
1427	Wine (*noted as very dear*) the pint	0	1	1¼
1440	" " "	0	0	3½
1448	Very good Wine, "	0	0	3
1470	White Wine, the pint	0	0	1¾
1492	Wine "	0	0	3
1493	Beaune Wine "	0	1	1¾
	Average price of ordinary Wine per pint	0	0	5¼
1426	Seven little Pigs and a side of Pork	3	7	0¾
1427	A young Pig	0	3	4
1470	" " "	0	3	5¼
	A young Rabbit	0	0	7½
	A Lamb	0	4	2
1390	A Carp	0	7	3
1405	" " (*noted as very dear*)	0	16	3½
1406	" "	0	10	2¼
1411	" "	0	7	4½
1450	" "	0	1	6¼
1372	A Salmon	2	1	10½
1406	A Whiting	0	1	4¾

Date.	Enumeration of Objects.	Cost in Modern Value. £	s.	d.
1426	Fifty fresh Mackarel, £1 19s. 0½d. .... each	0	0	9½
1340	One hundred salt Herrings	0	18	10¼
1426	,, ,, ,, ...	0	14	1½
1434	Twenty-five ,, ,, ...	0	1	5¼
1449	One hundred ,, ,, ...	0	9	2
1499	,, ,, ,, ,, ...	0	19	11¼
	Average price of a Herring	0	0	1½
1375	Thirty-four domestic Fowls (*noted as dear*)	3	17	11
	Each Fowl therefore....................	0	2	3¼
1458	A young Chicken	0	1	0¼
1493	A Capon....................	0	4	3½
1470	A young Chicken	0	0	6¼
1434	A Pheasant	0	13	9
1440	A pair of Pigeons	0	2	4
1449	,, ,, ,, ,, ...	0	1	0¼
1470	A Pigeon	0	0	6¼
1493	A pair of Pigeons	0	1	1¾
1449	A Gosling	0	3	0¾
1470	,, ,, ...	0	1	10¼
1476	Thirty-six Pigeons and three Goslings..........	0	19	5¾
1354	One hundred Eggs (*noted as dear*)	0	18	4
1372	,, ,, ,, ...	0	11	0¾
1376	,, ,, ,, ...	0	9	0¾
1427	Twenty-five ,, ...	0	1	8
1449	One hundred ,, ...	0	3	6¾
1470	,, ,, ,, ...	0	3	9
	Average price of one hundred Eggs	0	8	5¾
1427	Butter per pound	0	1	11¼
1434	,, ,, ,, ...	0	1	3½
1449	Salt Butter ,, ...	0	0	9¼
1470	Butter ,, ,, ...	0	0	10
1476	,, ,, ,, ...	0	0	10¼
	Average price of Butter per pound	0	1	2¾
1415	A Cheese (*noted as very dear*).	0	6	10¼
1426	,, ,, ...	0	0	7½
1427	,, ,, ...	0	0	8¼
1427	Hay—the Setier of 240lb.	1	1	4¾
1449	,, ,, ,, ...	0	15	3¼
1458	,, ,, ,, ...	0	15	6½
1498	,, ,, ,, ...	0	19	2

Date.	Enumeration of Objects.	Cost in Modern Value. £	s.	d.
1498	Average price of a Setier of Hay..................	0	18	2
1427	Barley—the Setier of 240lb.	1	0	0
1312	Beans—the Setier of 240lb.........................	1	4	10¾
1372	,, ,, ,, ...	1	13	2¼
1426	,, ,, ,, ...	2	5	0⅛
1427	,, ,, ,, ...	1	0	0
1443	,, ,, ,, ...	1	5	9½
1458	,, ,, ,, ...	2	5	10½
	Average price of a Setier of Beans	1	12	5⅓
	Beans, therefore, averaged per pound	0	0	1½
1341	Peas—the Setier of 240lb.	1	17	6
1372	,, ,, ,, ...	1	13	2¼
1411	,, ,, ,, ...	2	15	0
1426	,, ,, ,, ...	2	2	0½
1427	,, ,, ,, ...	1	0	0
1443	,, ,, ,, ...	1	5	9½
1458	,, ,, ,, ...	2	5	10½
1492	,, ,, ,, ...	6	0	3¾
	Average price of a Setier of Peas	2	5	4⅑
	Peas, therefore, averaged per pound	0	0	2¼
1372	Onions—the Setier of 240lb. (*noted as very dear*)	5	11	5
	The pound of these Onions therefore cost........	0	0	5½
1443	Onions—the bushel	0	0	3½
	Turnips—the bushel	0	0	7
1302	One thousand Pears (costing therefore 1½d. for four)	1	13	0
1440	Twenty-five large Pears	0	0	7
1426	Cherries, per pound	0	0	0¾
1437	,, ,, ,, ...	0	0	1½
1427	One hundred Apples (costing therefore 2d. for five)	0	3	4
	One hundred Plums................................	0	0	1¾
	One hundred Damsons..............................	0	1	0¼
1435	One hundred very fine Peaches	0	0	3½
1440	One hundred large Peaches........................	0	0	3½
1427	One thousand green Nuts (costing therefore 1d. for fifteen)..................................	0	5	6¾
1440	Setier of Nuts	2	9	6½
	The pound of these Nuts therefore cost..........	0	0	2¼
1372	Almonds per pound	0	2	1
1426	,, ,, ,, ...	0	2	0
1341	Rice, per pound (*noted as dear*)	0	1	3

Date	Enumeration of Objects.	Cost in Modern Value. £	s.	d.
1372	Rice, per pound	0	2	4¼
1476	" " "	0	0	11¼
	£ s. d.			
1375	Salt, per minot of 100lbs. 2 19 0[3] per pound	0	0	7
1376	" " " " " 3 0 0¾ " "	0	0	7¼
1390	" (Common) " " 1 13 10¼ " "	0	0	4
"	" (Fine) " " 2 10 3¼ " "	0	0	6
1470	" " " " " 0 14 7 " "	0	0	1¾
1492	" " " " " 2 9 10 " "	0	0	6¼
	Average price of Salt, per pound	0	0	6¼
1372	Sugar, per pound	1	3	8¼
1426	" "	0	12	0
1372	Ginger, "	0	18	11½
1450	" "	0	12	10¼
1328	Pepper, "	0	11	5¼
1372	" "	0	17	9
1450	" "	0	6	7¼
1372	Cinnamon, "	1	8	5¼
	Cloves, "	2	7	5
	Saffron, "	10	13	4
	Mace, per ounce	0	8	8½
1321	Incense, per pound	0	8	9
1323	Liquorice, " (*noted as dear*)	0	5	8¾
1450	Fine Gunpowder, per pound	0	19	9¼
1470	" " " "	0	13	4
1336	Candles, per pound	0	2	3½
1421	" " (*noted as very dear*)	0	3	3½
1434	" "	0	1	8¼
1499	" "	0	1	4
1476	Tallow "	0	0	9¼
1375	Oil—the Setier	9	3	4
1418	" per pint	0	4	9¾
1426	" " "	0	3	2
1440	" " "	0	3	6
1317	Wax, per pound	0	10	11¾
1350	" " "	0	11	6¾
1434	" " "	0	6	11
1336	Wax Candles, per pound	0	8	1¾
1428	Beer, per pint	0	0	1¾
1409	Rent of a small house in a country town, two stories high, with two windows, one above the other, looking out on the principal street—per annum	68	14	1¼

[3] It will be remembered that the tax on Salt constituted in France an important branch of revenue, and enormously augmented its price.

Date.	Enumeration of Objects.		Cost in Modern Value. £	s.	d.
1307	Woollen Cloth	per ell	5	13	9½
131[illegible]	Fustian	" "	0	5	8¾
1320	Cloth (Drap fin marbre)	" "	8	19	3½
	Various qualities of Cloth for the King's use—the highest price	per ell	8	17	9
	The lowest	" "	3	4	7¾
	Fine Cloth for the King's Physician	" "	4	13	8¾
	Stout Cloth (Bonne panne)	" "	7	2	7¼
1384	Fine Cloth	" "	3	0	9¾
	Cloth of coarser quality	" "	2	6	4¼
1463	loth for the King's Robe	" "	4	11	8
	" for the King's Mantle	" "	14	13	4
	Fine Black Cloth for Nobles	" "	6	8	4
	Coarse Cloth, used for linings	" "	1	0	10½
1498	Fine Black Cloth for the Queen's Mantle	" "	12	0	7½
1498	Black Serge, for hanging a room in the Hotel d'Etampes	per ell	0	7	7¾
1320	Green Velvet	per ell	9	15	7
1372	Black striped Velvet	" "	3	13	2¼
1461	B ue Velvet	" "	9	13	9
	Crimson Velvet embroidered with gold	" "	64	17	4¾
	Black Velvet, for a Pall	" "	15	3	9½
	" " for covering a Hearse	" "	9	13	9
1345	Silk, per pound		13	15	0
1461	Shot Florence Taffeta for the King's shirt	per ell	6	5	9¼
1483	Black Silk Ribbon	" "	0	2	6
"	Red and Green Silk	per ounce	1	0	3¾
1498	Black Satin	per ell	1	12	1
	Silk	per ounce	1	0	7½
	Wide Black Taffeta for the hangings of the Church of St. Florentin d'Amboise	per ell	2	5	10
1409	Two dresses of Cloth of Gold, bought of a Florentine Merchant by the King		797	10	0
1312	Linen (ordinary quality)	per ell	0	4	3¼
	" (coarser)	" "	0	3	8¾
	" (toile rondette)	" "	0	4	11½
1317	" (toile bourgeoise for Sheets[3])	" "	1	0	5

[3] The dimensions of the beds of this period may be judged from the fact that, in the example which has furnished this price, each sheet contained twenty-five ells of linen, and was eighteen feet four inches square. The sheets of Louis XI., according to the bill of the sempstress who made them, contained each sixteen ells, and were fourteen feet eight inches square.

Date.	Enumeration of Objects.	£	s.	d.
		Cost in Modern Value.		
1317	Linen (toile carrée)...........................per ell	0	12	3
1341	" (toile blanche deliée) .... " "	0	4	2
	" (toile à moulin) .... " "	0	2	11
1350	" (toile bourgeoise for lining the breeches of the Dauphin) ....per ell	1	1	6¾
1483	" (toile fine de Cambrai)............. " "	1	5	0
149	" (toile de Hollande).. ... . " "	2	5	10
1372	Two pair of Sheets, of which one, rather worn, was on the Queen's bed when she died	33	3	9
1314	Sewing Thread, per pound	0	6	10½
1336	" " " "	1	7	6
1329	Wool, per pound	0	10	3½
1341	A Sheep's Fleece	0	12	6
1320	Cotton, for repairing Matrass of the King, per pound	0	6	1¼
1372	Lamp Wicks	0	1	7
1350	Hat, of Otter or Beaver	8	7	9¼
	" (chapeau de paon à grand roe)	13	19	8
	" for the King's Fool, exclusive of pearls and fur	41	19	0
1372	Ladies' Hat of Beaver lined with cloth	2	7	5
1320	Shoes............. ... per pair....	0	10	2¼
	" .... " "	0	4	9
	" for a Duchess " "	0	8	1¾
1323	" .... " "	0	9	2
1350	Boots for the King—the pair	3	?	11
	Shoes " " " " "	0	13	11½
1442	Suit of Milanese Armour	64	1?	4½
1285	A Horse for the King's use	75	1	2¼
1287	A Palfrey	36	0	8¼
1317	A Horse	30	1	5
	" "	81	1	4½
1327	" "	29	1?	3
1427	" "	10	1?	4
1440	" "	14	17	4
1307	Horse Shoe—the largest size	0	3	2
	" " ordinary size.................	0	2	4½
	Steel, per pound	0	1	3½
	Best Vellum, per skin	0	3	10½
	Parchment " "	0	2	4½
1320	Ivory Flute for the King's Musician	7	4	6
1352	Knives, with ebony handles, gilt, and enamelled, for the King's Pages—the pair...................	5	7	5¾
1372	A Porcelain Jug	18	0	9

Date.	Enumeration of Objects.	Cost in Modern Value.		
		£	s.	d.
1372	A Gridiron	0	14	9¾
	Spit for roasting meat	0	9	5¼
1392	Playing Cards, per pack	2	7	6
1431	A Quire of Paper	0	2	8¾
1483	Painting of Our Saviour, the Blessed Virgin, St. John, and other Scriptural personages, painted for the towns of Amiens, by Simonnet Marimon .	29	6	8
	Curtain with rod and rings, to place before this picture..	1	4	5¼
1483	Medicines taken by Queen Charlotte during an illness of two months' duration....................	131	5	0

MODERN EQUIVALENTS OF ANCIENT FRENCH MONEY FROM THE EIGHTH TO THE FIFTEENTH CENTURY.

THE accompanying table, for which we are indebted to the researches of M. Leber, will serve as a guide in the reduction of the prices of various articles and the wages of labour recorded by French mediæval writers to their equivalents in modern value ; though it should be observed that the constant variation in the price of the Mark of Silver during the course of the same century, and even during the same year, arising chiefly from the depreciation of the value of money by the lowering of the standard of the coinage, renders it impossible, without following these variations year by year, and in some cases month by month, to frame a table which would enable the student to arrive in all cases at perfectly accurate results in the estimation of the actual equivalent of a sum stated by an ancient writer. The first half of the fifteenth century affords a striking example of these fluctuations in the value of the currency ; taking only the years embraced in the tables of M. Leber, we find that the Mark represented in 1405 and 1406 six livres fifteen sous, in 1408 eight livres, in 1409 seven livres ten sous, in 1411, 1413 and 1415 eight livres, in 1417 ten livres, in 1418 fifteen livres, in the first half of 1421 forty livres, and in the second half of the same year seven livres, in 1422, 1423, and 1424 seven livres ten sous, in 1426 nine livres three sous, in 1427 eight livres, in 1428 fifteen livres, in 1431 and 1434 eight livres, in 1435 ten livres, in 1437 nine livres, in 1438, 1440, and 1441 seven livres seventeen sous, in 1442, 1443 and 1448 eight livres, and in 1449 and 1450 nine livres. The equivalents given in the table are calculated from the average value of the Mark, and will be found sufficiently accurate for all ordinary purposes.

It is to be noted that the value of money, as regards its command over commodities, was in the eighth century eleven times, in the ninth century eight times, and in the fourteenth and fifteenth centuries six times that which belongs to it at the present day. This difference, and the price of the Mark of silver, whose present value is about £2 3*s.*, have served as the data by the help of which this table has been framed. The precise modern value of money in the tenth, eleventh, and twelfth centuries yet remains to be elucidated by future researches.

In the reduction of French money to English standard, the pound sterling has been taken at 25*f.* 30*c.*, which is, as nearly as possible, its exact value.

Period.	Average Price of the Mark of Silver.			Ancient Value.	Modern Equivalent: French.		Modern Equivalent: English.		
					Fr.	Ct.	£	s.	d.
VIII Century, after 779	The Livre at this epoch weighed 13½ ounces of fine silver			Livre.	957	00	37	8	7¼
				Sous.	47	85	1	17	5
				Denier.	2	98	,,	3	1¼
IX Century, beginning	The same as in the VIII Century.			Livre.	690	00	27	5	5¾
				Sous.	34	50	1	7	0¼
				Denier.	2	87	,,	2	3
	Mark of Eight Ounces.								
	Liv.	Sous.	Den.						
XIII Century, end . .	2	18	0	Livre.	113	79	4	10	8¾
				Sous.	5	69	,,	4	6¼
XIV Century,				Denier.	,,	47	,,	,,	4½
1st half	4	0	0	Livre.	82	50	3	5	2½
				Sous.	4	12	,,	3	3
,, ,,				Denier.	,,	34	,,	,,	3¼
2nd half .	6	0	0	Livre.	55	0	2	3	5¾
				Sous.	2	75	,,	2	2
XV Century,				Denier.	,,	23	,,	,,	2
first half	8	0	0	Livre.	41	25	1	12	7¼
				Sous.	2	06	,,	1	7½
,, ,,				Denier.	,,	17	,,	,,	1¾
2nd half .	11	0	0	Livre.	30	00	1	3	8¾
				Sous.	1	50	,,	1	2¼
				Denier.	,,	12	,,	,,	1

THE END.

J. BILLING,
PRINTER AND STEREOTYPER,
WOKING, SURREY.

Check Out More Titles From HardPress Classics Series In this collection we are offering thousands of classic and hard to find books. This series spans a vast array of subjects – so you are bound to find something of interest to enjoy reading and learning about.

Subjects:
Architecture
Art
Biography & Autobiography
Body, Mind &Spirit
Children & Young Adult
Dramas
Education
Fiction
History
Language Arts & Disciplines
Law
Literary Collections
Music
Poetry
Psychology
Science
…and many more.

Visit us at www.hardpress.net

CPSIA information can be obtained
at www.ICGtesting.com
Printed in the USA
BVHW081823120819
555665BV00016B/1727/P